Sharon Tate

Sharon Tate

A Life

Ed Sanders

Illustrations by Rick Veitch

Da Capo Press

A Member of the Perseus Books Group

Designed by Jack Lenzo
Set in 10½ point Caslon by The Perseus Books Group

Library of Congress Cataloging-in-Publication Data
Sanders, Ed.
  Sharon Tate: a life / Ed Sanders; Illustrations by Rick Veitch.
    pages cm
  Includes bibliographical references and index.
  ISBN 978-0-306-81889-9 (hardback) — ISBN 978-0-306-82240-7 (e-book) 1. Tate, Sharon, 1943-1969. 2. Actors—United States—Biography. 3. Models (Persons)—United States—Biography. 4. Murder victims—California—Los Angeles—Biography. I. Veitch, Rick, illustrator. II. Title.
  PN2287.T168S36 2016
  791.4302'8092—dc23
  [B]

2015034145

Published by Da Capo Press
A Member of the Perseus Books Group
www.dacapopress.com

Da Capo Press books are available at special discounts for bulk purchases in the U.S. by corporations, institutions, and other organizations. For more information, please contact the Special Markets Department at the Perseus Books Group, 2300 Chestnut Street, Suite 200, Philadelphia, PA 19103, or call (800) 810-4145, ext. 5000, or e-mail special.markets@perseusbooks.com.

10 9 8 7 6 5 4 3 2 1

Contents

"The idea of happiness is indissolubly bound up with the idea of redemption. The same applies to the idea of the past, which is the concern of history. The past carries a secret index with it, by which it is referred to its resurrection."

—Walter Benjamin

On the Concept of History, 1940

Thanks

The author would like to thank Paul Whiteley, Charles Guenther, Miriam Sanders, Evans Frankenheimer, Joanne Pettet, Sheilah Wells, Greg King, Shahrokh Hatami, Sharmagne Leland-St. John-Sylbert, Kristine Larsen, Michael McGovern, William Federici, Judith Hansen, Jim Fitzgerald, Paul Dostie, Ben Schafer, and others for providing help and information useful to this book.

Dedication

This book is dedicated to the memory of Larry Larsen, investigator extraordinaire, good friend, and exemplary person.

Larry Larsen and I had a long history together, beginning in 1970 and 1971 when he helped research my book, *The Family,* and then continuing through the 1970s and beyond. He was doing good work in 2009–2010 on the life of Sharon Tate when suddenly he was diagnosed with leukemia. Larry struggled mightily, with the help of his wife, Toni, and went into remission, after which Larry continued to help with research, but then it came back and he passed away in December of 2010. His daughter Kristine, also a private investigator, brought her skills and expertise helping with research while I completed this book, but then she too was struck with illness.

Larry Larsen was raised in Nebraska, he met his high school sweetheart, Toni, in Omaha in 1954, and they were married in 1958. He graduated from the University of Omaha in 1965. Then they moved to California, driving along Route 66 hauling a small trailer. "I wanted to go to theology school," he told me. He attended Claremont College in 1967–1968. At the same time as studying theology, he began working as a private investigator. He was a devout Christian. He was probably the only private investigator in the history of Western civilization to have been a fan of the writing of Søren Kierkegaard. It may have been the either/orness of the private investigator world. He and Toni had two daughters, Lynda and Kristine, both of whom became private investigators.

He was a brilliant investigator—firm, with a never-give-up technique, yet liberal and forgiving in his world outlook. Larry had the uncanny ability to hang out for hours and hours with crusty homicide detectives or even intelligence officers to pick up information no one else could have acquired. He was just plain amazing—he could generate literally entire bankers boxes full of useful data for the many cases he took on.

I knew he had strong feelings and didn't like to be rejected. As a private eye, he had many a door shut in his face, and many people were even rude in refusing to talk with him, yet he carried out his work always with a smile on his face. He told me once, "a no is always a qualified yes." His utter calmness under the most trying of circumstances during those years investigating the Manson group showed his profound sense of right and wrong.

Throughout his life Larry donated much time to working for a better world, for a more ethical and humane social structure. For instance, in the early 1970s Larry was one of the four founders of a nonprofit group, Community Information Project, to do pro bono public research to help good causes. Larry said, "One of the many concrete things we did was to write a city lobbyist registration and regulation municipal ordinance for the City of Los Angeles."

From around 1975 to 1981, Larry served as a Los Angeles County deputy supervisor, with responsibilities for the investigation of public corruption. One of his duties was to help his boss, Supervisor Baxter Ward, conduct a lengthy investigation into the assassination of Senator Robert Kennedy. Larry was active in alternate energy in the early 1980s as president of a company called Pacific Solar and Wind, and oversaw construction of a wind farm on a mountain ridge near Tehachapi, located in Kern County, California.

Later he wrote a series of articles for my and my wife's newspaper, *The Woodstock Journal*, on hydrogen fuel cells. Throughout the thirty years we knew one another, Larry hungered to write a book. Together we collaborated on a number of book proposals. Among them were proposals for books on computer crime, on the Unabomber, and one on possible ballot fraud in the 2004 federal election.

Here's a poem I wrote in 1974 for Larry Larsen, in the midst of our early investigations:

Homage to Data
The incoming data-torrent
bejewels the Investigation Lotus

and only one addicted to
clusters of information fresh
will know the thrill
to hear the doorbell buzz
    at 7:30 A.M.,

on a chilly winter morning
& the postman proffer

a 7 pound special delivery package
   teeming with data:

of tapes, of court transcripts, of xerox'd secret files
from secret filing cabinets, and hard-won photos,

from Larry Larsen, Private Eye

in the course of a tortuous
path of investigation,
looking far and near
upon a ruthless Secret Society,
say, or now a killer,
now a kill-cult, now assassination, th'
minutiae building in
   the manila binders:

               o fill up the files
               o river of Data!

Larry Larsen was a beacon of integrity and he always brought a
spirit of fun and good vibes to his work. Ahh Larry, we miss you.

—Ed Sanders

Foreword

In early September of 1969 I flew to Los Angeles from New York City to turn in my solo album, *Sanders' Truckstop*, to Reprise Records, and to take photos for the album cover. I saw my usual friends in California, including Phil Ochs, Janis Joplin, and Reprise executive Andy Wickham. People were talking about the murders the previous month of Sharon Tate, Jay Sebring, Abigail Folger, Wojtek Frykowski, and a young man named Steven Parent at Sharon's house high in Benedict Canyon.

The filmmaker/actor Dennis Hopper, I was told, was spreading strange tales about the putative murderers, and Andy Wickham also had heard some of the same stories. These rumors made an impression on me as I returned to New York to work on the liner notes for my album.

Then, in early December, the police announced that the case had been solved with the arrests and indictments of a group of communally-living young people led by a singer/songwriter named Charles Manson. Remembering the rumors I had heard back in September, I started clipping articles about the case.

An assignment to write an article on the arrests for *Esquire* magazine fell through, but by then I had several file folders of information gathered, and my curiosity thoroughly piqued. I decided to write a book on the Manson group. I obtained a book contract, closed up my Peace Eye Bookstore on the Lower East Side, and abandoned putting a band together to promote *Sanders Truckstop*. This led to *The Family*, which came out in 1971, and has been since published in a number of updated editions.

Thus the chance trip to California in 1969 changed my life profoundly, so profoundly that it has led to this book tracing the life of Sharon Tate over forty years later. I was assisted in researching *The Family* by Los Angeles–based private investigator Larry Larsen. Larry and I stayed in touch over the years, and when in 2009 I decided to write a biography of Sharon Tate, Larsen agreed to assist once again in the research, utilizing his extensive connections with law enforcement sources in California, some of them once associated with the strands of investigation into the Manson group and what came to be known as the Tate-LaBianca murders. However, after just a few weeks work on researching the life of Sharon Tate, Larsen tragically developed severe leukemia, and naturally gave up the project in his intense struggle to beat back the disease, which proved fatal about a year later.

Without Larsen's crucial help, I was faced with considerable problems. Not only had a good number of those involved in the case passed away, but memories of long-ago events had faded. For instance, when I spoke with Martin Ransohoff, Sharon Tate's original Hollywood sponsor, he could not recall many of the events of that association.

As for tracing Sharon Tate's exact life-path, while there may be thousands of photos of her, and though her father reported that she kept a large number of mementos of her life and career, there's not that much detailed day-to-day information, such as diaries. Sharon Tate apparently did not keep a written and annotated trail of her life. Therefore, there are gaps and lacunae in all parts of her life—early, middle, and late.

I have sequenced her history, comparing various sources, as a tapestry of America during the twenty-six years she was given, which concluded with the marvelous and bumpity turbulence of the late 1960s. I reached out to a number of people who knew her, always trying to avoid "the cruel inquisitiveness of biographers," to quote writer William Gaunt in his book on the Pre-Raphaelite painters. Sometimes it was difficult to discern actual reality, given disparate versions provided by various sources of the same time-tracks, but I have stitched together the sequence that seems most accurate.

When her life was severed, her Catholic mother Doris began grieving like ancient Demeter, who roamed the world in ancient times looking for her kidnapped daughter Persephone. I became very impressed with her work for victims' rights. Doris Tate's path and mine crossed when I visited her home in 1989, plus we were on a television show together. After she learned I was corresponding with Charles Manson and asking him questions, she strongly urged me to ask him for the real story about why her daughter was killed. She was not satisfied with the official time-track—she hungered to know the truth and wanted me to help in that search. Sharon's sisters also suffered lasting grief. The efforts of Sharon's family to keep her memory alive are to be found in books, in numerous articles, and on tribute websites.

So, the reader can ask why it was that I decided to write this book. It's mainly because of the mystery that still surrounds the close of her life, and what I learned from investigators over the years. And because of what the novelist Graham Greene once wrote, in the voice of the intelligence officer in his novel *The Third Man*—"One's file, you know, is never quite complete, a case is never really closed, even after a century, when all of the participants are dead." In addition, I believe that there is a secret index to the past, what the philosopher Walter Benjamin described in *On the Concept of History:* "The past carries a secret index with it, by which it is referred to its resurrection." By resurrection I think Benjamin means its substantially accurate reconstruction. For over forty years I have searched for the secret index to the life of Sharon Tate, and during those decades I have come to admire her and respect her dreams of triumph.

There are a number of mysteries still associated with the murders of Sharon Tate, Jay Sebring, Wojtek Frykowski, Abigail Folger, and Steven Parent. One of the main ones is why was the house on Cielo Drive and its occupants chosen for this horrible crime? Why why why? It may take a century of sorting out the loose strands, and weaving them into a cogent unity, to discover some of the answers. Or it may never happen.

Meanwhile, here is my tracing of the life and times of an American actress, cut off so cruelly from her husband, child, family, friends, and future films by the so far untraceable mechanisms of Fate and Evil.

—**Ed Sanders**

Chapter 1

Early Years

The United States was newly at war in early 1942, after the Japanese sneak attack on Pearl Harbor in Hawaii on December 7, 1941. The nation was mobilizing. President Franklin Roosevelt signed a law enacting price controls in January, and directed the auto industry to transform its output to fit the needs of the war.

Sharon Tate's mother and father knew each other in high school in Houston, Texas, in the early 1940s, but Paul Tate was too shy to ask Doris out. Finally, in late 1941 or early 1942, Paul gathered courage to ask her to dance. The place was the then freshly built Sylvan Beach Pavilion that overlooked Galveston Bay. Young Paul and young Doris danced together on the large, circular hardwood dance floor in the center of a glass-walled octagonal ballroom, with a triangular-shaped wooden deck that jutted out toward the Galveston Bay shoreline. The music at Sylvan Beach, according to an account by Paul Tate, was provided by big bands such as those of Artie Shaw and Glenn Miller. Tate has written that "from that first dance with Doris, I was a man smitten."

Doris Gwendolyn Willett was eighteen when she married nineteen-year-old Paul Tate on January 16, 1942, in Houston. Paul was just commencing a career in the military. Houston was the largest city in Texas, and its economy thrived, beginning in 1942, through shipbuilding to aid the war.

Also in January of 1942, unknown to most Americans, the Nazis held a conference outside Berlin to plan what was called the Endlösung der Judenfrage, "The Final Solution of the Jewish Question." The Final Solution entailed the transportation of all Jews to a number of camps, where they were to be killed. This would impact severely the life of an eight-year-old boy in Warsaw who later become a well-known film director.

On January 24, 1943, just over twelve months after getting married, Doris Tate gave birth to a daughter, whom they named Sharon Marie. Though the nation was convulsed with war that year, Bing Crosby had sung Irving Berlin's "White Christmas" in the film *Holiday Inn,* and bandleader Glenn Miller disbanded his band, after his "Chattanooga Choo Choo" had sold 1.2 million the previous year, and began leading the US Air Force Band. Right around the time Sharon Marie Tate was born, Rogers and Hammerstein's great musical *Oklahoma!* was preparing to open on Broadway. Others born in 1943 included fellow Texan Janis Joplin, George Harrison, Robert De Niro, and Catherine Deneuve.

Across Poland Jews were being rounded up and taken away. On February 13, 1943, when Sharon Tate was under a month old, the ghetto residents of Krakow were warned that another German raid was at hand. So, on Valentine's Day, Bula Polanski took her nine-and-a-half-year-old son Romek (diminutive for Roman) to the home of a family named Wilk, and left him there, with an envelope of money, promising to return for him when the situation improved.

A couple of days later, Roman's father, Ryszard, came to the Wilk house to retrieve Roman. "They took your mother," the father told the son. Bula had been removed by German soldiers from Krakow to Auschwitz, where she would perish. His father also was soon taken from the ghetto to the Mauthausen-Gusen concentration camp, located in Upper Austria, one of the worst of the concentration camps, intended for the "Incorrigible Political Enemies of the Reich," where extermination through unbearable labor of the intelligentsia was practiced.

Desperate parents gave all their money, when they could, to non-Jewish families to take care of their children. Taking in a Jewish child was punishable by death, but a good number of Poles went ahead and sheltered such children. Young Roman wound up in the care of a Catholic family in Krakow who, in the spring of 1943, sent him to a farm whose Catholic owners apparently did not realize he was Jewish. He slept in the loft of a barn and spent his days in farm work.

When Sharon was three months old, the Warsaw Ghetto Uprising began, lasting from April 19 till May 16. Since 1940, a half-million Jews had been living walled up in the Warsaw ghetto. In July of 1942, three hundred thousand were taken away, most of them to the Treblinka concentration camp, so that by early 1943 there were maybe sixty thousand left. The Nazis wanted the ghetto cleared of Jews as a gift for Hitler's birthday on April 20, so two thousand marched against the ghetto on April 19 to destroy it. Jewish resistance groups, including the heroic Jewish Fighting Organization (ZOB) fought for the ghetto's every inch with pistols, molotov cocktails, grenades, some rifles, and a couple of machine guns. By May 8 the uprising headquarters was overwhelmed. Tens of thousands of Jews perished, and maybe seventy escaped. A few were helped by Polish sympathizers. By May 16, everything was rubble, and the Nazis dynamited the Tlomacki synagogue so that the ghetto ceased to exist.

Meanwhile, in the summer of 1943, some photos of the six-month-old Sharon Marie Tate were entered into a beauty contest for babies in Dallas. In one memoir Sharon's mother, Doris, recalls that it was Paul's mother, Nannie Tate, who submitted pictures of Sharon to the toddler contest, which Sharon won, picking up a $50 savings bond and the title Miss Tiny Tot of Dallas. It's not known whether mother Doris harbored for herself a yearning for the modeling, performance, or acting which she cultivated in her daughter. Whoever submitted the photos to the Tiny Tot contest, Doris, as the young wife of a frequently absent military officer husband, used her excess time to promote her beautiful daughter first in beauty contests, then as an actress in bit parts in Italy, and finally with a full career in Los Angeles.

Sharon Marie Tate proved during her twenty-six years on earth to be supremely photogenic. Was there ever anyone who from six months to age twenty-six had so many hundreds and thousands of posed pictures tracing her prettiness? The Internet alone has thousands, maybe tens of thousands, of photos of Sharon.

The same summer that Sharon was selected Miss Tiny Tot, on a farm about one hundred miles from his home city of Krakow, Poland, a young boy, not quite ten years old, was living under an assumed name. That summer the nine-year-old was pressed into vigorous religious practice, including praying each day, services each week at a Catholic church, and nighttime sessions a few times a week at a Catholic school. According to one biography, he was given the name Raimund Borocowska. According to another, "for most of the occupation, Raymond Polanski was known as Roman Wilk." Also Romek Wilk. His full name, given him when he was born in Paris on August 18, 1933, according to another biography, was Rajmund Roman Thierry Polanski. He answered through adolescence to the diminutive Romek.

The past is often like a quicksand bog, with fragments protruding upward here and there. This we know for certain, his later name: Roman Polanski. 1943 saw the publication of Jean-Paul Sartre's long exposition of existentialism, *Being and Nothingness*, just in time for the secret work of the Manhattan Project, and the first use of the bazooka, napalm, and then flamethrowers against Japanese soldiers in caves in the war.

An opportunity arose in the spring of 1944 to bomb enough of the Auschwitz concentration camp to keep it from further operating. Hitler was losing the war, and the United Press reported in May that thirty thousand Jews were being railroaded to Auschwitz. The American war secretary had an assistant secretary named John McCloy who turned down a request to bomb the railway lines to Auschwitz. He also turned down a request to bomb the camps themselves so that in the "confusion" at least some of the camp inmates could flee. McCloy once again answered with a no, writing that the camps were "beyond the maximum range" of Allied planes in the United Kingdom, Italy, and France. A terrible lie. Long-range American bombers had flown from Italy over Auschwitz looking for a nearby IG Farben petrochemical plant. And so, on August 20, 1944, over one hundred Flying Fortresses with one hundred Mustang fighters escorting tossed down 1,336 five-hundred-pound bombs to the east of Auschwitz less than five miles away!

It would likely have been too late for Roman's mother, Bula, who was killed in Auschwitz.

Finally in 1945, when Sharon was two going on three, World War II came to an end, the atomic bomb was dropped on Hiroshima and Nagasaki, and the birth pangs of the Cold War began. Her father Paul remained in the military, so that the family was subject to quick moves. Little Sharon Tate lived in Pasadena, Texas, and attended St. Pius V Catholic School from kindergarten to the second grade, 1948–1951. Her sister Debra Ann was born in 1953.

Throughout her preteen and teenage years, Sharon lived the typical roaming existence of an army child, moving from Dallas to Houston, El Paso, Tacoma, Washington, DC, and Verona, Italy. This peripatetic and straitened lifestyle— with new residences all the time on a soldier's salary (though the government provided affordable housing), might have helped her mother's resolve to help her very pretty daughter onto a path of Hollywood largess.

In 1954, Sharon and her family moved to Richland, located in the Tri-Cities area of Washington State where her father was stationed at nearby Camp Hanford.

Hanford is located at the site of a huge facility along the Columbia River in the southeastern part of the state, featuring a plutonium production complex with nine nuclear reactors, providing explosives for American nuclear weapons. The Fat Man bomb, which destroyed Nagasaki, was made with plutonium from the reactors at the Hanford site.

Hanford's plutonium processing, key to the building of nuclear weapons, was protected in the 1950s by batteries of Nike-Hercules missiles. Nike missile systems were put in place to intercept Soviet bombers that might target the plutonium plants. From the early 1950s to the mid-1970s, the army deployed Nike, Ajax, and Hercules missiles here and there in the continental United States to protect major metropolitan areas and important military installations such as Hanford from enemy attack. It is thought that Officer Paul Tate, who worked in army intelligence, was involved in the military personnel protecting the

Doris Tate and her daughter Sharon. In an interview in 1989, Doris told the author she had had a "bad childhood" and had tried to make Sharon's better than hers had been.

Nike-Hercules missile batteries, which themselves were guarding the plutonium plants at Hanford.

The huge Hanford plutonium processing site by the Columbia River has left a blighted environmental legacy. Plutonium is one of the most lethal substances—and an extremely small particle can kill a human. To this day, there is large-scale nuclear contamination from large leaking tanks of nuclear waste, ever spreading, years after Hanford was officially closed. However, during Sharon Tate's residence in Richland during the late 1950s, nothing about contamination ever entered conversations.

Sharon attended Richland's Spalding Elementary School in 1954–1955, then Chief Joseph Junior High from 1955 to 1958. Then there was at least a brief stay of the Tate family in Alameda, near San Francisco.

I have seen a photo showing Paul Tate, handing a suitcase from the trunk of an auto to daughter Sharon, with mother Doris nearby holding one of her sisters, Debra. The caption on this photo reads: "S. Paul J. Tate and family moving into the first home of New Government Leasing Program at 2815 Otis Drive Alameda—13 February 1956—San Francisco—California."

Sergeant Tate and Doris's third daughter, Patricia Gaye, was born in 1957.

Sharon attended Columbia High School in Richland, Washington, in 1958–1959. The Columbia High athletic teams were called the Bombers, and had as their insignia an atomic mushroom cloud! Sharon showed her prettiness and popularity when she was voted a homecoming princess, and she served as a member of the student council.

Meanwhile in Poland in 1954, when Sharon Tate was eleven, Roman Polanski began to study at the Polish National Film School in Lodz, after much effort to get admitted. Postwar Poland had one of the finest film academies in the world. "Lenin said cinema was the most important art form that existed," Roman Polanski said in a later interview with *Cahiers du Cinéma*, "something that gave a lot of prestige to filmmakers. This meant the Communists didn't dare interfere too much with us."

In the spring of 1959, Roman Polanski graduated from the National Film School, thoroughly trained in the formal techniques of filmmaking. He had already filmed some strange short pieces. His first completed brief film, *Murderer*, lasted two minutes and showed an unknown killer stabbing a sleeping man with a penknife. Another early eight-minute film, *Break Up the Dance*, starred a group of youths arriving at a dance followed by a bunch of hooligans who climb a fence and begin to break up the festivities, shoving girls to the floor, tossing people into the water, and beating up the celebrants.

Sharon Winning Beauty Contests

Early in 1959, the same year that Polanski graduated from film school, Columbia High sophomore Sharon won a beauty contest in Richland, Washington. That is, she had a job as a hostess for the first Tri-City Autorama show where she was made "Queen of the Autorama." The show was conducted at the hangar at the Pasco, Washington, airport.

An article six years later in the *TriCity Herald*, Richland, Washington, September 5, 1965, read, "Sharon is no stranger to spotlights. At the age of 16, while a student at Columbia High, she was chosen both Miss Richland of the 1959 Atomic Frontier Days and Miss Autorama of 1958–59." The article also noted that in April 1959, as "Queen of the 1959 Tri-City Autorama," she "greeted crowds at the three-day grand opening event of Farley Chevrolet Co. at 3rd Avenue and Columbia Street." A home movie was made of pretty Sharon, sporting a tiara and resplendent in a saffron-colored full gown opening the trunk and front door of an automobile. There was a picture of her in the local paper under the headline, "Beautiful Girl, Beautiful Car Queen, Sharon Tate." The lure of renown was beginning its sparkle.

She was set to enter the "Miss Washington" pageant in 1960, and then would have competed, as her mother, Doris, later recalled, for the Miss America title, but before she could compete for Miss America, the Fates intervened and her father, Paul, was promoted to Captain and sent to the "G2 Southern European Task Force" at Passelaqua Army Base, near Verona, in northern Italy. Headstrong Sharon announced she was staying in Washington. Arguments ensued, but finally Sharon went with her family to Verona.

According to an article in the *El Paso Times*, Sharon spent the fall session of 1959, half of her junior year, at Irvin High School in El Paso, Texas. "Her parents, Mr. and Mrs. P. J. Tate, Miss Tate and two younger sisters, resided at 9303 Roanoke. Tate who was then a captain in the army, was later reassigned to Verona, Italy, and the family moved there in January, 1960. El Pasoans recalled Miss Tate as a very 'vibrant, happy and beautiful young lady with very strict parents.'" Very strict parents indeed. Her father especially, but her mother? Not so strict, but wary. Sometimes very wary.

It's possible that Captain Tate's work in army intelligence had to do with protecting a new generation of Nike-Hercules surface-to-air missiles, some equipped with nuclear explosives, which were placed in batteries near Verona.

In the spring of 1960, Sharon starred in a photograph published in the military newspaper, *Stars and Stripes*. The cover pic revealed her in a dark bathing suit wearing a cowboy hat and holding a lariat while sitting astride a long narrow white missile which bore the letters "U.S. Army."

It had already made her locally famous before her arrival at the American High School at Vicenza, near Verona. She was instantly popular and developed friendships among young people also from military backgrounds who had, like Sharon, felt alienation from frequent uprootings and being taken to new military locations, new streets, unforeseen houses, and unforeseen classmates.

The missile astride which the Western-attired, lariat-twirling young woman sat smiling may actually have been a Nike-Hercules missile, of the sort that

Seventeen-year-old Sharon Tate sits astride a missile.

protected the Hanford plant in the state of Washington, and the US installations near Verona.

The Vicenza American High School is run by the Department of Defense, and is located in Vicenza, Italy, on Caserma Ederle, an American military base within the US Army Southern European Task Force (SETAF). The Vicenza-Verona area is picturesquely beautiful, and has a long and complicated history leading back to the Renaissance, to Medieval times, then to Roman and Etruscan times. Vicenza was the birthplace of one of Italy's finest architects, Andrea Di Pietro Palladio, whose works in Vicenza include the city's museum, the Teatro Olimpico, and the Duomo.

That March of 1960, as Sharon was just about to settle in to the routines of Vicenza American High School, Roman Polanski set out for Paris (where

Nike-Hercules Missile

he had been born.) Roman's older half-sister Annette had survived Auschwitz, moved to Paris, gotten married, and invited Roman to visit. Polanski was determined to get out of Poland to the West just as young Sharon Tate was soon determined to get to Hollywood.

Roman was asked later about this first trip to Paris. He replied: "In those times you couldn't even dream of leaving Poland. It was like the Wall in Germany. No one was allowed a passport, no one was allowed to leave. I had my sister who went from Auschwitz back to Paris. You know, Paris was really her place. She lived there before. She was older than me. She got married after the war and I learned that she was alive living in Paris. We corresponded and she invited me to come. Then great changes happened in Poland and I finally got my passport. That was my first visit to this town and it was fabulous. You cannot imagine what it means for someone who lived in that gray, drab, communist reality to visit a Western city. Paris above all. But I was still at the film school, so I returned."

Roman went home to Poland, and with a complicated youthful enthusiasm, began his drive to make his first feature film, *Knife in the Water*. In an essay by Polanski in 1963, he described making films at that time in Poland: "There are eight production groups in Poland and I'm a member of the Kamera Group.

When I have an idea, I submit it to my group leader. If he likes it, he'll ask me to develop it into a script that can be presented to the commission. If the commission rejects it, I'm not able to make the film. The commission deals only with feature films—for shorts it's different because they're less expensive and fewer people are involved. My teacher was responsible for my work and gave his approval for two or three films I made at the Lodz Film Academy." The Kamera Group ultimately approved state funding for *Knife in the Water*, and filming commenced in the summer of 1961.

Meanwhile, Sharon became fairly fluent in Italian. One disturbing event occurred when she was raped, at age seventeen, apparently by a soldier on a date, about which she told Roman Polanski on their first date (in London in 1966). She confided in her future husband, in Polanski's words, that "it hadn't left her emotionally scarred." Otherwise, she kept quiet about the incident and didn't tell her mother and father. Perhaps she was afraid it might have gravely upset her father, and if it were spread abroad, might impinge negatively on his military career.

Her interest in becoming an actress led her, and some friends, to observe and even to participate in several Hollywood films being shot nearby. In 1960, Sharon picked up her first on-screen credit, appearing in an episode dated May 5, for the ABC series, filmed in Venice, of *The Pat Boone-Chevy Showroom*.

In 1960, after Sharon was spotted by the talent scout for the Pat Boone's special, Doris and Sharon went to Venice for a rehearsal. Pat Boone himself promised that he and his wife would be sure no harm came to Doris's daughter.

The scene in which Sharon was filmed took place in Venice's San Marco Square. The wind was severe and sloshed the waters of the canal over the boat's edge, soaking Sharon in her blue satin dress. The experience apparently was the one that hooked her into pursuing a show business career.

After the appearance on the Pat Boone special, Doris hesitantly allowed Sharon to work as an extra in various films, including *Vengeance of the Three Musketeers*.

"Sharon, I remember you so well when we were in Verona," recalled Vicenza High School friend Linda Franke in a posting on the Sharon Tate family website. "It was so wonderful knowing such a nice, warm person! I especially remember the prom when you doubled with Donna and Don and your summer job at the kiddie area at Lake Garda." (Lake Garda is the largest lake in Italy, formed by glaciers in the last ice age. It's located about halfway between Venice and Milano.)

Sharon was a cheerleader for the Vicenza Cougars football team, and in the fall of 1960 was selected queen of the homecoming dance. In the spring of 1961 she was queen of the prom.

There was an advertisement in the Vicenza High School newspaper seeking extras for the Anthony Quinn/Jack Palance movie, *Barabbas*. This Biblical epic starred Anthony Quinn as the thief pardoned in lieu of Jesus, and tracked his troubled life.

Also starring was Jack Palance as a sadistic gladiator named Torvald. Sharon won the job as an extra in a crowd scene viewing a fight.

In his autobiography, *Just Tell Me When to Cry*, director Richard Fleischer writes of shooting the climax of the gladiatorial fight between Anthony Quinn and Jack Palance before an audience of thousands. "Tony is victorious," notes Fleischer, "and the crowd calls for Palance's death. Nine thousand people screaming, with their thumbs down! What a shot! On the second day of shooting we were working closer to the crowd and I could scrutinize it. I was looking for good character faces I could feature in various reaction shots. There were some excellent types, but one face truly stood out, that of an eighteen-year-old girl of stunning beauty. She was gorgeous. A knockout. I pointed her out to my assistant and told him I wanted her in every close shot I could possibly use her in. And I asked him to find out who she was and where she came from. It turned out she was the daughter of an officer at the US military base in Vincenza."

The beauty also found the attention of Jack Palance, who sought her out, bringing her to Rome for a screen test, where she was accompanied by Doris, who was ever her willing urger. She also went out for a dinner date with Palance, which her mother allowed. Nothing came of all this attention, except perhaps the steeling of resolve to make it in the movies.

At the suggestion of Ernest Hemingway, Verona was set as the location in the summer of 1961 for *The Adventures of a Young Man*, a movie based on Hemingway's Nick Adams short stories. Hemingway himself wrote the opening and closing narration, and was scheduled to deliver it, but he killed himself at his home in Ketchum, Idaho, on July 2, 1961. While on location in Verona, cast and crew received word of Hemingway's suicide.

Directed by Martin Ritt and written by Hemingway biographer A. E. Hotchner, the film traces the life-voyage of a young man from Middle America coming to manhood after a cross-country journey followed by military service in World War I. This film sequences ten of Hemingway's Nick Adams stories into one complete whole, with the story sequence realized by various well-known actors and actresses. Richard Beymer starred as Nick Adams, with roles also taken by Dan Dailey, Arthur Kennedy, Ricardo Montalban, Paul Newman, Susan Strasberg, Jessica Tandy, Eli Wallach, and others. The latter portion of the film set in Italy is drawn from Hemingway's novel *A Farewell to Arms*.

By happenstance, Sharon and a group of her friends, while on an outing, came upon the crew filming *Adventures of a Young Man* in Verona. Sharon and some of her pals obtained parts as film extras. After the shoot, the youngsters were mingling with the cast, some of them seeking autographs from the stars. Beymer spotted the attractive Tate, introduced himself, invited her to lunch with the cast, and then they began to date during the time the production crew was in Verona. They became close, and he won the trust of Paul and Doris both. Paul Tate was known to grill potential beaus. (Also noticing Sharon was Susan Strasberg, who encouraged Sharon to study with her father Lee at his influential Actor's Studio in New York City. This encouragement led Sharon, later on in late 1963, briefly to journey to New York City to study with Strasberg.)

Richard Beymer's career was heating up around the time he began to date young Sharon Tate. He had a big role (as Tony) in *West Side Story*, which was released in October of that year. Leonard Bernstein's film was well received by the public and critics as well, and became the second-highest money maker of the year in the United States. The film was distinguished as being the musical with the most Academy Award wins (ten wins), including Best Picture. The soundtrack album made more money than any other movie track before it.

A few months after meeting Sharon, Beymer had a substantial role in *The Longest Day*, a World War II film based on the book by Cornelius Ryan that tells the story of the invasion of Normandy on June 6, 1944, from both the Allied and German points of view. This was followed by playing Joanne Woodward's youthful love interest in *The Stripper*.

Gossip columnist Hedda Hopper had a paragraph about Beymer in a piece published in late December in the *Los Angeles Times*, which mentioned Sharon. "It's all over between Richard Beymer and French sexpot Dany Saval after he gave her a ring and other attractive baubles. She must have been too flamboyant for his conservative upbringing. He's consoling himself in Verona, Italy, with 19 year old Sharon Tate who wants to be an actress."

As for film student Roman Polanski, that summer of 1961, he was filming his first feature, *Knife in the Water,* in the Polish lake country, paid for by the Polish Communist government.

Meanwhile, at her graduation dinner from Vincenza High, Sharon told her parents she did not intend to go to college. Sharon said, "Richard said he'll introduce me to his agent in California." And how would she survive? her parents wanted to know. On what money? Sharon replied, "I'll use my graduation money and savings bond."

Around that time her father received notice of a promotion and a transfer to San Pedro, California, south of Los Angeles. Sharon was persistent in her eagerness to get back to the States, so it was agreed that she would go to Los Angeles alone a few months ahead of her family, apparently on the ruse that she wanted to examine potential colleges. In fact, she had really two goals—to pursue work in films, and to continue her relationship with Richard Beymer, who had returned to Los Angeles after work on the Hemingway film was completed.

Upon her arrival in Los Angeles, she stayed temporarily at a friend's home in Nichols Canyon and looked up Richard Beymer. (Mr. Beymer refused an interview with the author in order to clear up the muddy time-track for Sharon during her time alone in Los Angeles in 1961.)

The true past can be like quicksand.

Her letters from Los Angeles back to her parents in Italy had disturbing mentions of her desires to become an actress, and thus precipitously to go her own path. Doris suffered great separation anxiety over Sharon's living in Los Angeles without her family. An anxiety that was ever increasing. She saw several doctors, one of whom diagnosed Doris with "acute separation anxiety disorder." Faced with her mother's increasing agitation, Sharon reluctantly returned to Italy.

One biographer of Sharon has written about Doris Tate's mind-state during the family's final months in Italy, pointing out that "she was using Sharon as a way to escape her life, as at that point her marriage was disintegrating and she was spiraling into depression and addiction as well. There was A LOT of tension in that house." At the same time, the biographer noted that the mother was very afraid of losing control over her beautiful daughter.

Things finally worked themselves out, and around February of 1962, the entire Tate family, including Sharon, sailed to the United States aboard the USS *Independence*. One account holds that Sharon befriended seventeen-year-old starlet Joey Heatherton on the cross-ocean voyage.

Sharon's father, now a major, was assigned to Fort MacArthur, a US Army installation in San Pedro, Los Angeles, California (now the port community of Los Angeles), named for General Arthur MacArthur Jr. (father of General Douglas MacArthur). During the early years of the Cold War, Fort MacArthur was a key part of the West Coast's anti-aircraft defenses, becoming the home base of the 47th Anti-Aircraft Artillery Brigade. A Nike surface-to-air missile battery was activated at the fort in 1954, remaining in service until the early 1970s. It is thought that Major Tate's intelligence work involved the protecting of Nike missile sites.

Sharon wasted no time in continuing her quest for triumph in the world of celluloid. Two or three weeks after returning to the United States, she called Richard Beymer's agent, Hal Gefsky, who, as a favor to Beymer, agreed to meet with her.

By now, Sharon Tate was fully evolved into what the nineteenth-century novelist Balzac called *la torpille*, a torpedo or stingray—a stunner who could astound someone or a group just with her entrance. Hal Gefsky was properly stunned by her beauty, and agreed to help get her work. Her parents provided some limited financial assistance. After all, they were not having to come up with college tuition.

In an article titled "Sharon Tate Leaves You Breathless" and written several years later, writer Robert Musel quotes Sharon on these early searching days: "You must remember," she said, tracing her breathless tale, "that I was shy and bashful when I reached Hollywood. My parents were very strict with me. I didn't smoke or anything. I only had just enough money to get by and I hitch-hiked a ride on a truck to the office of an agent whose name I had. That very first day he sent me to the cigarette commercial job. A girl showed me how it should be done, you know taking a deep, deep breath and look ecstatic."

"I tried to do as she said," Miss Tate explained, "but the first breath filled my lungs with smoke and I landed on the floor. The commercial required many takes. Just when they were ready for the final one, I passed out from taking too many puffs on my first attempt at smoking. That ended my career in cigarette commercials." She'd never before smoked anything, and began coughing nonstop.

In the summer of 1962, she cut a commercial for Chevrolet automobiles and one for Santa Fe cigars. Also she was employed as a wine hostess for Lipper Productions, serving Kelly / Kalani Wine.

She continued her friendship with Richard Beymer, including a love affair. After a while she saved enough so that she could move into her own apartment on Fuller Street, in a building managed by Richard Beymer's mother, Eunice.

Meanwhile, it would have been around early 1962, perhaps in the spring, just after Sharon had returned to California, that Richard Beymer went on location to various sites in France for *The Longest Day*. (The movie was released on October 4, 1962.)

Next for Beymer was a film initially titled *Celebration*. Columnist Hedda Hopper inserted another paragraph about Beymer on July 9, 1962, "Richard Beymer is smart. When he finishes *Celebration*, he's giving up his house here, selling his car, and hopping to New York to study acting for three weeks before starting *A Promise at Dawn* with Ingrid Bergman. 'Playing opposite Bergman is a wonderful opportunity, and I intend to be prepared,' said Dick. When they start filming in England, he'll be across the channel from Sharon Tate (daughter of an Army officer he dated while doing *The Longest Day*). As far as his romance with French actress Dany Saval, Beymer says it's over: 'She wasn't about to leave Paris—and my career is here.'"

William Inge, author of the hit Broadway plays *Picnic, Bus Stop,* and *The Dark at the Top of the Stairs,* won an Academy Award in 1961 for *Splendor in the Grass* (Best Writing, Story, and Screenplay—Written Directly for the Screen). He had a further Broadway play, *A Loss of Roses* (starring Warren Beatty, Carol Haney, and Betty Field), which became 1963's *The Stripper,* with Richard Beymer taking on Warren Beatty's part.

Filming for *The Stripper* (with the working title of *Celebration*) occurred in 1962 in the small town of Chino, California, about thirty-five miles from downtown Los Angeles. In the film, Lila Green (Joanne Woodward) is an insecure and aging showgirl for Madame Olga's stage shows. When her boyfriend, Rick, runs off with the show's money, Madame Olga lets Lila go, and Lila goes to live with her old neighbors, Helen Baird and her teenage son Kenny (Richard Beymer). Lila decides to go out and get a regular job and try and live a normal life. Then Lila and Kenny have an affair.

It's not clear whether Sharon Tate was with Beymer during the filming of *The Stripper.*

As for *A Promise at Dawn,* which gossiper Hedda Hopper wrote Beymer was so excited about, it met with the Fox axe. There was turmoil at Fox studios, and three pictures scheduled for production were cancelled. Among those given the zilch notice was *A Promise at Dawn,* starring Ingrid Bergman, based on Romain Gary's book of memoirs, and *Take Her, She's Mine,* with James Stewart.

While Sharon was jumping up and down to get to Hollywood, in the spring of 1962, in an aged Mercedes convertible, Roman Polanski drove from Poland on the way to Paris, with his worldly possessions aboard, including a print of his first full-length motion picture, *Knife in the Water.* It had been released without much fanfare in Poland on March 9. Even so, he had managed to complete a complicated project. It was quite a feat. The formidable tasks of making a feature-length film—raising the money; creating the script; doing the casting, the directing, and the costumes; inspiring good performances; thousands of decisions on the lighting, the sets, and locations; finding a good crew; editing; sequencing; adding music; dubbing—were all difficult, sometimes maddeningly difficult. But, he had completed a feature-length, professionally directed and filmed work.

At the 1962 Venice Film Festival, *Knife in the Water* received the Special Critic's Award, and it was commercially distributed in Italy, in Scandinavia, and in France.

While in Paris, Polanski was invited to the first New York Film Festival. A gigantic break! *Knife in the Water* was shown there on September 11, 1963, after which it was nominated for an Academy Award as the best foreign picture.

Chapter 2

Discovered by a Producer

Around April of 1963, Sharon's agent, Hal Gefsky, arranged for her to audition for a television series in preparation that was then called *Whistle Stop* but was soon to become *Petticoat Junction* and was produced by a company called Filmways for CBS-TV.

Filmways was a very successful producer of both movies and television series. The series *Whistle Stop* was to be a spinoff of another triumphant series called *The Beverly Hillbillies*. Filmways was casting for three unknown young women to appear in *Whistle Stop*, and Herb Browar, Gefsky's contact at Filmways, gave the go-ahead for Sharon Tate to come to the studio for an audition.

Set in the rural town of Hooterville, the show followed the goings-on at the Shady Rest Hotel, of which Kate Bradley (Bea Benaderet) was the proprietor. Her lazy Uncle Joe Carson (Edgar Buchanan) helped her in the day-to-day running of the business, while she served as a mediator in the various minor crises that befell her three daughters: Betty Jo, Bobbie Jo, and Billie Jo. The petticoat of the title is an old-fashioned garment once worn under a woman's skirt. The opening titles of the series featured a display of petticoats hanging on the side of a large railroad water tank where the three daughters are skinnydipping.

Just as Hal Gefsky had been blown away by Tate's stunningness, so too was Herb Browar. He was so stunned, he rang for Filmway's head Martin Ransohoff, who was in the midst of a shoot, and urged him to come check out the beauty in his office.

Ransohoff, then thirty-six, had been instrumental in developing the early careers of such screen stars as Ann-Margret and Tuesday Weld, and remained eager to "discover a beautiful girl who's a nobody, and turn her into a star everybody wants. I'll do it like Louis B. Mayer at Metro-Goldwyn-Mayer used to, only better. But once she's successful, then I'll lose interest."

Browar brought Sharon to Mr. Ransohoff, whose camera crew was still in place, and upon gazing at the stunning beauty, Ransohoff asked her to do an on-the-spot screen test. This she did.

"Marty saw me there," Miss Tate later recalled, "and he said 'Baby'—you know how Marty talks—'Baby, we're going to make you a star.' He took me to his legal department and he said, 'Sign this girl.'" (Quotes from an article by Robert Musel in *Stars and Stripes*, 1965)

"I thought he meant somebody else. I could not believe he was talking about me. I looked so awful. I was wearing an orange dress with big patch pockets and my hair was all over the place. I still can't believe all this is happening to me. It seems like a dream," she said.

The next day Sharon had a meeting at Filmways and brought along her mother from Fort MacArthur. Ransohoff, Sharon, and Doris watched the results of Sharon's screen test from the day before.

Ransohoff and his partner John Calley then negotiated an exclusive seven-year contract between Sharon and Filmways. Hal Gefsky represented Sharon, and secured around $750 a month for her.

"Up until then, I had been living on a tight allowance from my folks and what with my sheltered life and all I had never even driven a car. But when I signed with Marty the contract provided for a car and that was the first thing I got. That and a dog."

Sharon Tate was too timid and unskilled to take on a substantial role in *Petticoat Junction*. (On September 14, 1963, *Petticoat Junction* debuted at 9:00 p.m., following *The Red Skelton Hour* and just before *The Jack Benny Show*. Millions of viewers were introduced to the community of Hooterville for the first time. The show was an immediate hit.)

Meanwhile, young Sharon Tate submitted to Ransohoff's will, and immediately began various lessons, including working with a drama coach, singing lessons in Pasadena, and daily workouts at a gym. Ransohoff not only filled her days with classes in gymnastics and acting, but also she was coached on how to walk, dress, and even talk. He took care of even the smallest of details on eating, and eating techniques, and even the car she drove.

She was just twenty years old.

Sharon moved into the all-women Hollywood Studio Club, "a chaperoned dormitory," which existed to house young women in the motion picture business. The Studio Club existed from 1916 to 1975, was operated by the YWCA, and was located in downtown Hollywood. It was packed with karma; it had been the home at one time or another to Marilyn Monroe, Donna Reed, Kim Novak, Maureen O'Sullivan, Rita Moreno, Barbara Eden, and many others. The building was designed by California architect Julia Morgan, who also designed Hearst Castle.

At the Hollywood Studio Club, her first roommate attempted to lure her into a lesbian relationship, so she prevailed on her agent Hal Gefsky, who helped her to change roommates, and thus she moved in with a young actress named Mary Winters.

Leonard Lyons's column, "The Lyons Den," originating in the *New York Post*, was reprinted in newspapers all over the nation. Here's one with a couple of paragraphs about Sharon, from April 25, 1963: "Four weeks ago Sharon Tate, a 20-year-old blonde beauty, left her home in Verona, where her father is a US Army intelligence officer. She was intent on a career as an actress. Her father gave her the passage from Italy to Hollywood, plus $42 cash. The money was for two weeks' rent in Hollywood. He gave her the two weeks to launch her career.

"It took Miss Tate four weeks. She managed the additional rent and food money by doing a TV commercial. Then she was seen, and tested, by Marty Ransohoff of Filmways. He just signed her to a seven-year contract. She'll make her debut with Lee Remick and Jim Garner in *The Wheeler Dealers*."

This Leonard Lyons column tends to date the meeting of Ransohoff and Tate in the spring of 1963. The author spoke with Mr. Ransohoff during the writing of this book, and his memory was lacking as to the particulars of both his contract with Tate and the date of the contract.

Some Sharon Tate chronologies have her working as an extra that spring of 1963 both in Filmways's *The Wheeler Dealers* and *The Americanization of Emily*, a satiric anti-war comedy written by Paddy Chayevsky and starring Julie Andrews. It was Andrews's first movie after her Broadway run in *Camelot*; this was also the era in which Andrews made *The Sound of Music*.

Controversial upon its original release, *The Americanization of Emily* is a vanguard anti-war film, poking fun at mindless patriotism years before such films were fashionable or popularly accepted. Yet the film proved a commercial success, and earned Academy Award nominations for Best Cinematography, Best Art Direction, and Best Musical Score.

As for *The Wheeler Dealers*, it is a comedy film starring James Garner and Lee Remick and featuring Chill Wills and Jim Backus. In a fairly complicated and convoluted story line, stockbroker Lee Remick is assigned a task by an overbearing sexist boss (Jim Backus) so as to deliberately get her to fail and thus for her boss to be able to fire her. Along comes a "Texas millionaire" (really an Ivy League–educated easterner in disguise, played by James Garner) to her assistance. A romance ensues, bouncing along up and down between Remick and Garner, with a more or less happy ending through comedic plot twists.

There is no evidence of Sharon Tate anywhere in *The Wheeler Dealers* or in *The Americanization of Emily*, although it's possible that footage of her may have ultimately nested upon the cutting-room floor.

Nevertheless, all of these Ransohoff films made an impression on the newly-acquired Sharon Tate—they gave her the impetus to obey her new mentor, study hard, work out, take voice lessons, and Wait for Her Day in the Sun.

Meanwhile, that summer of 1963, Sharon met a young actor from Paris named Philippe Forquet, born on September 27, 1940. He, as she, was stunningly attractive. They met while Sharon was having lunch with her agent Hal Gefsky. A person from Twentieth Century Fox approached the table with the tall, handsome Forquet. Sharon and Forquet talked avidly, and agreed to meet later for dinner.

Now known as Philippe Forquet Viscount de Dorne, back in 1962, when he was a student in Paris, he was discovered by American director Robert Parrish, who gave him a role in the film *In the French Style* (released in 1963). Forquet took on the role of the gorgeously handsome younger boyfriend of Jean Seberg, known throughout the world for her work in the Otto Preminger film *Saint Joan* (1957).

His mother, Countess Forquet de Dorne, stoutly protested when her son left French Classical Academy to star in the hit movie *Take Her, She's Mine* (1963), also starring James Stewart and Sandra Dee, a huge teen star of the era (married to singer Bobby Darin). Producers at Twentieth Century Fox thought Mr. Forquet would join the stream of French movie stars in Hollywood, such as Maurice Chevalier and Yves Montand, so he was brought to Los Angeles and prepared to be transformed into the new Louis Jourdan or Alain Delon.

In this "generation gap" creation of 1963, Sandra Dee stars as teenage rebel Mollie Michaelson, fascinated with long-haired proto-hippies and radical anti-nuclear political causes. Her involvement makes her ultraconservative father Frank (James Stewart) very upset. Frank's wife is played by Audrey Meadows. Frank's anguish broadens when Mollie is sent to Paris on an art scholarship. Back in the United States, Frank spots the cover of a magazine on which his daughter has posed for a radical artist, Henri Bonnet (played by Philippe Forquet). Dad flies over the ocean to save his daughter from further disgrace, but he ends up in a café in Paris just as it is raided by police. They arrest him on false charges, and he spends a bunch of 35 mm footage to prove that he's not guilty.

Such was the movie in which Philippe Forquet was involved when he met Sharon Tate. One account of the young Forquet reads: "His dark good looks and

Gallic charm caused quite a flurry among the ladies. He received thousands of fan letters a week."

Sharon's relationship with Forquet blossomed forth.

On October 13, 1963, Tate had her first walk-on appearance in a Filmways production, an episode of *Mister Ed*, the saga of a palomino who could talk with his owner. The same week, she had her first speaking role in a Filmways production, a role in *The Beverly Hillbillies* TV show.

Beginning in the fall of 1963, Sharon Tate had roles in a sequence of episodes of *The Beverly Hillbillies,* including "Elly Starts to School," "Jethro's First Love," "Chickadee Returns," "The Clampetts Are Overdrawn," "The Clampetts Go Hollywood," "The Garden Party," "Elly Needs a Maw," and finally, "The Clampetts Get Culture." In most of these episodes Tate took on the role of secretary Janet Trego.

She also appeared in several *Mister Ed* episodes, including "Ed Discovers America" and "Love Thy New Neighbor."

During the autumn, just before the assassination of John F. Kennedy, while she filmed episodes of *Mister Ed* and *The Beverly Hillbillies,* Sharon attended classes with drama coach Jeff Corey, taking singing lessons in Pasadena and working out daily at the Beverly Hills Gym. Jeff Corey had been an established character actor, but his career was stymied in the 1950s when he refused to give names, and even ridiculed the House Un-American Activities Committee, and thus was blacklisted for around twelve years, unable to find work in Hollywood. He became a very successful acting teacher. His students included, besides Sharon Tate, James Dean, Jane Fonda, Peter Fonda, Rita Moreno, Jack Nicholson, Leonard Nimoy, Anthony Perkins, Rob Reiner, Barbra Streisand, and Robin Williams.

Another Tate coach was Charles Conrad, who had been trained as an acting coach under the far-famed Sanford Meisner, head of New York City's Neighborhood Playhouse, where he coached such famous actors as Robert Duvall, Jack Nicholson, Susan Sarandon, and Joanne Woodward, as well as counterculture hero Wavy Gravy. By the 1960s he had established the Charles Conrad Studio in Burbank, at which Sharon Tate studied. "Such a beautiful girl," he later commented. "You would have thought she would have all the confidence in the world. But she had none."

Right around the time Sharon Tate was performing in *Mister Ed*, in October of 1963 Roman Polanski's first feature film, *Knife in the Water,* opened commercially in New York City. *Knife in the Water* had been chosen as a Polish entry in the upcoming New York Film Festival. It was distributed by Kanawha Films, Ltd., a company formed by Archer King, the theatrical agent and producer, and Paul Peralta-Ramos, president of the Millicent A. Rogers Foundation.

An article by Eugene Archer in the *New York Times* on July 14, 1963, noted that "the aim" of Kanawha Films was to show "quality films of modest budget which might be overlooked by blockbuster distributors." *Knife in the Water* was described as "a drama about a sports writer, his beautiful wife and a young hitchhiker who joins them on a sinister yachting cruise."

A blurb in the *New York Times* on September 8, 1963 read: "September 11, 1963, New York Film Festival, at Lincoln Center, *Knife in the Water* (Polish *Nóz w Wodzie*) Critics' Award winner at last year's Venice Festival, a squarish couple pick up a beatnik boy, invite him aboard their boat. Soon the underlying tensions explode. First, the difference between generations, the sexual conflicts. A daring film by Roman Polanski."

On September 26, 1963, art director Richard Sylbert, whose previous art directions included *Lilith* and *The Manchurian Candidate,* was named art director of the forthcoming *The Pawnbroker,* which would start filming in October of 1963. Sylbert would also be the art director of Polanski's *Rosemary's Baby.*

In the *New York Times* on October 28, 1963: "Today's new film is *Knife in the Water,* a Polish-made drama with English subtitles, directed by Roman Polanski, which opens at the Beekman Theater, Second Avenue and 65th Street. The cast of the import, released here by Kanawha Films, Ltd., includes Leon Niemszyk, Jolanta Umecka and Zygmunt Malanowicz."

Bosley Crowther, *New York Times* critic, issued an opinion on *Knife in the Water* on November 3, 1963: "It is a slight and casual contemplation of the hostile behavior of the two men toward one another during the course of a day's outing, while the woman superciliously looks on. She's the wife of the older of the two contenders, the owner of the boat, who is ludicrously ostentatious and bullying toward his guest. So it isn't particularly surprising that eventually she, in her disgust, gives herself to the less successful show-off and then is spiteful toward both of them."

Not that many weeks after Polanski's triumph at the New York Film Festival, Sharon Tate was sent by Mr. Ransohoff to New York to take classes at Lee Strasberg's Actor's Studio. It was December of 1963. She and Philippe Forquet shared an apartment reportedly on Lexington Avenue and 78th Street. Another account had her living at 42nd Street and Third Avenue.

The truth of the past can be a bit like quicksand.

The teaching was not to Sharon's taste, so she stayed for just a few weeks studying with Strasberg. Forquet was also taking acting lessons. During dinner one evening, Forquet asked her to marry him, and she said yes.

A few weeks later they returned to Los Angeles. Ransohoff was not happy about the engagement, nor were her parents. (And Forquet's huffy mother,

Sharon and Philippe were engaged. Forquet left Hollywood for a while, and the relationship with Sharon went pffft.

Countess Forquet de Dorne, also weighed in with a no-no.) Ransohoff demanded Sharon break it off or he would dissolve the Filmways contract with her. Forquet recalled later that Sharon's mother, Doris, spoke of all the money that Sharon would not earn if she gave up her quest to become a successful actress.

Sharon seemed attracted to dominance. One biography of Roman states it like this: "The men she was attracted to were the dominant type, like her father. Unlike her father, they also tended to be brutal. (Forquet) once beat her up so badly, according to Sharon's mother, that she had to be rushed to a hospital for emergency treatment."

This much is true: they lived together, and became engaged. The rumors that he beat her, with Sharon requiring hospitalization, hit the tabloids. But was it true? Vague shadows in a vague timeline. There is indication that the Forquet-Tate romance was the victim of a pretty much made-up negative publicity campaign. Nevertheless, Forquet later claimed that Tate cut him in the chest with a broken wine bottle.

On May 27, 1964, Harrison Carroll, the gossip columnist for the now-defunct *Los Angeles Herald-Examiner*, wrote that Sharon and Forquet had announced their engagement. There was a photo of Sharon and Philippe Forquet from a magazine called *Cronaca*, dated September 12, 1964. The caption for the photo reads: "Sharon Tate, the new Marilyn of American cinema, offers the symbolic 'apple of sin' to a young partner (Philippe Forquet). How many problems arise in youth from 'flowers' and 'fruits' harvested before the wedding?"

During the summer of 1964, Sharon's agent Hal Gefsky introduced Sharon in a coffee shop to another of his clients, actress Sheilah Wells, who was under contract to Universal Studios, and they began sharing a one-bedroom apartment together at 1148 North Clark Drive as a money-conserving venture.

In an interview Sheilah Wells described meeting Sharon: "We hit it off immediately. In the conversation, she said 'I want to move,' and then I said, 'Gee, I want to move too,' and then she said, 'Maybe we could get a place together.' And this is only about after thirty minutes of this wonderful conversation, but you know how you know, especially when you're young, you know, the spark's there, the fun's there, and so she said 'where do you live?' and I said 'I live on Clark Street,' and she said 'Well, I live on Clark Street.' And it turned out we lived right next door to one another. And so she came over to my apartment at 1148, and she said, 'Well, what's wrong with this place?' You have to know that I am an interior designer, and that talent has been with me since my very beginning. So, it looked great to Sharon."

Sharon brought from her previous apartment next door an "ornate settee she had purchased, and a couple of other pieces," Wells recalled. The apartment had one bedroom, and a kitchen, and was adorned in "early actress," in Wells's words. "Sharon had her little dog, Love, and I had my afghan, Shad."

"It was full of a lot of fun times. We used to walk down to the Hamburger Hamlet, and we'd put our dogs together, and all these people would come up and start petting and talking. They were gentler, nicer times."

I asked if Sharon had already signed with Ransohoff. "Yes," she replied. "And I had just been recently put under contract by Universal, so we had a lot in common."

ES: "And she was through with Philippe Forquet?"

Wells: "That was just breaking up."

ES: "He was gone by then?"

Wells: "I think he was still around, because I met him, but I think she had asked him to move out, to leave."

ES: "What about the allegations that he had roughed her up?"

Wells: "I think there was that kind of contact."

ES: "You were still roommates when she met Jay Sebring?"

Wells: "Oh, absolutely."

ES: "Did you two go clubbing together?"

Wells: "Not like today. The girls didn't go out in groups like now. You would have a date."

The famous club Whisky a Go Go was located on the corner of Clark and Sunset, just down the hill from Wells and Sharon's apartment on Clark.

When the Beatles came to Los Angeles in late August of 1964, as part of their first triumphal swing through the United States, Paul McCartney announced at a press conference that the Hollywood actress he would most want to meet was Jayne Mansfield. The next day there was an overflowing party at the Whisky a Go Go in honor of the Beatles, with Mansfield on hand. Living just up the hill, Sharon and Sheilah attempted to attend the packed party. Wells recalled: "When the Beatles came, I remember we went down there and it was absolutely ridiculous and crazy, and we turned around and walked back up the hill."

Wells also recalled Sharon's amazing kindness: "The scene that was always so touching to me and to my mother, is when my mom would come down from Northern California, and when I was working, Sharon would take my mother out to the studios, and bring my mother on set, and take my mother to lunch, and she was so kind, and so sweet, and my mother never ever forgot that, how darling she was to her. And Sharon would ask 'are you okay for tomorrow, Mrs. Wells, what are you going to do?' Those kind of sweet kindnesses, when I think of her, that's exactly what I think about. Always there, and always, 'You okay?'"

Sheilah Wells remained Sharon's friend to the end—Sharon's mother thought that her daughter was staying over at Sheilah's the final night in the summer of 1969.

In 1964, Sharon acted in at least two episodes of *The Beverly Hillbillies*, as Janet Trego, the secretary: "The Giant Jackrabbit," and "Back to Marineland."

Meanwhile, while his future wife Sharon Tate was filming several episodes of *The Beverly Hillbillies*, a script Roman Polanski had written about a cult of cannibals was being filmed. Writing from Paris in the *New York Times* on March 22, 1964, Cynthia Grenier covered the seventeen films then being currently made in Paris and nearby: "One of the few of this batch to promise somewhat more international appeal is *Aimez-vous les Femmes? (Do you Like Women?)*, written by Roman Polanski, director of *Knife in the Water*. The youthful Polanski, who has become something of an international commuter between his native capital of Warsaw and Paris, his adopted home, is noted for his prankish, 'black' humor, as both his short and feature films have born witness. In *Do You Like Women?* Polanski gives full play to his dark imagination, producing an occult society in Paris that meets once a month to dine on the freshly roasted flesh of a beautiful young woman. Gleefully, Polanski has even gone so far as to work out the recipe for anyone interested in preparing such a dish for his own table.

"Sophie Daumer, a talented young comic actress who bears a marked resemblance to both Brigitte Bardot and Jeanne Moreau, plays a double role as the girl who gets eaten and one who escapes that fate."

Polanski's screenplay was based on a novel by Georges Bardiwill. This tome traces the activities of a cult of cannibals who collect at a vegetarian restaurant. This restaurant is a cover for the occult group that, as part of its full moon celebration, serves a gourmet-cooked beautiful young woman. It also features a romantic subplot about identical twin sisters, one of whom is the hero's girlfriend and the other, lunch.

Around this time a producer living in England named Gene Gutowski contacted Polanski. Born in Poland in 1925, Gutowski emigrated to the West after World War II. He was a fashion illustrator for a few years in New York, then became a television and film producer with a few productions to his credit, including the TV series *I Spy*. He moved to London in 1960 to produce a film titled *Station Six-Sahara* (starring Carroll Baker), and remained in London through the early 1960s.

Gutowski was ten years Polanski's senior and, of course, spoke fluent Polish. He proposed that he and Polanski become a producing-directing team. Gutowski would use his experience and contacts to put together American and English deals for films that Polanski would write and direct. Thus began Cadre Films, Ltd., the two-man company that would establish Polanski as a Western filmmaker and open the doors of big-money Hollywood to him. Gutowski took Roman around to meet film executives and threw a party for him in Los Angeles.

The 1963 Academy Awards were presented April 13, 1964, at the Santa Monica Civic Auditorium. Roman Polanski attended when his *Knife in the Water* was nominated as Best Foreign Film, but Federico Fellini's *8 1/2* won the prize. After that Polanski and his new partner went to New York to garner more publicity, and then in May 1964 they attended the Cannes Film Festival.

It was around this timeframe in Sharon Tate's life that she auditioned for the role of Liesl in *The Sound of Music*. Their paths—Roman's and Sharon's—were still far apart. Director Robert Wise and his casting consultants conducted more than two hundred auditions for the roles of the von Trapp children in the film. The winners were selected not only for singing and acting abilities but for personality and stage presence. In addition to Sharon, the role of Liesl von Trapp saw auditions by Mia Farrow, Lesley Ann Warren, Teri Garr, Shelly Fabares, and Patty Duke. Sharon was barely twenty-one, and the winner, Charmian Carr, was twenty-two—for the role of the sixteen-year-old Liesl.

The Sound of Music was the last collaboration between Rodgers and Hammerstein, and became a most beloved musical around the world. It tells the story of a nun who does not fit in with the quietistic life of a nunnery, and so she is sent to work as a governess for the seven children (including Liesl) of a widowed naval Captain.

The Captain (played by Christopher Plummer) is raising his children with excessive and dour strictness, and Maria the governess (played by Julie Andrews) wins over the children with her good spirit and pleasing vibes. Gradually she and the Captain fall in love, then, shudder shudder, they return from their honeymoon to Austria to discover it has been taken over by the Nazis, and a telegram informs the Captain that he must join the Nazi navy. The von Trapps' thrilling escape up and over the mountains to Switzerland just before World War II began added to the film's great popularity around the world.

Had Sharon Tate won a high-profile part in *The Sound of Music,* her career would have changed. She probably would not have met Roman Polanski and would not have embarked on an early cultic sequence of films—*Eye of the Devil* and *The Fearless Vampire Killers.*

Makeup-free Sharon Tate in the summer of 1964 during her time in Big Sur, which she always loved

Meanwhile, Martin Ransohoff produced a movie in 1964, *The Sandpiper*, starring Elizabeth Taylor and Richard Burton, which was filmed at Big Sur. The eminent photographer Walter Chappell was hired as a still photographer on the set, and around August of 1964 Chappell took pictures of Sharon. Tate, then twenty-one, had an uncredited bit part, and Ransohoff wanted Chappell to shoot a publicity portfolio of her. She took off her clothes for one or more of the photos. It's unknown whether Chappell, a well-known nudist, also took off his. Ransohoff demanded the negatives, but Chappell refused to turn them over.

When she headed back to Los Angeles in her new Triumph sports car, at night, she had a rollover accident, turning over four times down a hillside. Sharon was relatively unscathed, but with a totaled Triumph, and two little scars by her left eye as the only reminder of the wreck. She worried aplenty about how Ransohoff might be angry because of her screw-up.

(In Chappell's archive is a letter Tate wrote in November 1964 asking for some prints, and his response, which ended, "I hope you are lovelier than ever, as you have every possibility always to be.")

During the filming of *The Sandpiper*, Sharon fell in love with the beautiful coastline. According to one account, "In the years following, Tate would regularly escape to Big Sur. . . . Whenever she wanted to get away from Hollywood, she fled there. Scrubbed of makeup, she would check into rustic Deetjen's Big Sur Inn, often alone, sometimes with girlfriends, and walk the trails, sun at the beach, and blend in with the regulars at Nepenthe. Many did not know, until after her death, that she was an actress."

"The name is Sharon Tate," said Steve McQueen in an article dated December 19, 1964. "You've never heard of her, but you will. She has everything she needs for success, including two qualities that do not often go together—a wonderfully pure simplicity and very great beauty."

The article goes on: "Producer Martin Ransohoff, now shooting 'The Sandpiper' with Elizabeth Taylor and Richard Burton—discovered Sharon. As soon as Steve met her, he wanted her to play opposite him in 'The Cincinnati Kid,' which he is soon to make for Ransohoff.

"But Sharon's lack of experience cost her the part. Steve said: 'I even did the screen test with her.' A rare occurrence for a star. 'I was proud to do it. That girl looks really good. I'm sure she could have done the part, but of course I don't have the final say.'"

McQueen developed an affection for her. In an interview not long before his own death, he said, "Sharon Tate was a girlfriend of mine. I dated Sharon for a while." Colonel Tate later recalled how he kept a stern eye on McQueen during this period.

McQueen had taken a year off from acting, and by January of 1965, was, in his own words, "back in harness," signing with Ransohoff's Filmways for the title role in Metro-Goldwyn-Mayer (MGM)'s *The Cincinnati Kid*. The film was set in New Orleans, and it traces the story of Eric "The Kid" Stoner, a young Depression-era poker player, as he seeks to establish his reputation as the best. This quest leads him to challenge Lancey "The Man" Howard, an older player widely considered to be the best (played by Edward G. Robinson), culminating in a climactic final poker hand between the two.

Producer Martin Ransohoff had been green-lighted by MGM to proceed. Paddy Chayefsky penned the initial screenplay, which was turned down by Ransohoff. The project was then turned over to Ring Lardner Jr., who worked with Terry Southern to finish the final draft. (This pickiness on the part of Mr. Ransohoff did not bode well for his relationship with Roman Polanski just a little more than a year ahead.)

It was Lardner's first major studio work since his 1947 blacklisting as one of the Hollywood Ten. *The Cinncinati Kid* was directed by Norman Jewison, who replaced original director Sam Peckinpah just after principal photography commenced.

One version of the firing: "Sam Peckinpah was the original director, who for reasons only known to him decided to film *The Cincinnati Kid* in black and white. Peckinpah's deviation from the script, coupled with his drinking and marital problems, led to his eventual firing after only four days."

Another version: "Producer Martin Ransohoff felt compelled to fire Peckinpah after the beginning of principal shooting on *The Cincinnati Kid* due to disagreements over the conception of the film. The incident led to a physical altercation between the two. In the early 1970s, remarking on their fight, Peckinpah claimed Ransohoff got the worst of it: 'I stripped him as naked as one of his badly told lies.'"

A further rumor, contained in an internal memo at *Time* magazine (in the author's possession), has Ransohoff encountering Peckinpah getting too friendly with Tate on *The Cincinnati Kid* set as the cause of the firing.

The past is like quicksand.

Additional stars of *The Cincinnati Kid* were Ann-Margret, Karl Malden, Joan Blondell, Rip Torn, Jack Weston, and Cab Calloway; it was a combination Filmways/Solar Productions (Steve McQueen's company) production, distributed by Metro-Goldwyn-Mayer, with a release date of October 15, 1965.

Sharon was not cast in the role that was taken by Tuesday Weld. Both Sam Peckinpah and Martin Ransohoff agreed that her unsureness and inexperience would cause her to fail in such a demanding part. Instead, Ransohoff continued to burnish her experience with small roles in television shows.

Sharon Meets Jay Sebring: November 1964

There are two main versions of how Sharon met premier hairstylist-to-the-stars Jay Sebring in November of 1964. Sebring was one of Hollywood's most popular hair stylists and later the inspiration for the Warren Beatty film *Shampoo*.

The first, usually given greater credence, is that Sharon and Jay met on Thanksgiving evening, 1964, at a party given by the owner of the Whisky a Go Go, Elmer Valentine. During the 1960s, the Whisky featured important and rising acts such as The Doors, The Byrds, The Who, Buffalo Springfield, and The Kinks.

Writer Joe Hyams's autobiography, *Mislaid in Hollywood* (1973), depicts another version of how Jay Sebring met Sharon. Hyams, the former West Coast bureau chief for the *New York Herald Tribune*, was married to the actress Elke Sommer. He also wrote for various magazines such as *The Saturday Evening Post, Redbook, Ladies' Home Journal,* and the like, plus biographies of Humphrey Bogart and a later one about James Dean.

Sebring had spotted Sharon at a Paramount screening, and the next day, while cutting Hyams's hair, asked, "Do you know a girl named Sharon?" He didn't know her last name but badly wanted to meet her. Mr. Hyams then used Sebring's phone to call a publicist contact at Paramount who informed Hyams that Martin Ransohoff had a girl named Sharon Tate under contract. "She lives with a French actor, I think," the publicist added.

Two days later, according to Hyams's account, he arranged to have lunch with Tate at Frascati Restaurant, ostensibly to interview her. As prearranged, toward the end of the luncheon, Jay Sebring showed up. "I left them chatting happily together," Hyams wrote.

Quicksand of the past.

However they met, Sharon and Jay quickly became closely attached, so that Sharon moved out of the apartment she shared with Sheilah Wells on North Clark Street, and in with Sebring. "We lived together in 1964," but even after Sharon moved out, Wells noted, "she always kept her clothes here, and I was dating someone else—it was kind of a stops place, just in case things didn't work out, we always had our place on Clark." She chuckled.

Thomas John Kummer was born on October 10, 1933 in Birmingham, Alabama. His parents were Bernard Kummer, an accountant, and Margarette Kummer. He grew up with one brother and two sisters in a middle-class lifestyle in Southfield, Michigan. He graduated from high school in 1951, then served in the Navy for four years, apparently spending time in Korea.

When he moved to Los Angeles, becoming active in the hairstyling business, he changed his name to Jay Sebring: Jay, after the first initial of his middle name, and Sebring after the famous twelve-hour endurance race in Sebring, Florida.

In Los Angeles, Sebring's style of cutting hair proved popular. His clients included Warren Beatty, Henry Fonda, Steve McQueen, and many other renowned actors. In October 1960, Sebring married a model named Cami, a marriage that was in the process of a divorce by the time he first became fascinated with Sharon Tate.

By his late twenties, Sebring had already made a name for himself at the apex of hairstyling. For instance, Kirk Douglas in his autobiography praises Sebring for his work for the 1960 production of *Spartacus:* "I went to see Jay Sebring, a genius with hair. Jay was a charismatic, tiny little fellow. Good-looking. Well built. Quite a ladies' man. Jay came up with the distinctive look for the slaves—hair cut butch on top, long in back with a tiny ponytail."

Around the time that Sharon and Jay met, he purchased a house that was located on a private dirt road at 9810 Easton Drive off Coldwater Canyon and that once had belonged to movie producer and writer Paul Bern, who had married movie star Jean Harlow on July 2, 1932. Two months later Bern was found dead, totally unclothed, with a gunshot wound in the head.

The death was ruled a suicide, though several later books analyzed it as a murder by Bern's "mentally deranged" ex–common law wife, Dorothy Millette, who killed herself two days after Bern's putative suicide. Sebring's new house was believed to be haunted by the ghost of the suicided or murdered actor.

Sharon Tate herself referred to it in an interview conducted during the filming of *Eye of the Devil* in 1965: "At night in the area people swear they see and hear Paul Bern's ghost. . . . It's a house where you get scared. . . . The Harlow house is lugubrious but the day I brought over my little sisters they had so much fun. Life was back to normal," she said as she laughed.

In early 1965, however, Sharon had a grim, ghostly experience when aroused from sleep one night in her room on Easton Drive. She spotted a "creepy little man" whom she believed to be Paul Bern entering her bedroom apparently looking for something while ignoring her. When she ran from the room, she encountered an entity with its throat slashed, tied with white cord to the stair railing. The next morning she departed back to her own apartment. After her death, columnist Dick Kleiner wrote about the event, supposedly told to him by Sharon early in 1966.

Did it actually happen?

Jay Sebring was very well organized, with a rising career, but he had some strange sexual practices. According to the LAPD homicide report after he was killed: "He was considered a ladies' man and took numerous women to his residence. He would tie the women up with a small sash cord and, if they agreed, would whip them, after which they would have sexual relations." (A woman who lived with Jay Sebring not long after Jay and Sharon had split up told the author: "Jay liked to tie his lovers up and pretend to whip them. He liked to blindfold them. He liked to do all sorts of dominating things to make you sort of prove your love.")

Meanwhile, Sharon sent a steady stream of imprecations and beseechings—telephone calls and letters—to Mr. Ransohoff, demanding more prominent work.

Late in 1964, a producer named Sy Weintraub wanted Sharon to co-star in *Tarzan and the Valley of Gold*, the fourteenth Tarzan movie, and it appeared she had agreed to take on the part. On January 2, 1965, the *Los Angeles Times* featured a photo of Sharon Tate, plus a seven-year-old lion named Major, and co-star Mike Henry, with the following text: "The new Tarzan is Mike Henry, handsome, black-haired twenty-six-year-old linebacker for the Los Angeles Rams and a native of Boyle Heights. Tarzan and principals of Banner Productions, which will film a new Tarzan series, went aboard the SS *Theodor Herzl* when she docked at Los Angeles Harbor from a run to Acapulco. The company will set sail with the *Herzl* Sunday to begin shooting in Mexico. Jane will be played by Sharon Tate, 22-year-old blonde, and her name isn't Jane any more. It's Sophia."

Two days later in the *Los Angeles Times*, there was a small article by Philip Scheuer, "James Bond Image for Tarzan in 1965": "The new Tarzan—No.14—will be Mike Henry, ex-Rams footballer, who joked that he'd rather face African Lions than Detroit Lions. The heroine is Sharon Tate. 'We have a screenplay by Clair Huffaker and we're giving it the James Bond approach. . . . without the sex! With each film we've been bringing Tarzan a little more up to date, making him more literate.'"

There must have been some mixed signals between Filmways's Martin Ransohoff and Sharon's agent Hal Gefsky. The articles were dated just before the cast was due to sail for Acapulco to begin filming, yet Ransohoff, at the last minute, insisted that Tate pull out of the project. An actress named Nancy Kovack replaced Sharon Tate in her role as Sophia Renault (formerly Jane).

Accordingly, Sharon was still trapped in 1965 appearing as Janet Trego in a continuing sequence of episodes of *The Beverly Hillbillies*, with titles such as "Dash Riprock, You Cad," "Double Naught Jethro," "The Clampetts vs. Automation," "Possum Day," and "The Possum Parade."

She also was loaned out to *The Man from U.N.C.L.E.*, a television series broadcast on NBC from 1964 to 1968. The series follows the shenanigans of two secret agents, played by Robert Vaughn and David McCallum, who work for a secret international law-enforcement agency called U.N.C.L.E. (the United Network Command for Law and Enforcement). The episode in which Sharon Tate performed was titled "The Girls of Nazarone Affair."

Fellow actress Kelly Kersh recalled *The Man from U.N.C.L.E.* episode in which she and Sharon Tate played the two malevolent THRUSH girls. The episode called for Kersh and Tate to beat up Napoleon Solo. "Sharon and I had never done a fight scene before. The stunt people choreographed it," Kersh told an interviewer much later.

She and Tate rehearsed the fight scenes with actor Robert Vaughn and the stunt men. "At one point, Sharon was supposed to hold his arms back and I was supposed to punch him in the stomach," recounted Kelly Kersh. "In the rehearsal I didn't hit him very hard. I didn't have a lot of experience doing this so he stopped the scene and said, 'Now look, you can hit me as hard as you want. Hit me as hard as you can.' He was holding his stomach in tight. So I hit him and he said, 'See, you can't hurt me.' He was a little annoying the way he carried on and on.

"Before we actually went before the cameras, I said to Sharon, 'When you grab his arms from behind rather than just grabbing him—I want you to grab his arms and snap him back. And then quickly stick your knee right in the small of his back. Then I'll hit him in the stomach.' Sharon was very athletic and she thought it was a great idea. And that's what we did. Sharon snapped him back, which he totally did not expect and I punched him good in the tummy. He doubled over. We really didn't hurt him—that wasn't the point—it was his pride

Sharon Tate and David McCallum in an episode of *The Man from U.N.C.L.E.* Sharon also was in *The Beverly Hillbillies.*

that was injured. I remember some of the cast and crew turning away so as not to laugh in front of him. After he got up he said something like, 'Maybe you shouldn't do it like that.' Sharon and I had a good laugh about that one."

Sharon Wants Bigger Roles, and Becomes Engaged to Sebring

Sharon confided to Kelly Kersh that she was unhappy with her career to date, and was anxious for her discoverer, Martin Ransohoff, to land her bigger roles. By early 1965, after being shoved from the Tarzan movie by Marty, she was tired of slots in *Mister Ed*, *The Beverly Hillbillies*, and *The Man from U.N.C.L.E.* She was sick of not being in any of Filmways's movie projects, such as *The Americanization of Emily*, *The Sandpiper*, and *The Cincinnati Kid*. She wanted in the Big Game, and reportedly hounded Ransohoff for a feature role, feeling she was more than ready.

Jay Sebring was in love—very much in love—with Sharon, and when his divorce from his wife Cami became final, he began to press for marriage. He arrived early at Doris and Paul Tate's house the day before he proposed. He asked them, "May I have your blessing to take your daughter's hand in marriage?" Colonel Tate gave his assent. The next day Sharon and Jay came to her parents' house for dinner. While steaks were being grilled on the barbecue, Jay dropped onto a knee and asked Sharon to marry him. She said yes.

Jay and Sharon spent a week in Hawaii with Steve and Neile McQueen. It did not lead to any agreement on a marriage date, although Sharon gave Jay her high school ring, which he may have been still wearing when they were murdered four and a half years later.

When he proposed to Sharon, Jay Sebring was a very successful barber to the famous, and an entrepreneur of hairstyling supplies. His shop was eagerly visited by stars for gossip and excellent hair care, which inspired confidence, especially in Hollywood, where the face and hair are vitally important. Almost magically, he kept thinning hair from swirling down the shower drain. And he arrived to help the transition in hairstyles from short to longer modes.

His main shop had a stained glass window and an Egyptian ankh sign on the door. "They shampooed," an employee later recalled. "No one had ever shampooed men before. The problem was how to dry the hair. You couldn't put men under those helmets. Heat lamps were slow. Then someone heard about a handheld plastic contraption from Europe. They began blow-drying hair, and selling the dryers to clients at cost."

Sebring was not cheap; when many barbers charged around $1.50 for a haircut, Sebring charged $25.00. "Henry Fonda would be there when I went in," wrote his friend Joe Hyams. "There'd be starlets shampooing hair. It was the hottest place in Hollywood in the afternoon. There was gossip, coffee, pretty girls and the haircuts were damned good."

When Sharon started dating Jay Sebring, Martin Ransohoff threw up obstacles. "You shouldn't be dating a barber," he reportedly said.

In mid 1965, urged on by Sebring and her friend Steve McQueen, Sharon changed agents, signing with Stanley A. Kamen, Steve McQueen's agent, who was with the William Morris Agency. Kamen, one of Hollywood's best-known and most successful talent agents, was executive vice president and member of the board of directors of the agency, and was renowned for making a leading man out of McQueen. Over the years, he also represented Barbra Streisand, Warren Beatty, Walter Matthau, Joan Collins, and Gregory Peck.

Sharon was hesitant to leave Hal Gefsky, and she insisted that Gefsky keep on getting his 10 percent agent's fee, while also paying Kamen a percentage. Thus she was double-paying. This emphasizes something good about her character.

She was anxious to get going. To make her move. To start the Triumph. But it was more secretary Janet Trego on *The Beverly Hillbillies.* . . .

Meanwhile, Roman Polanski's movie *Repulsion* opened in London on June 10, 1965. The audience stood when Polanski appeared in his box, and then they chanted his name at the end. It had the ambience of a rock-and-roll concert, with exclusive T-shirts and other accessories on sale in the lobby.

Polanski had been approached by Twentieth Century Fox with a hot idea: direct a remake of *Knife in the Water,* but this time it would star Richard Burton, Elizabeth Taylor, and Warren Beatty. Polanski turned it down. Instead, his partner Gene Gutowski had found a soft-core porn company called the Compton Group whose two owners had been eager to make a film with Polanski, but they'd wanted it to be a horror movie. Gérard Brach and Polanski then created the script for *Repulsion* in seventeen days.

It was a trajectory of triumph for the young director, just three years past turning out a Polish-state-sponsored film. The Compton Group approved a £120,000 budget for his follow-up movie, titled *Cul-de-Sac,* with a director's fee of £10,000.

Principal photography for *Cul-de-Sac* began in August of 1965, off the northeast coast of England in a tiny place called Holy Island. *Cul-de-Sac* was released in Britain in February of 1966, and in the United States nine months later.

Chapter 3

Early Films: *Eye of the Devil, The Fearless Vampire Killers, Don't Make Waves*

Instead of *Tarzan and the Valley of Gold* or *The Sound of Music,* Sharon Tate's first big role was in a movie about human sacrifice titled *Eye of the Devil.* The film was originally known as *13,* with a screenplay by Dennis Murphy and Terry Southern. Tate and Sebring traveled to London to prepare for filming, which commenced on September 13, 1965, at locations in France.

Many, if not most, of the film's scenes had been shot, when one of the stars, Kim Novak, fell from a horse and was injured, and couldn't continue. Filmways considered cashing in its insurance policy for the flick, but in the end, even with 85 percent of the filming completed, Ransohoff decided to redo the project and hired writers to rewrite the script. He cut back on Novak's part, and made Sharon's role more featured.

Forty-four-year-old Deborah Kerr, famous for her beach-romping with Burt Lancaster in *From Here to Eternity,* and for such films as *The King and I,* and *Tea and Sympathy,* was hired to take over the role of Catherine de Montfaucon, and every scene that had shown Miss Novak had to be reshot. Filming rebegan in November 1965 with a new cast and director. (The movie progressed through three directors—Sidney Furie, Arthur Hiller, and Michael Anderson—before J. Lee Thompson was chosen by Martin Ransohoff.) During the winter of 1965–1966, there was filming at the Chateau d'Hauteford in France, and the newly revised project was completed.

The plot consisted of a rather humdrum human sacrifice (for the good of the crops) narrative, revealing how, uh oh, the grape crop was suffering another bad season, the third in a row, so that the owner of the vineyard at the castle Bellenac, one marquis Philippe de Montfaucon (played by David Niven) had to be summoned from his home in London back to the castle in the countryside. It becomes evident that the ritual sacrifice of Mr. Niven has to occur in order to bring back the health and vigor of the vineyard. He very much wants to spare his wife and children the spectacle of his ritual demise, and asks them to remain in London, but nevertheless they still trail after him. But, uh oh, his wife Catherine de Montfaucon soon learns that not only is her husband, the marquis, acting in a weirdo mode, but that the castle staff is utilizing ancient pagan rituals that portend a knife job for hubbie, to save the grape.

Catherine (Deborah Kerr) is treated rather menacingly by castle residents, among them Christian de Caray (played by David Hemmings) and his eerily chilly sister, Odile de Caray, played by Sharon Tate. Her husband, the marquis, she is told, has gone to a nearby town.

As Odile de Caray, Sharon proved quite effective, with her presence on the screen described by one critic as "effortlessly mesmerizing." She is attired in black tights, with high boots and a witchy stone medallion around her neck. Her cultic, hypnotic movements are followed closely by the camera, although at least one account states that Sharon Tate's voice was dubbed.

Catherine, wandering around the chateau, views Philippe (Mr. Niven) with twelve other men taking part in some sort of ceremonial ritual, and shortly thereafter she is further frightened by twelve hooded men in the nearby woods. She learns that Philippe's/Niven's father, believed previously to be dead, is living in a turret in the house. The father informs Catherine/Kerr that whenever the vines are barren for three years, the head of the family must be sacrificed to improve the quality and quantity of the grapes.

Catherine hurriedly splits from the castle to raise an alarm, but a local priest (uh oh, another cult member) prevents her. Christian/Hemmings shoots an arrow through the heart of Philippe/Niven in the fulfillment of the sacrifice.

The next day Catherine and her children leave the chateau, unaware of the attention the priest is giving her young son Jacques. He is the next Marquis de Bellenac, and the film makes clear that he is aware of his sacrificial fate, should the crops fail again for three straight years.

Even though she did not have as many lines as the other actors—just over a dozen spoken—Tate came through as crucial to the film, setting an otherworldly, cultic ambience. Niven described her as a "great discovery," and Kerr said that with "a reasonable amount of luck," Tate would be a great success. In interviews, Tate mentioned her good fortune in working with such professionals in her first film, and said that she had learned a lot about acting by watching Deborah Kerr in front of the camera. The *New York Times*, when the film was released finally after two years, wrote of Sharon's "chillingly beautiful but expressionless" acting.

While filming took place in France, Sebring returned to Los Angeles to see to his business obligations.

When parts of *Eye of the Devil* were being filmed in London, the company hired an English magician called Alex Saunders, the so-called "King of the Witches," as technical advisor. Alex Saunders, aka the High Priest Verbius, claims that Aleister Crowley tattooed him as a tenth birthday present, and further claims to have initiated and trained people in two hundred covens of witches in the British Isles. He also claimed that he became a friend of Sharon Tate on the set of the *Eye of the Devil*. Before filming ended, Saunders claims he initiated Miss Tate into witchcraft. He has photos purporting to show Miss Tate standing within a consecrated magic circle.

"Do you fuck?" Sharon is reputed to have asked Mr. Saunders at their time of meeting, thinking perhaps his witchcraft practices involved celibacy.

Life magazine gave the photographer Shahrokh Hatami an assignment to cover Sharon Tate at around the time of the filming of *Eye of the Devil*. Hatami has pictures in his archive from snapping Kim Novak, David Niven, and Tate. Hatami was already a well-known photographer, having covered, for instance, the overthrow by the CIA of the democratically elected Mohammed Mossadegh in Iran in 1953, and for *Paris Match* he had taken some famous early photos of the Beatles in the dressing room of the Cavern Club in Liverpool. His portfolio would include shots from the sets of films such as Truffaut's *Fahrenheit 451*, Chaplin's *A Countess from Hong Kong*, and Woody Allen's *What's New Pussycat?*

Around the time *Eye of the Devil* was completed, Hatami flew with Sharon from London to Los Angeles. And then Paul Newman provided his plane for a trip with Jay Sebring, Sharon, and Hatami to Las Vegas. Good times for all, and the beginning of a friendship between Hatami and Sharon Tate that was to last the rest of her life.

In January 1966, noted columnist Earl Wilson wrote that Sharon "left the London set of *13* to say goodbye to her father in Hollywood; he's an Army officer off to Viet Nam."

After filming was completed, Sharon hung out in London, where she tasted the nightclubs and the fashion world. She invited close friend Wende Wagner, who lived with Robert Mitchum's son Jimmy, to visit her in London. Wagner had had roles in two episodes of the TV series *Flipper* in 1965, as well as one episode of *Perry Mason* the same year. She too came from a military family: her father was a navy commander and her mother was a champion downhill skier. Wagner has been described as "very much a free spirit, . . . more interested in surfing and traveling around the world than a career. She combined both passions when she earned work as an underwater female stunt double for Lloyd Bridges on his hit series *Sea Hunt* (1958) as well as the TV series *The Aquanauts*."

It was while hanging out with Wende Wagner that she met by Fate her future husband, which very likely wouldn't have occurred if she had won either the part in *The Sound of Music*, or that of Tarzan's love interest in *Tarzan and the Valley of Gold*.

As part of Ransohoff's promotion of Tate, he arranged the production of a short documentary called *All Eyes on Sharon Tate*, to be released at the same time as *Eye of the Devil*. It included an interview with director J. Lee Thompson, who expressed his initial doubts about Tate's potential with the comment "We even agreed that if after the first two weeks Sharon was not quite making it, that we would put her back in cold storage," but noted that he soon realized Tate was "tremendously exciting."

The fourteen-minute film consisted of a number of scenes showing Tate filming *Eye of the Devil*, dancing in nightclubs and sightseeing around London, and also contained a brief interview with her. Asked about her acting ambitions she replied, "I don't fool myself. I can't see myself doing Shakespeare." She spoke of her ambitions to find a path in comedy, and in other interviews she expressed her desire to become "a light comedienne in the Carole Lombard style." She mentioned two contemporary actresses that were influencing her—Faye Dunaway and Catherine Deneuve. Of the latter, she said, "I'd like to be an American Catherine Deneuve. She plays beautiful, sensitive, deep parts with a little bit of intelligence behind them."

The documentary *All Eyes* showed David Niven walking with an arm around the back of Sharon, and Sharon with her arm around his back. In a brief piece written for the *Los Angeles Times*, March 27, 1966, John Scott noted: "David Niven gazed seriously at blonde Sharon Tate in MGM's movie, *13*, and said 'Every time I look at you, Sharon, it reminds me of a line from The Taming of the Shrew.' No slouch at quoting the Bard herself, shapely Sharon asked: 'The one that goes, "twas told me you were rough and coy and sullen"?' Niven grinned. 'Oh, no,' he said, 'Kiss me, Tate!'"

Polanski purchased for a putative £40,000 (with a low-interest loan set up by his partner Gene Gutowski), a small, elegant house at 95 West Eaton Place Mews, on a cobbled road close behind Sloane Square. Sharon Tate, as it turned out, was staying around the corner in an apartment rented for her by Filmways. The Fates were soon to bounce them together.

During this time Polanski and Gérard Brach were working on a script about vampires. It was titled *The Fearless Vampire Killers*. Polanski: "Our basic aim was to parody the genre in every way possible while making a picture that would, at the same time, be witty, elegant, and visually pleasing."

Polanski was doing well—he was pulling £250–£300 a week from his company, Cadre Films. He cut an upbeat swagger. He wore mod attire, had a haircut resembling rocker Mick Jagger's, drove a souped-up automobile, often placed a lit joint upon his lips, and was obviously propelling himself Up Up Up. Beautiful women abounded at his beck after *Knife in the Water*, then *Repulsion*, then *Cul-de-Sac* saw him strutting in the so-called "youthquake" that hit London and Britain in the mid to late 1960s.

He could Get It Done! He was a picture-per-year triumph. "While editing *Cul-de-Sac*," he later wrote, "I was promoting *Repulsion;* while promoting *Cul-de-Sac*, I was preparing *The Fearless Vampire Killers*. That made me a film-a-year director."

Polanski was dating torrid young starlet Jill St. John. According to a St. John timeline, she flew with Polanski to New York in October of 1965 to see the film *Bunny Lake Is Missing*. The Fates intervened, as columnist Walter Winchell succinctly reported in February of 1966: "Jill St. John, who said 'This is it!' about *Repulsion* director Roman Polanski, decided that it isn't."

"Jill St. John was wary of Ransohoff from the first," Polanski later claimed in his autobiography. "Bright as well as beautiful, she observed him closely through her long lashes when the three of us had dinner together during one of my exploratory trips to L.A. 'I think he's a phony,' she told me."

Polanski naturally was eager to locate funding for the vampire script he was working on with Gérard Brach, and Cadre Films began to troll for funding sources. Polanski met an American producer named Ben Kadish who had moved to London and was connected to Filmways's Marty Ransohoff and his coproducer John Calley. Polanski had never heard of Ransohoff.

Right after *Repulsion* was released, and while *Cul-de-Sac* was in a rough-edit form, Roman Polanski had a meeting with Calley and Ransohoff at the Dorcester Hotel in London. Ransohoff expressed a desire to view the rough cut. Upon viewing the cut, he was impressed enough to buy American distribution rights. Polanski mentioned to Ransohoff the vampire flick he was then writing. There were additional meetings between Polanski and Mr. Ransohoff. Filmways had a multipicture distribution arrangement with MGM, with the result that the Polanski/Gutowski company, Cadre Films, signed a three-picture deal with Ransohoff's company.

Filmways allotted a $1.7 million budget to what was originally titled *The Dance of the Vampires*. Polanski was so enthralled by the prospect of big money from a fairly big Hollywood deal, that the contract he inked with Ransohoff allowed Ransohoff to edit and change at will the films Polanski would direct for Filmways (and MGM), at least for versions shown in America.

Sharon Tate Meets Roman Polanski

The Fates had their say when Sharon decided to stay on in London after *Eye of the Devil* wrapped. Clack clack, measure measure, snip snip, went the three ancient Greek Fates—Clotho, Lachesis, and Atropos. When Ransohoff and his Filmways partner, John Calley, arrived in London, Filmways threw a welcoming party at the Dorchester Hotel. Polanski was introduced to Sharon Tate. They exchanged phone numbers.

Sharon was living in an apartment on Eaton Place rented for her by Filmways. Polanski recalls that its walls featured paintings by David Hockney. Also living in the apartment was Sharon's voice coach, who was a woman, and a Yorkshire puppy named Guinness.

Polanski's Mews house was just around the corner from Sharon. On an evening soon after they met, they had dinner together, then headed back to his place. He wrote that Sharon said she felt guilt coming back to his house with him. She was still involved with Jay Sebring. On the way there, as Polanski wrote in his autobiography, he stopped at an actor friend's to pick up some acid. One cube, he wrote, which he and Sharon split. Sharon had already taken LSD several times, and said it wasn't "necessarily scary." He noted that Sharon tended to bite her nails—something, over the years, he would chide her about.

At dawn they made love. Then he had to fly to Sweden, to speak with students at Lund University. "What had impressed me most about her, quite apart from her exceptional beauty," he later wrote, "was the sort of radiance that springs from a kind and gentle nature; she had obvious hang-ups yet seemed completely liberated. I had never met anyone like her before."

Another version of how Polanski and Tate met is contained in Greg King's biography of Sharon Tate, pages 39–40. When Sharon decided to hang out in London, and asked her pal Wende Wagner to join her, somehow, the manager of the London Playboy Club, Victor Lownes, took upon himself the overseeing of their fun, taking them to parties and to exclusive night spots in Soho and Knightsbridge. "They were having a lot of fun," Mr. Lownes later recalled, "enjoying the shopping during the day and the party scene at night."

As part of his duties, Lownes hosted a luncheon for Tate and Wagner, and brought to the gathering about a dozen of his friends, including Roman Polanski. Also invited was actor Skip Ward, a friend of Sharon's, in Europe for the filming of *Is Paris Burning?* "I was delayed," Ward later recalled, "and I didn't arrive at Victor's until nearly three in the afternoon. By then, the party was almost over. When I walked in, I said hello to Wende, and then noticed that Sharon was sitting next to Polanski. They were deep in conversation. I watched them for quite a while, as they talked and laughed. At the time, I made a mental note that Jay wasn't going to like this."

Martin Ransohoff wanted Sharon Tate for the part of Sarah Shagal, the daughter of the innkeeper in the film. Polanski had in mind his recent girlfriend Jill St. John. Filmways kept urging Polanski to test Sharon for the role, so he arranged a screen test at MGM's London studio. Polanski, Jack MacGowran, and Sharon filmed some test footage in costume. When Polanski got her to wear a red wig, covering her ash blonde hair, "She suddenly looked the part," as he later wrote.

Polanski spoke about the Filmways deal in an interview in early 1966 with Philippe Haudiquet:

Q: You've just signed a contract with the American producer Martin Ransohoff. What film will you be making with him?

RP: *The Fearless Vampire Killers,* a period comedy set in Transylvania and starring Jack MacGowran. I wrote the scenario with Gérard Brach. I just spent two days in Hollywood talking the film over with Ransohoff, and I've already found the locations on the Austro-Italian border in the Dolomites. We start filming in February.

Sharon Tate played a young beauty transformed into a vampire during the film. On the set of *The Fearless Vampire Killers,* she posed for publicity pictures, flashing her vampire incisors, shiny and fanglike. Tate was the main female character, who attracts the love of both the bloodsucking count in a Transylvanian castle (played by Ferdy Mayne) and a young and rather blank-minded vampire hunter, played by Polanski. As we have noted, the filmmaker had Tate wear a red wig to cover her Prom Queen all-American appearance. As one reporter later described it: Sharon was cast as the luscious woman "with the bitable neck."

The shooting was a challenge for Tate, because Polanski was a notorious taskmaster and strove for perfect takes from the fairly inexperienced actress. But Tate worked hard, eventually pleasing her director. Polanski said: "Though devoid of the natural performer's self-confidence, she burned to do well—to prove to herself that she could accomplish something in her own right. Giving her the necessary reassurance wasn't easy. *Vampire Killers* was behind schedule, but my tendency on such occasions is to become more exacting rather than less. I started doing more and more takes with Sharon—on one occasion as many as seventy."

Gene Gutowksi and Hans Möllinger had scouted locations, and located Valgardena, located high in the Dolomites near an Italian ski resort called Ortisei, where there was an extended period of filming. Ortisei was an hour's drive up through the mountains from Sharon's high school turf in Verona.

It was filmed during the snowy and tourist season. Locals and tourists alike were treated to the spectacle of numerous coffins for vampires which Polanski ordered constructed for the film, not to mention the two wolves brought from the Rome zoo, eighteen thousand bulbs of garlic, and twenty gallons of imitation blood made according to an undisclosed Polanski recipe.

"It was at Ortisei that my relationship with Sharon progressed beyond the casual stage," Polanski noted in his autobiography. "We hadn't made love since that one first night in London, and there were butterflies in my stomach when she joined us on location. We dined together soon after shooting had begun. Then I walked her back to her hotel. When I asked, rather haltingly, if she wanted me to come upstairs with her, she gave me one of her uniquely dazzling smiles and said yes. That marked the real beginning of our love affair."

It was a complicated production, with castles, snowy chases, a formal dance of ballroom-attired vampires, lots of scenes on castle parapets, tens of thousands of decisions for the director, both at Ortisei in the Italian mountains and on the sets constructed at the MGM studios in London.

In the course of writing this book, I watched a DVD of *Fearless Vampire Killers* (the Polanski version). The film is largely a visual spectacle, with a number of scenes of voyeurism—Polanski and his cowriter Gérard Brach did not write any riveting lines for anyone, including Polanski, to say, although there were a few memorable instances of humorous dialogue. The film stars *Tom Jones* alumnus Jack MacGowran as Professor Abronsius, Polanski as his assistant, Alfred, Alfie Bass as Shagal, an innkeeper, Sharon Tate as his daughter, ex-boxer Terry Downes as Koukol the lurching hunchback, Ferdy Mayne as the head vampire, Count von Krolock, and Iain Quarrier as the count's gay son, Herbert von Krolock.

In the opening, Polanski and his boss, the obsessed academic MacGowran (in role as Professor Abronsius), are in a horse-drawn sleigh that is being attacked by a wolf. They pull in at a tavern. They rub the professor's frozen limbs with snow; then there is footage of a large-bosomed woman leaning over, washing or heating their feet in a tub of hot water. Polanski's eyes bulge with amazement—it's Sharon Tate. The professor, coming awake, notes the garlic cluster above them, dangling from the ceiling. The professor asks the folk at the inn if there is a castle in the neighborhood. They say no. Obviously they're both afraid and lying. Polanski/Alfred and the professor are escorted to their room, the only one with a bathroom; they open the door to the bathroom, and there is Sharon Tate taking a bath in a metal tub.

The door is shut quickly. Then, a minute or so later, sounds of a spanking. Polanski looks through the keyhole, and enjoys the sight of Sharon Tate (as

Sarah Shagal) being spanked by her father, who is apparently upset over her compulsion to take baths.

The dialogue is as follows:

Shagal, the innkeeper (as he spanks her): I told you, every day you are having baths!

Sarah Shagal, as she yells and kicks: I won't!

Shagal: I told you, no bath! No bath! No bath! No bath!

Then, night scene, tavern owner Shagal and wife asleep in bedclothes; he awakens. Cut to Polanski putting cups onto the back of the professor. As an interlude; innkeeper Shagal sneaks up into an upper room where a maidservant is mending his nightgown; his wife comes after him, but he hides behind the door. Then a morning scene—innkeeper Shagal tries to nail boards blocking off the bathroom.

Polanski is making a snowman outside the tavern, while Sharon Tate watches from the pane of an upstairs window. He views her watching, and she slides from view.

Then children pelt him with snowballs and run away. Next Polanski enters the tavern. The hunchback Koukol arrives from the count's nearby castle; a woman tavern server cowers in fright beneath the table.

They pull up a trap door, and give him some bundles of something. He departs, and the professor asks Polanski to follow him. Polanski/Alfred surveils the hunchback while hiding behind the snowman; the hunchback watches Tate viewing him behind the upper window pane; Alfred notices this, and waves her out of the way. The hunchback's sleigh, pulled by horses, departs, with Alfred grabbing on behind.

After that there is a scene of the professor in the kitchen, complaining about getting hit on the head in the night. Meanwhile, the hunchback's sleigh confronts a lone wolf—the hunchback gets out and races up a hill after the wolf. There's a yowl. The hunchback returns to the sleigh with a bloody mouth and face. The sleigh continues, dragging Alfred behind it.

Then there is a scene at the tavern. Professor Abronsius is asleep, snoring, at a desk, papers in front of his sleeping face, a single candle lighting the scene. Meanwhile Alfred searches quickly through the professor's leather valise, finding a crucifix, garlic, and a sharply pointed stick.

There is a knock on door—it's Sharon Tate, to whom the script gives the following lines to deliver: "I'm not disturbing you, am I?" And more: "I just don't know what to do with myself. I get so bored. You can't imagine how bored I get." And: "I'm just not used to being locked up the whole time."

To this Polanski/Alfred replies, "You mean you're always locked up?"

Tate: "At school, we had fun there . . . did all kinds of things. You know what I mean." Then, "Papa, I don't know what happened to Papa." And, "My room, is FULL of garlic. He says it looks pretty." She drops a sponge she is carrying; Polanski picks it up. She's preparing for a bath. "Once a day, it's good for your health. Do you mind if I have a quick one?"

"I don't mind at all."

"Thank you, you're being very nice." Enters bathroom, turns, "Could you get me some hot water?"

There is a scene of Dracula (Count von Krolock) and the hunchback on a horse-pulled sleigh on a snowy road. They are headed toward Shagal's inn. Then a scene of Alfred preparing the hot bath. Then Count von Krolock, the vampire, looks in through an open window. Tate: "Thank you." Then Alfred departs the bathroom.

Tate is in the bathroom taking a bath. The count comes down through an open skylight and bites her in the neck. She struggles as he does the neck-suck. Polanski/Alfred views it through the keyhole, then awakens the mad professor—they go into bathroom, but she's gone. There's bloody neck-froth in the bubble bath.

Her father arrives, looks up to the open skylight, shouts "Your excellency! Give me back my daughter. Give her back to me!" as he hangs/dangles from the skylight. Then he falls back down into the full bathtub, all wet and weeping. His wife shows up—both are weeping.

In the next scene, Polanski and the professor are in the kitchen. The innkeeper's lifeless body, frozen, pocked with vampire suck-marks, is brought into the kitchen from outside. His wife is howling. The townspeople blame it on a wolf. The professor protests. "Open your eyes! You know perfectly well who has been at work!" Shagal the innkeeper of course is now a vampire; the professor hands a very sharp stake to Mrs. Shagal, saying that she can save her husband's soul by sticking it in his heart. She refuses.

Then there is a scene with Polanski/Alfred attempting to hammer a stake into Shagal, with the professor holding it in place. It fails when Alfred smacks the professor in the hand. Big ouch. They return to finish the job, but the fresh vampire Mr. Shagal runs off, after first biting the neck of the sleeping chamber maid.

The young woman tries to fend off Shagal with a cross, but Polanski and his cowriter Gérard Brach have created the first Jewish vampire, who says "Oy vey, have you got the wrong vampire."

Next MacGowran/the professor and Polanski take off on skis across the snowy vastness following the freshly vampired tavern keeper. They arrive at a substantial stone mansion, with a graveyard, which they explore. First they are locked up in a subterranean room; then they are brought into the castle to the rooms of the head vampire, Count Von Krolock. The professor hands the count his biz card, "Professor Abronsius."

The count asks Professor Abronsius to sign one of his books, *The Bat,* which he owns. The two visitors jive the count with the story that they were following a bat through the winter landscape, which is why they arrived at his castle. A very big bat.

A cock crows; the count conducts Alfred and the professor to his musty library. "It's at your disposal." Professor Abronsius is very excited by the many books. The hunchback arrives—"Your beds are prepared"—and he conducts them to their bedroom. On the way, out of a door comes a young man. Count Krolock introduces: "Herbert, my son." Herbert shakes Polanski/Alfred's hand. The professor and Alfred are given separate rooms. A cock crows again. "Good night, gentlemen." The count heads for zzzz in his coffin.

There is a scene of Koukol the hunchback coffining up the count and his son. Shagal tries to drag his box into the same place, but, in a show of class delineation, the hunchback carries Shagal's coffin out to the stable. Then sunlight.

The professor and Polanski/Alfred awaken, and the hunchback brings in bread and a drink. Polanski thinks he has heard Sarah, Shagal's daughter, during the night. He dresses the professor, who stands up on the bedstead then jumps down into his trouser legs in one swoop. They go forth and peep into a room where the hunchback is making a coffin. Uh oh.

Then they are heading toward the count's crypt room when the hunchback, with a big broad axe, crouches to stop them, and they turn back. Polanski and the professor go up to the roof, then work their way around across snow-crusted parapets, to a small entrance to the coffin room, which they slide down into. But the professor gets stuck in the entry hole, his legs dangling from the window down the castle wall, so he charges Polanski/Alfred with the task of driving the stakes into the hearts by himself.

The professor orders him to open the count's coffin. Polanski/Alfred raises the hammer in one hand, and places the stake, sharp end down, upon the sleeping count's heart, but quails and cannot go through with it. Then the professor orders Alfred to go around to the outside and pull him out.

Alfred then wanders through the castle, and encounters Tate/Sarah taking a bath. "Sarah!" "Hugh!" she replies. He kisses her, "I'm going to save you. We'll go away together."

"Where do you want us to go?" "I don't know." "To your parents, perhaps." "Papa will be coming to see me, soon." "They said that?" "Yes." She asks him if he'd seen the beautiful dress (on the bed). Yes. "They gave it to me for the ball tonight." It begins at midnight. "They'll all be there."

"Sarah," Alfred says, "You must follow me." She gets out of the tub, asks him to turn away. He draws a heart in the frosty window pane, spotting the professor's legs wiggling, protruding from the tight hole in which he is stuck on the side of the castle, which reminds him to get back to work. He races forth to pull out the professor.

Next the count's gay son, Herbert, tries to vampire Polanski/Alfred in his own room, as a girl draws a bath. He attempts to bite Polanski's neck, but bites instead into a little book on love that Polanski has filched from the count's library. Polanski/Alfred races thence with Herbert chasing him. Then the son catches him, and tries to bite his neck, but is unsuccessful.

Alfred warns the professor, and they escape to the parapets just in time to watch the crypts below, as their lids rise, and the vampires awaken and emerge. Count von Krolock approaches and says Polanski will be, in the centuries to come, a good companion to his "sensitive" son. "It will be extremely difficult for you to get away from here, unless of course you have wings, like a bat."

Next the count addresses the throng of vampires gathered in the ballroom. He notes how just a year ago, "we were assembled here. . . . I your pastor, you my flock. With hopefulness in my heart, I told you then, with Lucifer's aid (flashing a two fingered Devil sign) we might look forward to a more succulent occasion." Now, a year later, even though travelers rarely arrive, he has a big surprise, regarding neck-slurp, for them.

Big groan of arousal and expectation from the assembled crowd. He pulls back a curtain and reveals Sharon Tate. And announces "two more humans are in our hands." Much groaning excitement.

Then to the roof where the professor and Alfred have rigged the cannon to fire and blast open the locked door (which will enable them to attend the ball of the vampires.) Next is the formal dance scene, for which Polanski has been praised for the "macabre beauty" of its perfectly timed sequences. Sharon is resplendent in a red gown, dancing with the count in front of the others. Polanski/Alfred and the professor sneak into the ballroom, attired in formal bewigged garb, both joining the actual dancing circle—a formal bow and curtsy dance, changing partners, to chamber music. Alfred dances into contact with Sarah. "Life has meaning once more," he whispers. "We're going to save you."

The professor announces that when he gives a signal they'll "run for our lives" out the door. Then Polanski/Alfred, Abronsius, and Tate/Sarah attempt to escape. The count shouts to the throng, "Catch the girl!" Alfred and the professor make the sign of the cross together, with each holding a sword in a crisscross cruciform manner, which causes the cross-fearing crowd to draw back in fear. Then they place the two long swords into a cross pattern on the floor by the door, thus blocking the path of the attacking vampires.

The trio flees down some spiral stone steps, whereafter, to Krzysztof Komeda's mournful soundtrack they wend through a bat-ceilinged wet-walled "cave." They locate a trap door leading upward, and the trio scampers off to their horse and sleigh to flee. The count orders Koukol the hunchback to catch them. Koukol takes off down the snowy hill using a coffin as a sled, on the heels of the horse and sleigh, but he overshoots them and flies in his coffin down a precipice, after which loom sounds of wolves attacking him.

Then Tate/Sarah is resting in the sleigh, with visible vamp' twin bite marks on her neck; Polanski/Alfred is sitting next to her and notices how cold her hand is. It was quite shocking to see pretty Sharon Tate wake up and suddenly open wide her perfect mouth, revealing vampire fangs, which bite lasciviously into Polanski's neck. It surely provided the archetype for all future horror movies in which a beautiful woman chomps into a victim's neck.

So, at the close of the film, the obsessed professor vampire hunter has departed the castle of neck-suck, thinking he has thwarted them all, not knowing that two recently infected neo-vampires, played by Polanski and his new lover Sharon Tate, rest in the same coach.

The film concludes with a narrator declaiming a Polanskian message of Abandon All Hope Against Organized Evil: "That night, fleeing from Transylvania, Professor Abronsius never guessed he was carrying away with him the

Sharon as a cuddly vampire

very evil he had wished to destroy. Thanks to him, this evil would at last be able to spread across the world."

Thus passed before my eyes *The Fearless Vampire Killers,* a fairly good spook or spoof of horror/neck-suck films, with some interesting well-filmed scenes and vignettes (though with rather measly dialogue) done with considerable satiric wit, which would give twenty-three-year old Sharon Tate, raised a Catholic, a one-two opening in the world of films in the form of one movie about a cult that commits human sacrifices, and a second movie about class-based blood-drinking among Transylvanian townspeople and nobility.

Moving in with Polanski Shortly After Easter of 1966

At first Sharon remained at her apartment on Eaton Place, with additional filming on *The Fearless Vampire Killers* at various MGM studios in London, till it was concluded. In April of 1966 Jay Sebring complained to friends that he'd been bird-dogged by Roman Polanski. Sharon moved in with Roman shortly after Easter 1966, when filming was halted for a few days. He wanted to take her to St. Tropez, but his passport problems prevented it. They went instead to the south coast English resort, Eastbourne. It didn't work out, so they spent the rest of the brief vacation at his Mews house. She showed herself a fine cook and homemaker, well-schooled by her mother, Doris.

"She began to make a tremendous difference in my life," he later wrote. "We took to spending more evenings at home and entertaining more people, some of them Hollywood friends like Warren Beatty, Dick Sylbert, and Yul Brynner, others 'locals' like Victor Lownes, Andy Braunsberg, Simon Hesera, Larry Harvey, and Michael Sarne, who had just finished directing his first feature, *Joanna.*"

"When she was out in public with Roman, she never felt adequate enough to open her mouth. She could only talk to him alone. Her problem was that she had always been beautiful, and people were forever losing themselves in fantasy over her—electing her a beauty queen, imagining her as a wife, dreaming of a caress. Most people had fantasies. But a few people, like Polanski, took charge," or so John Bowers wrote, in *The Saturday Evening Post,* May 6, 1967, in an article titled "SEXY LITTLE ME—This is how Hollywood turns a pretty Texas girl into Sharon Tate, the star."

Took charge indeed. Polanski exerted great control over Sharon Tate, as her friend Joanna Pettet described in an interview with the author: "I just knew that he did control Sharon. He told her how to dress; he told her what makeup he liked, what he didn't like. He preferred her with nothing, no makeup. And she was exquisite with no makeup. But he ruled her entire life from the time she met him."

Sheilah Wells recalls that Sharon "actually had written me a beautiful letter that she had just met this wonderful man, and said 'I hate to hurt Jay.' My boyfriend was Ron Roth. He was a young producer at Universal, with *Bob Hope Presents the Chrysler Theater* (which ran on NBC from 1963 through 1967.) Sharon was very fond of him and wanted to know how we were doing. And then she went into 'I just met someone, a fascinating man by the name of Roman Polanski, and I think it's serious,' and that she didn't want to do anything to hurt Jay, and she was really concerned about that, how she was going to handle it. It was just a simple, sweet letter. She was a very caring, sweet, sweet girl. People say, 'Oh, she's so nice, she's so sweet,' but Sharon truly truly was."

After Sharon and Roman began living together, Jay Sebring flew to London, apparently aware of the new situation. Sharon wanted the three to have lunch. It was at a place called Alvaro, just around the corner from Roman's Mews house. Jay accepted that it was pffft for him and Sharon. Even so, Roman and Jay got along, and even became friends, though Sebring still loved the delicate beauty whose class ring he wore on a chain around his neck for all the years left to him.

Not long after her breakup with Sebring, Sharon was interviewed by a writer for a French magazine. The writer said, "I'm pretty sure you were engaged to someone the last time I saw you." "With Jay Sebring," was Sharon's answer. "Now it is finished. He was trying to dominate me too much. When I was filming a nude scene in *The Vampire Killers,* he telephoned me and tried to dispute it." (Translation from the French.)

"However, we have stayed friends. I called him the other day to find out how he was doing. He told me that now he was going out with a fifteen-year-old girl. I found that totally immature.

"I told Jay he should be ashamed—a fifteen-year-old! When I was fifteen, I was still looking for red and white striped flannel nightgowns. I was dead scared of men. Jay told me, 'But she's very much advanced for her age. She knows just about everything.'"

"I'm dating Roman Polanski now," Sharon continued. "I have to admit that I never thought that one day I would date someone so intelligent. He is teaching me a lot of things and shares confidences with me."

The article mentions that she was biting her nails, then suddenly stopped. "I should stop doing that. It's edginess or something like that. I have a mass of energy inside me that I'm not using."

The reporter asked, "Do you feel you have gained some maturity in dating Polanski?" "Oh yes, absolutely." Sharon answered. "When I arrived in London last year I was terribly shy. Leslie Caron invited me to a party and I was thinking: What can I say to people that would be interesting?"

The fifteen-year-old friend of Sebring was Catherine James, an emancipated young woman who had a varied career as an upper echelon rock-and-roll fan, and who later wrote of her life in an autobiography entitled *Dandelion*.

Also hanging out at Sebring's Easton Drive place was another young woman, Sharmagne Leland-St. John. "I honestly cannot remember exactly when I moved in," she e-mailed me. "First of all a few weeks after I met Jay my parents had me committed to Camarillo because I had sort of 'co-hosted' a sweet 16 party for his then girlfriend Catherine James. My former boyfriend had driven us to the Sebring house because for some reason Catherine's mother and boyfriend were late. Neither one of us had a car. (This was when he loaned me Sharon's car.) Anyway we walked in the door at Jay's and were offered punch which had acid in it. We drank the punch, were having a great time, and my former boyfriend got jealous that I was hanging out in the kitchen with George Hamilton and told me to get my purse because we were leaving. I didn't really want to go.

"He told me, 'You came with me, you are leaving with me!' So I said, 'NO! You chauffeured me, I'm staying!' It got ugly and I didn't want to spoil Cathy's party so I went to say goodnight to Jay. . . . He asked me why I was leaving so soon, and I said my ex boyfriend is demanding that I leave. 'Do you want to?' 'Well, no!' So he told me to go lock myself in the upstairs bathroom . . . and he would take care of Myron. Apparently a group of guys threw him out bodily. There was a fist fight and everything. So at 3 a.m., he went to my parents' home, got them out of bed, and told them that I was on drugs at a Hollywood orgy! Catherine's mother was there at the party! It was hardly an orgy. That was probably May 31, 1966. So I dated him steadily, and then they had me committed, and I spent over a month incarcerated in a mental institution. I escaped in July of 1966. Jay found me a safe house . . . way out in Tujunga or Sun Valley because he knew if I went to Easton they'd look for me there." St. John recalls she finally moved into Sebring's house on Easton Drive in late August of 1966. Jay loaned her Sharon's automobile, which was still parked there while Sharon was in England.

The quicksand of the past.

Actress Joanna Pettet Recalls Meeting Sharon

"I can tell you exactly the very moment I met her. I was bowled over by her beauty. My partner at the time was Victor Lownes, who was part of the Playboy conglomerate; he ran the Playboy Club in London. I was with Victor, and Roman Polanski was a very good friend of Victor. One afternoon Sharon and Roman came in and I came downstairs, and Sharon was watching Roman and Victor play backgammon. And she had absolutely no makeup on, and I was just astounded; I had never seen anyone more beautiful. And we became very good friends.

"It was while I was doing *Casino Royale*. I think it was probably 1966. Then, we stayed friends. I was working, she was working, so it came in and out."

Pettet recalls how Victor and Roman would watch pornographic movies at Lownes's place in London, but that she and Sharon would leave the room when that type of movie was shown. "I was very young," Pettet recounted during an interview in 2010, "and I had never been exposed to that, and I just wouldn't watch them, and whether or not Sharon just played along with me, and then when she was with Roman it was different, I don't know. But, she knew how I felt about that."

Sharon on *The Merv Griffin Show*

Merv Griffin, the star of the popular American TV talk show, took a walk with Sharon Tate on a "tour of swinging London's Carnaby Street" on August 5, 1966. This walk was filmed and shown on *The Merv Griffin Show*. The footage shows Sharon and Merv strolling side by side, Sharon gesticulating with her sunglasses in her right hand, first along Carnaby Street, then down Kings Road, where the most "in" fashions were on display in stores. Sharon then sat in chairs with Griffin and was asked about this part of London. Sharon's spontaneous reply was interesting: "Actually, Chelsea is—you can't say it's like our Greenwich Village—but it's where the artists and painters and a lot of actors live. Actually, this is one of the best areas to live in, because it's kind of kooky, and the houses are unusual, you know. Saturday down here," she told Griffin, "is the time to come to Kings Road."

Griffin asked, "What happens on Saturday?"

Tate: "You see all the strange people in all the strange clothes."

Griffin: "Tell me about you. We have yet to see you in motion pictures in America, but from what we hear, you're going to be a smash. And now, you have a monster movie."

Tate: "Not really."

Griffin: "What's it called?"

Tate: "*The Vampire Killers*. It sounds terrible, but it's a satire on horror films. It's like a live Walt Disney film. Roman Polanski."

Griffin: "It's funny, we all thought you were an English girl, and most everybody does here, but you were born in?"

Tate: "I was born in Dallas, Texas.

Griffin: "And lived all your life in America?"

Tate: "Not really, I lived in Italy for four years."

Griffin: "Why was that?"

Tate: "My dad's in the army."

Griffin: "An army brat made good! Where's he stationed now?"

Tate: "Right now he's in Vietnam."

Griffin: "In what capacity?"

Tate: "Intelligence, between Vietnam and Korea."

Griffin: "He's an officer?"

Tate: "Yes."

Griffin: "Well, they must be proud, or do they know what you're doing?"

Tate: "They were a little skeptical at first."

Griffin: "They haven't seen you yet, have they, as an actress?"

Tate: "No, no, they haven't seen anything. They'll laugh, I'm sure, they'll laugh" (breaks into a laugh herself).

Around the time Sharon was on *The Merv Griffin Show,* Filmways and Martin Ransohoff were producing a movie called *Don't Make Waves,* based on the Ira Wallach novel, *Muscle Beach.* It starred Tony Curtis and Claudia Cardinale. Julie Newmar was slated for an important role, but suffered a back injury and had to bow out of the project. PR releases stated that it was because she couldn't lift leading man Tony Curtis. Ransohoff summoned Sharon Tate from London that August of 1966, to take over Newmar's part as Malibu, a sky-diving bikini-clad beach-peach who performed her own stunts.

In *American Prince,* his 2009 autobiography, Tony Curtis wrote of making *Don't Make Waves:* "The plot was utterly ridiculous, but I agreed to appear in the film because I got a percentage of the gross. When Martin Ransohoff asked me to recommend a director, I suggested Alexander Mackendrick, with whom I'd worked on *Sweet Smell of Success.*" Curtis's first wife was the actress Janet Leigh, to whom he was married for eleven years, 1951–1962, and with whom he fathered actresses Jamie Lee and Kelly Curtis. Curtis left Leigh in 1962 for Christine Kaufmann, his seventeen-year-old German costar in the film *Taras Bulba.*

During *Don't Make Waves,* four years into this second marriage, Curtis was having marital troubles with Christine Kaufmann, which Sharon apparently helped him deal with through friendly advice. Sharon and Tony would become friends, but not lovers.

A famous seducer of costars, Curtis later wrote about the women in *Don't Make Waves:* "Claudia Cardinale was gorgeous, but her boyfriend at the time was rumored to be an important politico, so Ransohoff delicately told us, 'Hands off.' Sharon Tate was living with Roman Polanski. . . . and I was a good friend of Roman's. We would meet at parties, after which I would go over to their house and make myself comfortable there."

Ransohoff was very hands-on in his relationship with productions. Curtis wrote: "Ransohoff complained that (director) Sandy (Mackendrick) wasn't working fast enough (i.e., going over budget—as Ransohoff had complained about regarding *The Fearless Vampire Killers*), and Ransohoff also didn't like the way the picture was coming out." (Shades of Ransohoff fiddling with *Vampire Killers*.)

"I was growing rather wary of MGM," writes Polanski in his autobiography. "I was also growing suspicious of Ransohoff, particularly when I found that Sharon's agent was his agent, too, and had helped renegotiate her contract downward. Ransohoff summoned her to Los Angeles to play opposite Tony Curtis in a comedy—*Don't Make Waves*—at a paltry $750 a week."

An article in the December 1967 issue of *Muscular Development* traces the involvement of the muscle-building community in the film: "The new MGM-Filmways production has Tony Curtis and Claudia Cardinale as the top featured performers with Sharon Tate and Dave Draper in the co-starring roles. The $4,000,000 film is based on Ira Wallach's novel, *Muscle Beach*. The movie can be described as a 'sex and flex' gala spectacular featuring blondes, bikinis and bulging biceps.

"The big surprise of the movie to Tony Curtis, Claudia Cardinale and the other pros in the cast of Martin Ransohoff's comedy was the big blond giant, Dave Draper. Dave plays the part of Harry, winning the role from forty-two others who were tested for the part. The film brass at Filmways were so pleased with the terrific job Dave did in the movie that they signed him to an exclusive long-term contract, and have high hopes for his future as an actor. The publicity chief for Filmways Productions, Fred Baum, said, 'Dave did such a great job he surprised everyone. In fact, he just might steal the picture.' One of the cast, beautiful Joanna Barnes commented, 'Honestly, he's so appealing in the picture you want to hug him.'

"Co-starring as Draper's girlfriend is the very lovely Sharon Tate, one of the most beautiful girls these eyes have ever seen!"

Dave Draper, who plays Malibu's boyfriend Harry, was the 1965 Mr. America and the 1966 Mr. Universe.

One of the film's highlights was The Byrds' pleasing title track, composed by Chris Hillman and Jim McGuinn:

If you're looking to get a good thing going for yourself
House and pool, a new Rolls Royce and some degree of wealth
Don't make waves, don't make waves, don't make waves
Take a ride out West to find that freedom that you crave
Kick that nine to five, don't let them make you a slave
Don't make waves, don't make waves, don't makes waves

As we have noted, Sharon Tate was the buzz story of the movie, as the always-bikinied skydiver, Malibu. Here's the plot: When impulsive and reckless Laura Califatti (Claudia Cardinale) totally wrecks a sports car belonging to tourist Carlo Cofield (Tony Curtis), she invites the unhappy young man to spend the night on the couch of her Malibu Beach apartment. But he is thrown out by Laura's "lover," Rod Prescott (Robert Webber), a self-important businessman who operates a swimming pool company owned by his wife (played by Joanna Barnes). After sleeping on the beach, Carlo goes for a swim, nearly drowns, and is saved by a beauteous skydiver-surfer Malibu (Sharon Tate), who gives him mouth-to-mouth resuscitation. Captivated by the girl, Carlo decides to settle down in the area. Since he has failed to get any compensation for his sports car, he plies his knowing of Rod's affair with Laura to con for himself a well-paying gig as a pool salesman.

To enhance Carlo/Curtis's romance with Malibu/Tate, Carlo bribes an astrologist, Madame Lavinia, into telling Malibu's bodybuilder boyfriend, Harry, that sex is bad for his body. Rod's wife, Diane, declares that she is suing for divorce, naming Laura/Cardinale as correspondent.

Eventually, all six become trapped in Carlo's cliffside house during a rainstorm. As it tips over and slides down the incline to the muddy beach below, Malibu/Tate is rejoined with the ultramuscular Harry/David Draper, Diane agrees to drop her divorce proceedings against Rod, and Laura/Cardinale and Carlo/Curtis unite in permanent love.

The Long Beach, California, *Independent Press Telegram,* on August 21, 1966, published an article titled "Just a Pretty Girl in San Pedro—Now Look!" by Margaret McKean. The article provides a slice of time for Sharon Tate as she began filming *Don't Make Waves:* "A few weeks ago Sharon's mother got a phone call from the studio, 'Sharon wants you to meet her plane and we'll go from there to the Beverly Wilshire.'"

Doris Tate thought a meeting would give her a chance to catch up on Sharon's recent life. "But stardom," the article continued, "does not have much time for girl talk. After arriving, Sharon fell into bed to get a few hours' sleep before a 9 a.m. wardrobe call. Since then she's been on the set of *Don't Make Waves* with Tony Curtis in Malibu. A stage mother Doris Tate is not. 'This is the life Sharon wants, she can have it. She was always kind of pretty and I'll have to admit that she's worked hard. She'll be 24 next January and it would seem she's behaved herself and come through all this glamour pretty well.'

"There are no raptures or glowing gushiness from the star's mother or kid sisters, Debbie, 13 and Patti, 9. Her father is now stationed in Korea and tape recordings of the family exchanges center on such important things as 'how mother and dad can take another long separation' and 'is the yard work getting done?' 'We've got a new house in Palos Verdes and Sharon hasn't even had a chance to come see it yet,'" her mother commented.

"'In some ways, Sharon is disillusioned—'She hates what studio beauticians do to her hair and recombs every set.' She recently wrote her dad, 'I finally own a Christian Dior and now I don't like it. Mother dressed me better from her sewing machine at home.'"

Writer Norma Lee Browning described visiting the set of *Waves:* "The last scene I watched at Malibu involved Sharon and Tony Curtis doing a dangerous sky diving scene into the swimming pool. Sharon insisted on doing the stunt herself instead of a stunt girl. There was one take when something went amiss; Sharon got trapped under water and almost didn't come up. There was slight panic on the set. First aid was summoned. Sharon was fished out. She was okay, and she still insisted on doing the rest of the takes herself instead of using a stunt girl. I remember thinking then, Wow! That girl's got guts!"

The set featured a lot of mud, as the article, "Mud Not a Lark for Film Stars," by Philip Scheuer in the *Los Angeles Times,* October 4, 1966, traces: "A more miserable, bedraggled bunch of glamorous people you never saw. All in the name of art or if not art then box office, they have been sloshing their way through mud for some three weeks—the real thing on location in Malibu and the homemade kind on a sound stage at MGM, this for Filmways' production in color of *Don't Make Waves.*" The article noted how the stars were trapped in slime, with the house trapped in the mudslide built in triplicate, two times on Stage 30 at MGM, and one at the foot of a cliff in Malibu, on the remains of a real mudslide that had occurred several years in the past. The first house on the stage was fairly right side up, and mounted on the old *Mutiny on the Bounty* rocker, so that it was capable of being tipped 18 degrees. The second house built at the MGM soundstage was scary indeed, resting on its flat roof, with the floor above at an extreme angle.

For *Don't Make Waves* Sharon rented a house in Los Angeles "from a friend," as Roman described it. Sharon suffered during the filming of *Don't Make Waves,* in good part because she missed Roman, who was deep into postproduction work on *The Fearless Vampire Killers,* and because she was disappointed with her career-path as determined by Martin Ransohoff. She and Roman kept in touch by phone. Polanski later saw fit to report that it was at that time, alone in Los Angeles, that Sharon acquired her first vibrator, urged to it by a woman friend. Many publicity stills of Sharon in a bikini were released during the film's promotion. There were life-sized cardboard lobby displays of Sharon as Malibu. She also became the spokeswoman for Coppertone suntan lotion, posing for an ad in a bikini lying on a surfboard held by several young men, and a radio ad with *Variety* columnist Army Archerd. Her shapeliness would later serve as the inspiration for Mattel's popular "Malibu Barbie" doll.

Sharon's wondrous physique was featured early in the film, with a shot of her hauling Tony Curtis across the beach, in her role as the lifeguard Malibu, flashing her pretty bikinied derriere.

Though Tate had already shot two films, *Waves* was the first to be released into theaters, and reviews were largely negative.

While Sharon was filming *Don't Make Waves,* Roman flew to Los Angeles for a week in order to show John Calley and Martin Ransohoff the rough cut of *The Fearless Vampire Killers.* In his memoir, Roman reported much love making with Sharon during his visit to Los Angeles, rekindling their strong feelings toward one another. Ransohoff didn't dig the rough cut of *Vampire Killers.*

Polanski then had to rush back to London to mix onto the film's track the music composed by Krzysztof Komeda, and to complete the film. After *Don't Make Waves* was finished, Sharon returned to London. Then Roman flew to New York City in October 1966 to show *The Fearless Vampire Killers* to MGM executives. The film had cost more than $2 million—around $300,000 beyond the budget. Mr. Polanski had difficulty finding suitable MGM executives to watch it, as he later noted: "The company was in . . . a complicated proxy fight when I got there, and the energies of its top executives were directed elsewhere. . . . No one had time to see my film." Finally a vice-president of MGM took a gander, though he received a sequence of phone calls during the screening, and excused himself for around ten minutes while the reel was rolling. Polanski called Martin Ransohoff in Los Angeles to get a release date for the film, but Ransohoff said it was too long, and needed work.

In parallel with Polanski's rush to complete the film, Ransohoff ordered around twenty minutes of Polanski's version excised which were, in Polanski's words, "replaced by an interminable cartoon trailer," in actuality an animated prologue which had to be added to explicate some jokes because Ransohoff's recut had made the jokes incomprehensible. The voices of the actors were dubbed to make them sound "more American," and Ransohoff gave the picture a new title, changing from *Dance of the Vampires* to *The Fearless Vampire Killers.* He replaced Polanski's voice with actor David Spencer's. And Polanski also complained that he had moved the music around.

Roman Polanski may have been ravingly angry, but he was powerless, since Filmways had the right to cut the film in the western hemisphere. After viewing Ransohoff's reworking, Polanski spoke out to *Variety,* "What I made was a funny, spooky fairy tale, and Ransohoff turned it into a kind of Transylvanian *Beverly Hillbillies.*"

The Fearless Vampire Killers, Polanski's version, was released in Britain in February of 1967, and in the United States, in Ransohoff's version, in December, over a year after his trip to Los Angeles to screen the rough cut. The uncut Euro version was successful at the box office, but Ransohoff's cut and redubbed job bombed in America.

Writer John Bowers, in an article in *The Saturday Evening Post*, sketched a remarkable slice of Sharon's life in late 1966: "Sharon has a quarter-inch scar under her left eye and one beside the eye, the result of accidents which she keeps having. As Polanski drove with her one night in London, meticulously keeping on the left in the custom of the land, an Englishman with a couple of pints under his belt hit him from the right. The only one hurt was Sharon, whose head bounced off the dashboard, spraying blood on slacks, boots and fur. An angry red wound appeared at the start of her scalp, and it will leave another whitish scar on her head. With blond hair combed down over her forehead to hide it, she skied at St. Moritz. And then she caught a jet for Hollywood because Ransohoff had called." Sharon had to reshoot a few scenes for *Don't Make Waves*. She complained a bit, and discovered that now she could grumble to Ransohoff. She disliked Hollywood and wanted to remain in London with Polanski. Bowers reported that Sharon hated to fly, and that "she had to be drugged to endure it."

Bowers noted that Sharon was seated beside Mr. Ransohoff at La Scala restaurant in Beverly Hills, wearing an outfit that was "more like a slip than a dress, and her blond head caught glints of movie-star light as she turned this way and that. 'Oh, there's David! David Hemmings. David, David!'" Hemmings had been the star of Antonioni's *Blow-Up* after appearing with Sharon in *Eye of the Devil*. In the restaurant various celebrities glanced at Tate, but also at one another, and not neglecting quick peeps at the LaScala entranceway, checking what marvelous entity might be entering, and only now and then staring down at their drinks or meals.

The Saturday Evening Post caught an interesting colloquy between Ransohoff and Tate on what he intended to do with *The Fearless Vampire Killers:* "Ransohoff wore an open-neck sport shirt and shapeless coat, and he talked business. 'Listen, sweetie, I'm going to have to cut some stuff out of *The Vampire Killers*. Your spanking scene has got to go.' 'Oh, don't do that. Why would you do that?' "'Because it doesn't move the story. The story has got to move. Bang, bang, bang. No American audience is going to sit still while Polanski indulges himself.'

"'But Europeans make movies differently than Americans,' she argued. '*Blow-Up* moved slowly. But wasn't it a great film!' 'I'll tell you something, baby. I didn't like it. If I'd have seen it before the reviews, I'd have said it'd never make it. It's not my kind of picture. I want to be told a story without all that hocus-pocus symbolism going on.'

'Oh, I want to do a complete nude scene,' said Sharon. 'Say you'll let me!' 'OK, OK,' Ransohoff said, bored, looking toward the door."

Bowers then described how in an early morning shoot, Tate was filmed on the Malibu beach, redoing a scene for *Don't Make Waves:* "In a sequence with an undraped David Draper, 'Mr. Universe.' Sharon stuck out her backside and shot out her front. Magically, a button or two came undone on her polka-dot blouse, and after close examination of camera angle, director Sandy Mackendrick decided to leave it that way. He gave Sharon guidance in rubbing mineral oil over Draper's bare back, as the scene called for. 'Treat him like a horse,' he said. 'Pat him just as you would an animal. That's the way.'"

Sharon Tate rubbed the mineral oil upon Mr. Draper's well-formed back, but when the camera stopped, she said, "Ugh." Then in her rather small dressing room in a trailer on the set, she smoked a cigarette, and said, "I'm happier when I'm working. I don't have time to think too much that way."

Bowers described a visit to Doris and Paul Tate's house in Palos Verdes Estates, about an hour from the film location. Paul Tate was stationed at the time in Korea. Doris was taking care of Sharon's two sisters: "Her mother—a pleasant, plump, dark-haired woman—turned Sharon's face this way and that. 'Have you had your blood count recently, honey? You look so pale to me.' What did she think of Sharon's becoming a movie star? What did she think of Roman Polanski? 'You know,' she said, in the voice of every middle-class American mother, 'I don't care—just as long as she's happy.'"

Back in Hollywood, Bowers noted how Sharon moved among various hotels, and stayed at various friends' homes. And in the background, as she talked often by phone with Roman, was the fact that "So many things were unresolved, shadowy. Ransohoff was sore at Polanski because Polanski had gone way over the budget on *The Vampire Killers.* Polanski was mad at Ransohoff because Ransohoff was cutting away at his film and postponing its release in the States."

One night Sharon, attired in aviator's leather jacket, slacks, and tinted Ben Franklin glasses, visited the private discotheque in Beverly Hills called The Daisy. Without comment, she quietly viewed young actresses of her generation go through their dance motions. Among the dancers were Suzanne Pleshette and Patty Duke, plus Linda Ann Evans in a miniskirt. Sharon gazed at Evans and commented, "I've worn a much shorter mini in London. That's nothing."

Sharon was photographed by the renowned Richard Avedon in New York on October 31, reportedly for a magazine spread on "The World's Most Beautiful Women."

Chapter 4

1967: The Year of Love, Dolls, Rosemary

Playboy magazine published a photo series in its March 1967 issue called "The Tate Gallery" featuring Sharon with bared bosom, shot by Roman Polanski. The article about her began, "This is the year Sharon Tate happens. A screen newcomer with three films to be released in 1967, Sharon shows best in Roman Polanski's *The Vampire Killers,* a slap-stick unreeling of macabre carryings-on. Says director Polanski, who last year shocked moviegoers with *Repulsion,* 'What kind of film is *The Vampire Killers?* It's funny!' A man of many talents, Polanski, who co-stars in his new movie, personally photographed Sharon for the pages of *PLAYBOY.* Depicted here is her sudsy tête-à-Tate with a frightening film ghoul who, like us, finds Sharon a tasty dish, indeed."

The *Playboy* text continues: "*The Vampire Killers* displays Sharon's formidable form in two tub-thumping scenes. Signed by Martin Ransohoff to a Filmways contract four years ago, she received a half-million-dollar Hollywood non-buildup: continuous courses in everything from diction to dancing to dress—even bodybuilding. Says Miss Tate, 'Mr. Ransohoff didn't want the audience to see me till I was ready.' As Polanski's photos reveal, Sharon's ready now."

The Playmate of the Month for March of 1967 was Fran Gerard, photographed by Mario Casilli and Gen Trindl. The issue also featured an interview of Orson Welles by Kenneth Tynan, and several articles, such as "Executive Salaries" by Vance Packard, and "The New Aristocrats" by Paul Goodman. Plus a pictorial spread on the Bunnies of Missouri.

Meanwhile, in March of 1967, a movie production began for Jacqueline Susann's controversial book, *Valley of the Dolls,* which had been on the bestseller lists for sixty-five weeks. Sharon decided to test for the role of the doomed star-let Jennifer North. All actresses, even Academy Award winners such as Patty Duke, had to undergo screen tests. Sharon's test, shot March 8, 1967, featured the following lines:

"What about your career?"

"Bah, my career. You must be joking. I haven't got two cents worth of talent. All I've got is a body."

Sharon won the part. In the film, Jennifer works in soft core French "art movies" to pay her husband Tony's medical bills. Sharon would win praise for her acting of her character's suicide.

Jacqueline Susann approved of Sharon: "When I was told she had been cho-sen over several other girls, I leaped. She was exactly what Jennifer should have been . . . She was perfect. Marvelous. Out of the whole picture she was the one girl who was cast as I saw the part."

Shooting began with location work in New York, plus some interiors, on March 13.

Jacqueline Susann herself described the plot in a promotional documentary: "*Valley of the Dolls* is actually the story of three girls who come to New York to look for fulfillment of their dreams. Each makes it to the top in her own way, and finds emptiness and loneliness; and the longest and loneliest hours are in the night. A child fears the loneliness of the dark, and clutches at its rag doll. A lonely star also clutches for a doll, a little red or yellow doll, a sleeping pill. It hap-pens to so many girls, the mad scramble to reach the top; they never know what is really up there, but the last thing they expect to find is the Valley of the Dolls."

Three up-and-coming women come together in New York at the inception of their careers. Sharon Tate is the beauteous blonde Jennifer North, who is in the chorus of a Broadway play starring Susan Hayward as famous actress Helen Lawson. (Judy Garland was originally cast in the Lawson part, but behaved excessively temperamentally, refusing to leave her dressing room, for instance, and was sacked about a month into filming.)

Tate was optimistic: *Eye of the Devil* and *The Fearless Vampire Killer*s were each due for release, and now she had been signed to play a major role in *Val-ley*. There was much media hoopla swirling around the production, and while Tate acknowledged that such a prominent role should further her career, she confessed to her lover that she did not dig the script, or the book itself for that matter.

Barbara Parkins, then the star of the TV series *Peyton Place,* played Anne Wells, who recently arrived in New York and became a famous model (after initially working for a theatrical agency representing the Broadway star

Sharon in one of her most famous roles, Jennifer North in *Valley of the Dolls*

Lawson/Hayward). Patty Duke played the aggressive and hyper-emotional Neely O'Hara, who is a rising singing star.

The three, Duke, Tate, and Parkins, in their respective roles, become friends, and all three find themselves involved with troubled men.

Neely O'Hara/Duke's career streaks upward; she moves to Los Angeles for a successful film career, but, uh oh, starts taking "Dolls" such as Seconal and Nembutal, plus stimulants also. She begins to act bonkers and erratic, and is sent to a sanatorium.

Jennifer North/Tate also heads to Hollywood. She marries a successful nightclub singer, Tony Polar. Soon she is pregnant, but then opts for an abortion when she learns Tony has Huntington's chorea, a fatal disease (which in real life afflicted the great Woody Guthrie) that often attacks offspring. Jennifer/Tate begins working in French soft-core porno "art films" to pay for her husband's ever-increasing medical bills. Then Jennifer/Tate is diagnosed with breast cancer and told she must have a mastectomy. She commits suicide with an overdose of Dolls. Jennifer's on-screen suicide, as an example of Sharon Tate's good acting, is one of the shining sequences in the film.

Anne Wells/Parkins, having become a highly successful model, also succumbs to the attractiveness of Dolls to overcome her sad relationship with two-timer Lyon Burke, who has an affair with Neely/Duke.

Neely is released from the sanatorium and given a chance to resurrect her career, but she re-succumbs to the lure of Dolls and alcohol, and she heads into a shrieking decline. Anne gets rid of drugs and her unfaithful lover and returns to New England. Lyon Burke ends his affair with Neely and asks Anne to marry him, but she says no.

And thus it was Curtain Time in the Valley of Seconals, uppers, and mood-depressing downers.

Patty Duke later wrote how it was "miserable working with Mark Robson, the director. . . . He was someone who used humiliation for effect, who could be insulting about your physical appearance and who wouldn't hesitate to bite your head off in front of everyone . . . Sharon Tate, however, got it even worse than I did. She was a gentle, gentle creature—you could be mean to her and she would never retaliate . . . Robson however, continually treated her like an imbecile, and she was very attuned and sensitive to that treatment. . . . He just picked on her. . . . Finally, after hours of this nonsense, Sharon wound up in tears. . . . We were always making faces at Robson and giving him the evil eye behind his back."

Polanski later quoted Robson as remarking to him, "That's a great girl you're living with. Few actresses have her kind of vulnerability. She's got a great future."

An article, "The Dames in the *Valley of the Dolls*," which *Look* magazine ran on September 5, 1967, captured Sharon Tate in a scene: "'Roll over and over and over,' purrs *Dolls* director Mark Robson, as the camera rolls behind him. The lady on the bed obliges. She's Sharon Tate, she's gorgeous, she doesn't have any clothes on, and from every indication, she knows how to roll over. 'Cut!' belts Robson. Then, one-two-three, smiling madly for no apparent reason, Sharon springs out of bed. (She's not naked after all. She's wearing lovely little bikini panties.) Blithely, she reaches into a terry cloth robe, held out by a wardrobe lady, plucks her wiglet off and hands it to a hair lady, and turns to see some scantily clad photographs of herself given to her by a publicity lady. 'I want none of these to go out. None, none, NONE,' says Sharon, who tends to repeat words for emphasis. 'Sharon's very sensitive,' explains one of the more serious minded 20th executives.'"

Sharon further said, "People look at me . . . and all they see is a sexy thing. I mean people see sexy, I mean sexy is all they see." The article continues, "She sighs deeply, sweetly—voice all baby's breath. 'When I was put under contract, I thought, "Oh, how nice," but'—She stops, as if holding back a sob—'I was just a piece of merchandise. No one cared about me, Sharon. People expect so much of an attractive person. I mean people are very critical on me. It makes me tense. Even when I lay down I'm tense. I've got an enormous imagination. I imagine all kinds of things. Like that I'm all washed up. I'm finished. I think sometimes that people don't want me around. I don't like to be alone though. When I'm alone my imagination gets all creepy.'

"'If you just take it down to bare facts, the reason for living is the reason you make it. I mean the brain was made to create. I'm trying to develop myself as a person. Well, like sometimes on weekends I don't wear makeup.'"

A slice of honesty from a young actress who wanted to be recognized for skills beyond her body and sexuality. In interviews during production, Tate expressed an affection for her character, Jennifer North, an aspiring actress admired only for her curves. Tate, Duke, and Parkins developed a close friendship that went on after the completion of the film. Even though the filming had been less than fun, the good-natured Sharon Tate promoted the film enthusiastically. She brought up her admiration for Lee Grant, with whom she had played several dramatic scenes. Tate was asked to comment on her nude scene, and she replied:

"I have no qualms about it at all. I don't see any difference between being stark naked or fully dressed—if it's part of the job and it's done with meaning and intention. I honestly don't understand the big fuss made over nudity and sex in films. It's silly. On TV, the children can watch people murdering each other, which is a very unnatural thing, but they can't watch two people in the very natural process of making love. Now, really, that doesn't make any sense, does it?"

Patty Duke's take: "By the close of shooting, everybody hated everybody. War zones had been set up all over the place. On the last night there is traditionally a wrap party. You do the final shot, the chips and dip are already set up, everybody has a drink, and sometimes people hang around until morning. On this picture I had to go around begging grips and electricians to stay so that there could be any kind of celebration at all."

Unlike Patty Duke and Barbara Parkins, Sharon would not live to see the day of *Valley* as a cult classic, with fans holding *Valley of the Dolls* parties on Halloween and participants dressing up as Duke's Neely O'Hara and Sharon's doomed Jennifer North.

Filming locations for *Valley of the Dolls* included the 48th Street Playhouse and Gracie Square in New York City; suburban Katonah, New York; the LA County Music Center, plus scenes in Malibu; Redding Center, Connecticut; the Santa Monica Courthouse; and exteriors at Yale University in New Haven, Connecticut.

During the same season, on April 2, 1967, in the midst of filming *Valley of the Dolls*, the masterwork *Sergeant Pepper's Lonely Heart's Club Band* was completed and the next day Paul McCartney flew to the United States to surprise his love

Jane Asher (who was touring in the Rockies in *Romeo and Juliet*) on her birthday. He first stopped in San Francisco, where he met with Jefferson Airplane, then flew on Frank Sinatra's Learjet to Denver on April 5, then on April 7 back to Los Angeles where he met with Cass Elliot and John Phillips, and went to a Beach Boys recording session to watch Brian Wilson working on his "masterpiece," the "Elements" suite.

Regarding Frank Sinatra and his Learjet—we shall run into Mr. Sinatra again farther down the road.

In the late winter of 1967, Roman Polanski went skiing in Vermont. Polanski and Cadre Films, the company he had formed with Gene Gutowski, were not doing very well by the early months of that year. After the hassles with Ransohoff over cutting and reworking *The Fearless Vampire Killers*, Filmways and Cadre had ended their three-picture deal.

What had begun in a mode of triumph and splendor a year earlier was now in danger of dissolution, and Polanski was feeling depressed. He was on his way to a skiing trip in Vermont, when he took a call from Robert Evans, the thirty-six-year-old vice president in charge of production at Paramount Pictures. Evans asked Polanski to meet him to discuss a script set in the world of competitive skiing called *Downhill Racer*. Polanski's answer was that he intended first to do some actual skiing.

The Fearless Vampire Killers of course, was set in northern Italian ski country, and so *Downhill Racer*, a pet project of up-and-coming Robert Redford, would have been a continuation of the snowy movie theme. Ten days later Polanski was on a plane to Los Angeles. When he arrived, Evans apparently told him that *Downhill Racer* had just been an excuse to get him there. What he really wanted Polanski to read was an unpublished novel by Ira Levin called *Rosemary's Baby*.

Rights to the novel had been purchased by William Castle, a producer of horror movies, who then brought the galleys to Robert Evans, newly installed as head of Paramount. Castle initially had plans to place Vincent Price in the lead role, and to shoot the film in 3-D, but was bought out by Paramount for a hefty fee and a profit split, plus a producer's credit.

In his hotel room in Los Angeles, Polanski read the novel nonstop through the night and called Evans the following morning to tell him, "I want to do it."

Polanski worked out a budget of $1.9 million, out of which, through Cadre Films, he would receive a flat fee of $150,000 to write and direct, with no cut of the profits. Sharon's agent at William Morris, Stan Kamen, negotiated the contract between Cadre Films and Paramount.

"Characters and utmost fear are the most important things in cinema," Roman Polanski once said. No doubt keeping that in mind, when he was back in London, Polanski began working on a script drenched in fear, cultnoia, and modern marriage. He dictated a preliminary draft to a Cadre Films secretary named Concepta. Then he worked in his little study on the top floor of his Mews house, day upon day, to perfect the script.

In an interview with Michel Ciment, Michel Perez, and Roger Tailleur, in 1969, Polanski said, "They asked me which screenwriter I wanted and I said I'd try to write it myself, seeing at the end of the week whether it was working out or not. I went back to London and began writing. I was very enthusiastic and after three weeks had a finished script of 260 pages. Then I returned to Hollywood to start trimming it down." It was his first adaptation of a novel to film.

According to another biography, in just over three weeks of dictation and then polish, polish, polish, he completed a 272-page screenplay.

Roman asked for the renowned Richard Sylbert to be production director. According to Sylbert, "I spent 30 days at the Beach House (in Malibu) with Roman working on that script after his first draft. First he did his draft." It was Sylbert's idea to film at the Dakota apartments in New York City. Filming began in September of 1967.

What a moil the casting of a film so often is! Polanski viewed Rosemary as an "All American Girl"-type, and so hankered to have Tuesday Weld named to the critical role. Weld turned it down, and so did Jane Fonda because she was making *Barbarella* with her husband Roger Vadim in Europe. Other actresses considered were Julie Christie, Elizabeth Hartman, Patty Duke, Goldie Hawn, and Sharon's good friend Joanna Pettet.

Robert Evans suggested television star Mia Farrow, and brought to Polanski some footage of *Peyton Place* episodes so he could view Farrow in action. Polanski was not impressed, but he finally screen-tested her, and she won the part. It didn't hurt that she was married to the much older star, Frank Sinatra—which would guarantee a high-level buzz in the media.

As for the role of Guy Woodhouse, husband of Rosemary/Farrow, both Evans and Polanski wanted Robert Redford. Redford had a starring role with Jane Fonda in *Barefoot in the Park*, released in 1967 to great acceptance. He then was scheduled to star in the Silvio Narizzano's Western, *Blue*, a Paramount production, but just one week prior to shooting he quit the film, and there were some lawsuits against him as a result. During negotiations over Redford starring in *Rosemary's Baby*, attorneys for Paramount apparently served Redford with a subpoena in the middle of a luncheon meeting with Polanski. This brought the negotiations to a close.

According to a biography of Jack Nicholson by John Parker, Robert Evans suggested Jack Nicholson to Polanski but, after their meeting, Polanski stated that "for all his talent, his slightly sinister appearance ruled him out."

Other actors considered were Richard Chamberlain, James Fox, and Laurence Harvey. Warren Beatty turned it down. Finally the part was offered to John Cassavetes. For Minnie and Roman Castevet, producer William Castle suggested Alfred Lunt and Lynn Fontanne, the famous Broadway acting duo—parts which went to Ruth Gordon and Sidney Blackmer. Castle even asked Polanski to give him the part of Dr. Saperstein, a role eventually filled by Ralph Bellamy.

Everybody gives advice in a film project.

Polanski met with producer William Castle. Castle himself was eager to direct the film, but he was impressed with Polanski's vision for the film, and assented to Polanski directing. After Polanski returned to London, had completed a script, and sent it back to Castle, Polanski called and said he would like Castle to locate a house for him, near the ocean. "His fiancée, Sharon Tate, would contact me," as Castle wrote in his autobiography.

"On Sunday morning, the doorbell rang at our home on Alpine Drive in Beverly Hills. I saw a strikingly beautiful woman. 'I'm Sharon Tate.' Her voice was soft and musical. Introducing her to Ellen and the girls, I found they were delighted with her unaffected simplicity. 'I think I've found a house for you and Roman,' I said. 'Right on the beach. The owner, Brian Aherne, is going to Europe and wants to lease.'

"Sharon loved the house and felt that it would be just right. Later that afternoon, Sharon Tate, barefoot, stood on the beach gazing at the ocean. Sunlight filtering through her honey-colored hair; her eyes danced with excitement. 'It's perfect,'" he recalled her saying, 'Roman and I will be so happy here.'"

Cadre Film co-owner Gene Gutowski, his wife Judy, Polanski, and Sharon Tate moved in mid-1967 to the place Sharon so glowingly approved.

Actor Brian Aherne's mansion was located on Ocean Front Highway, at 1038 Palisades Beach Road. Its chief allure was the fact that actor Cary Grant had once lived there with his friend Randolph Scott. Overlooking Santa Monica Beach, it featured a walled garden with a corner tower and a swimming pool. The mansion had a history: it had been built in the 1920s for silent screen siren Norma Talmadge. An important feature was that the house had many rooms suitable for putting up the wide assortment of guests attracted by Sharon's and Roman's openness.

Actress Joanna Pettet was a houseguest at the mansion. In an interview with the author, she said, "When I came to California to do a film called *Blue* with Terence Stamp, we were in Moab, Utah most of the time, on location, but we came back to do a few shots that they hadn't got, at Paramount Studios. So, I stayed with Roman and Sharon at Cary Grant's house in Malibu that they rented. The one thing they went on about was, 'It's Cary Grant's house.'"

The Summer of Love

What a summer of fun, surprise, and good vibes! They called it the Summer of Love, during which, throughout the nation, young people celebrated psychedelia, rock and roll, the wearing of primary colors, communal living, hitchhiking, traveling around in brightly colored vans and converted school buses, sexual experimentation, and the use of pot and LSD. The seeds of the Summer of Love were planted during the Great Human Be-In at Golden Gate Park in San Francisco on January 14, and the prototype outdoor music event, the Monterey Pop Festival June 16–18—featuring Jimi Hendrix, The Who, Ravi Shankar, Janis Joplin, and Otis Redding. On June 25, the Beatles sang "All You Need Is Love" live to a worldwide audience of four hundred million over the BBC, thanks to the "Early Bird," "Lana Bird," and ATS-1 satellites. Another great Beatles song, "Lucy in the Sky with Diamonds," which many considered an anthem to LSD, was on everybody's turntable. It seemed as if peace and love might overcome violence—except, well, there was the ever-continuing war in Vietnam, with President Lyndon Johnson in August sending 45,000 additional troops, adding to the 464,000 already there. Also, during the summer of 1967 there were riots, beginning in late June in Buffalo, and then in Newark in July, where 26 died, 1,500 were injured, and 1,000 arrested. Detroit caught fire on July 23, in a wave of destruction which killed 43 and left whole sections destroyed for the next forty years and beyond.

So while "flower power" and Sharon and Roman's friend John Phillips's tune, "If you're going to San Francisco, be sure to wear some flowers in your hair" suffused one part of the American psyche, war and violence commanded another.

During the Summer of Love, Sharon and her boyfriend Roman adopted the cutting-edge style for the year that was known in the media as "rich hippie." Sharon was famous among friends for her cool hashish brownies and her calmness and sweetness, and out in public for her micro-micro miniskirts.

The summer of 1967 saw the release of the first film in which Sharon had a starring role. It was not *Eye of the Devil* from 1965, nor *The Fearless Vampire Killers*, but rather it was *Don't Make Waves*. There was much publicity focusing on Sharon as Malibu, queen of the surfers. The lobbies of theaters were festooned with life-sized cardboard photos of Sharon in a polka-dot bikini.

Filming of *Rosemary's Baby*

> I like a good scare in the theater. . . . I know that I've had many great moments watching horror movies.

—Roman Polanski

Polanski later contended that he had wanted Tate to star in this tale about a young Manhattan woman who gradually discovers that she has been tricked by her husband into having a child with the Devil, and had hoped that someone would suggest her, as he felt it inappropriate to make the suggestion himself. The producers did not suggest Tate.

There were ten days of filming in New York City. Sharon was a frequent visitor to the film set. She gave ideas for some of the scenes, including the one in which Rosemary is impregnated. She also appeared uncredited as a guest in a party scene. She was photographed on the set by *Esquire* magazine and the resulting photographs generated considerable attention both for the film and for Tate.

During the filming, Sharon became friends with Mia Farrow. Roman and Sharon accompanied Mia and Frank Sinatra to dinner on several occasions. Mia remembered that Sharon and Roman took her in and made her part of their high-flying group of pals. "She was like a princess in a fairy tale. As kind as she was beautiful," Farrow later commented.

Director Roman Polanski filmed the exteriors for *Rosemary's Baby* at the Dakota; however, the interiors were created in a Hollywood soundstage, because the Dakota does not allow filming inside. The Dakota is a landmark building, built circa 1881–1884, and located at 1 West 72nd Street, just off Central Park. Its designer was Henry J. Hardenbergh, who managed elegantly to combine German Gothic, French Renaissance, and English Victorian styles. Its brick and sandstone walls are adorned with balconies, corner pavilions, and terra-cotta panels and moldings. It has a steeply pitched slate and copper roof featuring ornate railings, stepped dormers, finials, and pediments, perfect for an occult thriller.

Polanski's directorial style was firm, firm, firm. He gave forth a sense of authority and he knew what he wanted at each moment in great exactitude. He was demanding, sometimes abrupt and terse, even yelling and scoffing, but the proof was in the daily rushes. During the New York filming, Roman had a suite at the Essex House on Central Park South.

Polanski was one of the first directors to use a video camera to help block scenes. Mia Farrow once described it in an interview with Tom Burke, who asked, "Did Roman Polanski rehearse *Rosemary's Baby*, or if not how did he work?"

Farrow replied, "We did some blocking. Then we got tired and started to play, because Roman had this machine, a home television taping machine, so we were all on home television and that was fun. John Cassavetes and me and Roman, we made all kinds of silly television commercials. That was fun."

Filming continued in Los Angeles, and the meticulous Mr. Polanski saw the project fall behind schedule. Mia Farrow had agreed to take part in her husband

Frank Sinatra's new production, *The Detective*, but it became obvious that the schedule for *Rosemary's Baby* was going to cut into *The Detective*.

Mia painted her pink trailer on the Paramount lot with big letters, white, "PEACE" and "LOVE" plus a large flower with a smiling face. Roman also painted images on Mia's Love trailer. It was appropriate—after all it was the far-famed Summer of Love which saw brightly painted hippies, some holding sticks of burning incense, flock to big cities, holding Be-Ins in places such as Central Park in New York City and Griffith Park in Los Angeles.

During the filming of *Rosemary's Baby*, Sharon and Roman socialized with Frank Sinatra and his young wife on weekends in Palm Springs at Frank's luxurious compound with detached guest bungalows.

Steve McQueen and his wife, Neile, lived in a house near the Sinatra compound, and Steve took Roman, Mia, and Sharon out one night in a Land Rover outfitted with oversized tires. Recounted Roman: "Then he proceeded to race across the desert in the total darkness, through clumps of scrub over bumps, into the occasional sickening void. I could hear what sounded like girlish giggles but later found out were squeals of genuine alarm. Steve McQueen was an old friend of both girls so I didn't say anything, but the sight of Sharon's bruises afterward convinced me that he was an asshole."

Twice in his autobiography Polanski expresses dislike of McQueen. As we have noted, McQueen in an interview late in his life stated, "Sharon was a girlfriend of mine. I dated Sharon for a while." Is it possible that Roman was jealous of the attraction that may have existed between Sharon and Steve?

One version of how Roman at last met Sharon's father, Paul Tate, goes as follows. Sharon called her dad's sudden unannounced visits "surprise attacks." One such surprise occurred in September of 1967 at the Cary Grant house in Pacific Palisades. The colonel sat chatting on the deck of the house with Sharon. Roman was not yet home—the two had not yet met.

Then Roman arrived from work. Paul Tate remained on the deck, while Sharon greeted Roman, announcing that her father was outside. Her father could hear the conversation. Roman, according to the father, was not that eager to meet Sharon's dad, complaining that it had been a difficult day on the set, and that he just wanted a hot bath and then an opportunity to relax.

Sharon told Roman that the colonel was only remaining through dinner. "You need to get to know him." Roman then, for some reason asked if there was any "bu" in the house.

"Please don't do this," was Sharon's reply.

Roman then surrendered to the event, and, holding hands with Sharon, went out to the deck to meet Paul Tate, "nice to meet you."

The phone rang, and Roman urged Sharon to answer it. Then, with Sharon gone, Roman realized that the colonel was upset that he and Sharon were living together.

"You know," said Roman, "She's too nice. I've been trying to toughen her up, but she won't fight back."

"I wouldn't try too hard," the Colonel replied. "She doesn't get mad very often, but when she does, oh, son, you better watch out. And when she's done with you, then you've got me to reckon with."

Roman then said, "I'd better go see who's on the phone."

Here's another version of how Polanski met Sharon's parents, from the quicksand of the past. It seems that Roman was a bit nervous for this first meeting. The colonel was back from war duty, working on the Vietnam War while at the same time being stationed in Korea. The parents showed up one day unannounced. Uh oh. But all went well. They no doubt were impressed with the opulence of the mansion on Palisades Beach Road and the obvious money being earned by the high-flying director who chatted with them in halting English. The thread goes back to 1964, and Sharon's enforced breakup with actor Philippe Forquet, who recalled in a later interview that Doris was much concerned about the loss of money if Sharon should give up an acting career for marriage.

Roman later wrote that "any qualms I may have felt about this first meeting with them were soon dispelled by their warm and friendly acceptance of my relationship with their daughter." The Tates brought a Yorkshire terrier as a present, which Roman named Dr. Saperstein, after the character in *Rosemary's Baby*.

The photographer/filmmaker Shahrokh Hatami was hired to film a documentary on Mia Farrow and the making of *Rosemary's Baby*. As we have noted, Hatami had enjoyed an extensive career in photojournalism. He had already taken numerous photos of Sharon Tate for *Life* magazine back in 1965, and subsequently became a confidant of hers, as we shall see.

In the midst of *Rosemary's Baby* came conflict. In the early fall of 1967, with filming days behind schedule, Frank Sinatra was on the phone. He wanted to speak with Paramount Pictures head Bob Evans.

"I'm pulling Mia off the fuckin' film, Evans, if it ain't finished by November 14. She's starting my picture [*The Detective*] on the seventeenth."

"Sorry, Frank. She won't be finished with *Rosemary's Baby* until mid-January."

"Then she's quitting."

Mia came to Evans's office. "I'm going to have to quit. I love him."

"Screen Actors Guild will enjoin you from doing his picture, too, Mia." said Evans. He screened for her about an hour of *Rosemary's Baby*. He claimed in his autobiography he assured her she was a shoo-in for an Academy Award.

"Suddenly, she didn't take a hike," recounted Evans. "Just as suddenly, Frank served her with divorce papers, right on the set, delivered by Mickey Rudin, his attorney."

In another interview Evans remembered: "She wanted to leave to be with Frank. She was madly in love with Frank, and I took her in and I showed her an hour of cut footage, and I said, 'You're going to win the Academy Award for this. . . . Suddenly she didn't want to get on the plane to leave.'"

Peter Sellers and Roman Polanski met in an Italian restaurant near the Paramount lot during filming of *Rosemary's Baby*. "My first impression of him was of a sad, shy man who hid his essential melancholy behind a fixed smile that revealed his rather prominent teeth," noted Polanski in his autobiography. Sellers's "manner conveyed profound depression," wrote Ed Sikov in his book on Sellers, *Mr. Strangelove* (p. 272).

Sometime in the next few weeks, Sellers became involved with Mia Farrow.

There was a brief article on Sharon in the *Los Angeles Times* on October 24, 1967. It was published in the run-up to the release of *Valley of the Dolls*. "Men are attracted to women who seem to have solved their problems, who face life with self-assurance," Sharon told the reporter, Lydia Lane. When asked about the beautiful attire she wore in the upcoming *Valley of the Dolls*, Sharon commented: "I go to the Paris collections often, but I do not make mistakes since I've learned not to be hypnotized by a name. The enthusiasm for a creation is one thing. What the dress will do for you, how well it suits your needs is another. When I buy I try to picture the whole outfit. You must co-ordinate, if you want to look your best. Some clothes are designed to be sex symbols, but the girls who wear them have to have other things going to find success with men."

Topanga Canyon and the Spiral Staircase: The Fall of 1967

Topanga Canyon, an enticing and beautiful place in the counterculture sixties, twists up from Topanga Beach for a few miles to a summit overlooking the San Fernando Valley. The canyon was easily accessible to Hollywood along roadways across the San Fernando Valley.

There is a creek that runs its pleasant boulder-strewn and cabin-sited way down Topanga Canyon into the Pacific. Following along the creek is Topanga Boulevard, which runs from the ocean up over the top of Topanga and down into the San Fernando Valley and then north a few miles in a straight line to Santa Susanna Pass Road, near the location of the Spahn Ranch, the future home of a roaming band of young people led by a charismatic singer and guitar player.

Woody Guthrie once lived in the canyon, and his cabin still stands. In spite of the mutant sprawl of Los Angeles, the canyon maintained a form of rustic beauty and its inhabitants were among the most experimental in lifestyles to be encountered anywhere.

While Roman was busy shooting his movie about a satanic coven, Sharon introduced him to the joys of Topanga Canyon. He described it in his autobiography: "Our life together was a sheer delight. Sharon introduced me to the America she knew: not only junk food, drive-ins, and popcorn at the movies but the California coast, Big Sur, and Topanga Canyon. Some friends of hers lived in Topanga, and we used to spend whole afternoons there. In their garden, which overlooked a cliff, they had a crude swing—a tire at the end of a long rope—and I shall never forget the thrill of soaring higher and higher through the branches, over the cliff, glimpsing the extraordinary view, hearing the wind whistle around us."

That fall of 1967 a converted school bus painted black, with the words "Holywood [sic] Productions," arrived in Topanga Canyon. It held a roaming group of young people led by a man named Charles Manson. Manson was determined to record his songs and to become famous.

Manson's target was a man named Gary Stromberg, who was employed at Universal Studios in Los Angeles. Stromberg was a friend of Phil Kaufman, whom Manson had befriended earlier in the 1960s in prison. Through Kaufman, it was set up that Manson would record a couple of sessions for Universal Records, with Universal to pay for the recording costs.

When Manson and the group first arrived, they lived at a secluded house at the mouth of Topanga Canyon near the Pacific Coast Highway. The house was called the Spiral Staircase, after a spiral staircase at its entrance, and it had slid off its foundation and rested askew. Apparently its first floor had a creek flowing through it. The place was located behind the Raft Restaurant on Topanga Canyon Lane, and according to Manson there were windows that opened out onto the hill in back and some doors opening on a twenty-five-foot drop straight down into the creek. The Spiral Staircase has since been torn down, but in 1967 it was a citadel of dope, fucking, and worship of devilish deities.

It was at the Spiral Staircase that Manson, by his own admission, had his first meeting with the So-Cal variety of devil worshippers and Satanists. Manson met the owner of the Spiral Staircase in San Francisco. "She was a trippy broad, about forty-five years old," Manson describes her, "who experimented with everything. When I met her, she was pumped up about devil worship and satanic activities."

He says she gave him complete crash privileges. For a few months, the Spiral Staircase became a scrounge-lounge for the Family. They parked the bus there between peregrinations and were exposed, according to Manson, to all sorts of blood-drinkers and ritualists. Of course, many other types of people congregated at the spiral house, including an occasional starlet driving a Rolls-Royce.

Patricia Krenwinkel in a later interview told how it was at the Spiral Staircase that she'd first met members of an English-based satanic group that had migrated to the United States, led, as she termed it, by a "blond-haired Englishman."

In one report written by an officer with the LA County sheriff's office, he describes a conversation with a fellow officer stationed in the Topanga Canyon area in 1970. The officer "stated that he had knowledge of a purported English-woman living at 'The Castle' in Topanga Canyon." He then listed the name of the woman, one of the founders of the English satanic cult. The officer stated that he had never met the cult-woman, "but that he has met a tall male Negro with an English accent at The Castle." The officer further "said he could not recall the male Negro's name since this incident occurred approximately two years ago but that he thinks it was Roberts or Robertson."

The officer also "said he understands from his informants in the Canyon that Roberts or Robertson is the personal representative" of the English cult-woman's group "which does witchcraft and that the woman is the money behind the operation." The officer said "that to the best of his knowledge 'The Castle' is owned by the (English) woman and that a large tree in the front of the location was preserved for the purpose of some type of witchcraft rites."

"Light shows" were a feature of the late-sixties counterculture, utilizing projections of films, photos, pulsing lights, and blobby images from colors mixed in petri dishes and projected on screens and walls to the music of guitars, drums and other instruments. At one such "light show party" held at the Spiral Staircase, a twenty-year-old actor/musician from Santa Barbara named Robert Beausoleil arrived sporting a pointed beard and smoking a hand-carved skull pipe. The man known as Charlie and his female followers were singing together, so he joined in and began playing along. Beausoleil later told me that a few days later, Charlie came to see Beausoleil, wearing an old tweed jacket, a tweed cap and a walking stick. Beausoleil was staying at the home in Topanga Canyon of a music teacher named Gary Hinman, whom Beausoleil would murder in the summer of 1969. (In an interview with the author in prison Beausoleil told me that the Manson group had met the English Satanists at the Spiral Staircase that 1967 fall.)

Sharon as Matchmaker

Sharon's good friend Joanna Pettet was having an affair with Terence Stamp, her costar in the Paramount picture *Blue,* when she was staying at the Cary Grant house rented by Sharon and Roman. After final work on the film was completed, Pettet flew home to New York City, where Sharon Tate's skill as a matchmaker bore fruit. Joanna Pettet described how she met her future husband, the actor Alex Cord, in New York City in October of 1967: "Alex," she said, "had dated Sharon long before she married Roman. I remember Sharon and I talking in London, and she said to me, 'If there is one man I could see you really falling for, it would be Alex Cord.' I didn't know who he was at the time. Then I met him in New York. I believe she was in London. And I called her, when I was sitting with Alex, and I said, 'You'll never believe who I am with.' I said Alex Cord. And she was just amazed."

Meanwhile, the chopped and channeled *The Fearless Vampire Killers* was released in the United States in November. *Time* and *Newsweek* both panned it. Polanski carried on a public feud with Ransohoff for "butchering" his creation, plus it was not profitable. Tate's performance was largely ignored in reviews, and when she was mentioned, it was usually in relation to her nude scenes.

"Ransohoff is a perfect example of a hypocrite," Polanski stated in an interview with Michel Ciment, Michel Perez, and Roger Tailleur in 1969. "He's a philistine who dresses himself up as an artist."

Eye of the Devil was released shortly after, and Metro-Goldwyn-Mayer (and Filmways) attempted to build interest in Tate with its press release describing her as "one of the screen's most exciting new personalities." The film failed to make its mark among the ticket-purchasing public, although the *New York Times* wrote in its review that Tate's "chillingly beautiful but expressionless" performance is a high point of the film.

Premiere of *Valley of the Dolls* on the Cruise Liner *Princess Italia*: November 1967

Valley of the Dolls had its world premiere aboard a docked cruise liner, *Princess Italia*, on November 14, 1967, in Venice, Italy. The cruise liner was filled with the international press to see one of the most anticipated films in history. Patty Duke, Barbara Parkins, and Sharon Tate at last got to view the completed film—oi oi oi. Somehow the production had inadvertently become a comedy.

Afterward the good-natured Sharon willingly met for press interviews, while some of her costars attempted to elude the press. There are reports that Jacqueline Susann hid herself in her suite aboard the *Princess Italia* in disgust. Nevertheless, she remained aboard during the voyage.

The studio hired writer Army Archerd, and his associate Bill Burrud, to narrate a documentary tracing the multiweek world premiere trek. Sharon Tate is shown in the film answering questions; she apparently stayed aboard for the total voyage from Venice to the Canary Islands to Miami Beach, then to Nassau in the Bahamas, thence to Cartagena, Colombia, then through the Panama Canal to another premiere in Acapulco. The twenty-eight-day journey ended December 10 in Los Angeles, where the ship was greeted by a mariachi band.

Archerd interviewed Sharon for the documentary. She looked, as usual, very well turned out, in a black dress showing a lot of bare shoulder, long dangling earrings, and her hair pulled back, with a center part, into a bun in back.

Army Archerd asked, "The part calls for someone who is beautiful as well as talented. . . . Can you tell us how one gets in the mood to do something as daring as the disrobing you do in the film?"

Sharon replied, "Well, I don't think there's any mood. I think if you try to prepare yourself, you fall flat on your face. Actually it's very good, you know, it's something so difficult to do, and I found that if you FORGET more what you're doing, you know, and try not to be so self-conscious about things that are so normal, people don't notice you as much, as if you're trying to be so shy about everything."

One anecdote, told by Sharmagne Leland-St. John, involves the husband of one of the stars of *Valley of the Dolls*, with whom Leland-St. John later briefly lived. Sharon Tate, the story goes, asked the husband, who accompanied his wife on one leg of the cruise liner voyage, whether she should get married to Polanski. The husband advised against it, and Sharon purportedly thanked him profusely, saying something like, "Thank you, I really appreciate it, you saved my life, I'm not going to throw my life away." It has to be said that the husband has denied giving any such advice.

While Sharon was on the SS *Princess Italia* for the *Valley of the Dolls* promotional voyage, Roman was busy concluding work on *Rosemary's Baby*.

Once back in Los Angeles, Sharon and Judy Gutowski, wife of Cadre Films co-owner, Gene, took a mini-vacation to Big Sur, during which time Roman balled a young model at the Santa Monica beachfront mansion. When they returned, Mrs. Gutowski learned about the balling and told Sharon.

The poet Czeslaw Milosz and his wife were among the torrents of Polanski pals who enjoyed the mansion. He warned Polanski, according to Roman's autobiography, "If I were you, I would get them out of here. They're trying to turn Sharon against you." The former Polish diplomat, Milosz, who had broken with the Communist government, was then fifty-six, and would win the Nobel Prize in Literature in 1980.

Another version of the mini-vacation in Big Sur, according to another biography of Polanski, says this: "Tate's indulgence had already been put to a severe test in the period, some weeks before their wedding, when she and Polanski were living together in Santa Monica. During a weekend when Tate was away relaxing at a spa some 300 miles up the coast in Big Sur, the director had invited a young Balinese model over for the night. Gene Gutowski and his wife Judy also happened to be staying at the house for several weeks. Polanski had apparently thought nothing of it—the girl was gone again by Sunday evening, in good time for him to welcome Sharon back at the airport. . . . Judy told Sharon about the model as soon as she got back."

About two weeks before Christmas, 1967, Polanski, Mia Farrow, the producer William Castle, cameraman William Fraker, and the crew returned for final filming of exteriors in Christmas-shopper-dappled New York City. Polanski refilmed the opening shot from the ledge of the rooftop of the building across from the Dakota. It had been the first thing filmed the previous summer, but the director, always a perfectionist, didn't dig the results, so had it redone. After that, it was back to Los Angeles for final work. Shooting for *Rosemary's Baby* at Paramount Studios was not finished until after Christmas.

Not afraid to shoot and reshoot and reshoot certain scenes, Polanski saw *Rosemary's Baby* go $400,000 over its $1.9 million budget, just as *The Fearless Vampire Killers* had gone over by $300, 000.

End of 1967: Getting Out of Her Contract with Martin Ranshohoff

Not long after the *Princess Italia* docked in Los Angeles, Sharon went to Martin Ransohoff, stating that she wanted out of the remaining three years of her contract in order to retire from filmmaking and become a full-time wife. She told Ransohoff she wanted to start a family with Polanski.

Mr. Ransohoff agreed, as he later recounted, "conditioned on her intention to retire." One apparent provision of the let-out was that she turn over twenty-five percent of her earnings the next four years. Sharon agreed to those terms. That way, she'd be Free Free Free to seek out roles that would offer her the best chance to show her true abilities for comedy and acting.

Another account has it occurring around the time of the release of *Valley of the Dolls*. "Around that time," Ransohoff recalled in an interview, Sharon asked to be freed from her contract. "She told me she really wanted to have kids and didn't want to continue her movie career," he said. Ransohoff must have realized that it was a fib, because Sharon soon continued her film career.

Sharon was featured in a pictorial spread in the December 1967 issue of *Esquire* magazine, along with quotations from Chinese leader Mao Tse-tung. The spread bore the title, "A Beginner's Guide to Mao Tse-tung." It began: "The little red book which contains highlights from The Thought of Mao Tse-tung is the most influential volume in the world today. It is also extremely dull and entirely unmemorable. To resolve this paradox, we, a handful of editors in authority who follow the capitalist road, thought it useful to illustrate certain key passages in such a way that they are more likely to stick in the mind. The visual aid is Sharon Tate and, to give credit where credit, God knows, is due, she will soon be seen in the Twentieth Century-Fox motion picture, *Valley of the Dolls*.

1. Every communist must grasp the truth, 'Political power grows out of the barrel of a gun.' 'Problems of War and Strategy' (November 6, 1938). [This caption was accompanied by a photo of Sharon on one knee, flashing a lot of bare chest, her right hand grasping the top of a rifle, and her left hand grasping a pointed pistol.]

2. Our fundamental task is to adjust the use of labor power in an organized way and to encourage women to do farm work. 'Our Economic Policy' (January 23, 1934) [This was accompanied by a shot of curvy Sharon curled atop a bale of straw.]

3. How is Marxist-Leninist theory to be linked with the practice of the Chinese revolution? To use a common expression, it is by 'shooting the arrow at the target.' As the arrow is to the target, so is Marxism-Leninism to the Chinese revolution. Some comrades, however, are 'shooting without a target,' shooting at random, and such people are liable to harm the revolution. 'Rectify the Party's Style of Work' (February 1, 1942). [With this was a shot of Sharon in a wet T-shirt, holding a bow.]

4. The world is yours, as well as ours, but in the last analysis, it is yours. You young people, full of vigor and vitality, are in the bloom of life, like the sun at eight or nine in the morning. Our hope is placed on you. The world belongs to you. China's future belongs to you. Talk at a meeting with Chinese students and trainees in Moscow (November 17, 1957).

5. The flattery of the bourgeoisie may conquer the weak-willed in our ranks. There may be some Communists, who were not conquered by enemies with guns and were worthy of the name of heroes for standing up to these enemies, but who cannot withstand sugar-coated bullets. We must guard against such a situation. 'Report to the Second Plenary Session of the Seventh Central Committee of the Communist Party of China' (March 5, 1949). [This was adorned with a photo of bare-chested Sharon, whose bosom tip is covered by a dangling bandoleer packed with bullets.]

6. Whoever wants to know a thing has no way of doing so except by coming into contact with it, that is, by living (practicing) in its environment. . . . If you want knowledge, you must take part in the practice of changing reality. If you want to know the taste of a pear, you must change the pear by eating it yourself. 'On Practice' (July, 1937). [This had a shot of Sharon, in a very open blouse, holding a bitten-into pear.]"

All in all, this *Esquire* spread combined a satiric putdown of Maoism with the gun-toting open-bosomed eroticism of a rising actress, befitting the daughter of an Army Intelligence officer serving in Korea during the Vietnam War.

Meanwhile, the reviews for *Valley of the Dolls* must not have been pleasant to read for the movie's key players, including Sharon. Bosley Crowther, for instance, in the *New York Times*, began his review: "Bad as Jacqueline Susann's *Valley of the Dolls* is as a book, the movie Mark Robson has made from it is that bad or worse. It's an unbelievably hackneyed and mawkish mish-mash of back stage plots and "Peyton Place" adumbrations in which five women are involved with their assorted egotistical aspirations, love affairs and Seconal pills. It's every bit as phony and old-fashioned as anything Lana Turner ever did, and all a fairly respectful admirer of movies can do is laugh at it and turn away."

He mentions, without praise, "Sharon Tate as a no-talent showgirl who gives up when she has to have a breast removed." Even with poor reviews, however, the movie did very well at the box office. As columnist Joyce Haber noted, on January 29, 1968, "*Dolls*, which has to be among the worst movies of all times, is somehow breaking box office records across the country. If it continues at this pace, it bids to be among the top grossers in movie history. *Dolls* is exceptional, a bad movie gone berserk. Bad reviews and worse word-of-mouth seem only to enhance its appeal for audiences. And this, with a cast headed by Sharon Tate, Patty Duke, and Barbara Parkins!"

Chapter 5

1968: Marriage and Rising in Hollywood

Sharon and Roman were married on January 20, 1968. Polanski later wrote this about the decision to get married: "Sharon made no secret of her strong desire to have a child. Although she never mentioned marriage, and despite her liberated California life-style, I knew that her Catholic upbringing made marriage important to her . . . I proposed off the cuff, over dinner in a restaurant. . . . We decided to get married in London; that was my real home and the place where most of our friends lived."

Off the cuff in London meant that her mother, Doris, and father, Paul, could not attend. Telegrams were sent out to friends. The wedding was at 11 a.m. at the Chelsea Registry Office on Kings Road. There was a civil ceremony followed by several celebrations. Sharon's costar in *Valley of the Dolls*, Barbara Parkins, was her maid of honor. Roman's business partner, Gene Gutowski, was the best man. There was a crowd of reporters and gawkers.

It was a mod wedding, and Sharon and Roman were dressed in the height of fashion for the time, rich hippie. Roman was attired in a green Teddyboy jacket he had purchased at a Hollywood boutique. Sharon, with the spirit of her mother's home economics skills in the fore, had designed her own wedding dress, a cream-hued taffeta ultra minidress. "It's Renaissance until you get below the knees," as Sharon humorously described her design to the press.

On again/off again Sebring girlfriend Sharmagne Leland-St. John flew over to London for the wedding. She was on hand working on an album by actor Richard Harris. "Sharon was especially beautiful," recalls Leland-St. John. "Carrie White did her hair, Carrie and I were on the plane together flying over.

She had sprinkled little flowers throughout Sharon's curls. Sharon wore a puff-sleeved mini wedding gown."

It was just before her twenty-fifth birthday.

"Sharon and I are very happy," Polanski proclaimed. To which Sharon added "I'm so happy I can't believe it!"

Press from London and around the world covered the wedding. The marriage brought the couple vast oodles of ink and attention, for few events are more adored by show business than an unusual and even improbable marriage of hot young stars. This filled the bill, and filled it to overflowing. Peter Sellers was there for the wedding and the several celebrations. One was held at the Playboy Club. Among the attendees were Brian Jones, Sean Connery, Rudolf Nureyev, Princess Radziwill, Leslie Caron, Candy Bergen, Joan Collins, Michael Caine, and many others.

The author of *Valley of the Dolls*, Jacqueline Susann, also attended one of the wedding parties, at a doctor's house (probably Polanski's neighbor Dr. Green-burgh). She recalled it later: "It was quite a thing. She was very happy, but she was completely under Roman's domination. He doesn't look it, but he must be a dominating man. Many little men, Billy Rose, Napoleon for example, were dominating with women.

"At the reception, there were people like Warren Beatty, Leslie Caron, some of Warren's ex-girlfriends, Tony Curtis's ex-wife, the German one, came floating in. And Sharon came in a black chiffon dress, a 1930s thing she had bought in a thrift shop. It was a kind of maxi-dress. Roman took one look and he didn't like it. He told her so, and she went back to where they were staying and changed to a miniskirt." And this: "She was a very vulnerable girl, and she wanted to do whatever Roman wanted."

Roman fed Sharon part of a piece of the wedding cake, and given all the up-beat ebullience, the future seemed as brightly illuminated as ever a wedding could have predicted. Their honeymoon was spent skiing in the Swiss Alps.

Under the headline, "Mini Skirt Brawl for Roman and Sharon," the *Daily Mirror* of London on February 9, almost three weeks after the wedding, reported: "Film Director Roman Polanski came back from his honeymoon recently with an arm bandaged and three stitches on his lip. And the cause of the injuries, it seems was a mini skirt worn by his bride of eleven days—actress Sharon Tate, who is pictured with him at Heathrow Airport, London. Sharon, 24, and Polanski were walking to see a film in Paris when her eye-catching suede mini proved too much for a passerby. The man looked . . . and looked again . . . and then made a grab for Sharon. Polanski, 34, took a swing at the man, a Spaniard. The Spaniard punched back. 'It was quite a fight, all over the pavement,' Polanski said at the airport, after flying in from Paris. 'I got a few kicks as well as punches. But I gave him something to remember.' Finally, the stranger ran away. Polanski who married Sharon at Chelsea Register Office, London, went to the hospital to have his badly cut lip stitched. Sharon is star of the recently released film *Valley of the Dolls*."

When Sharon and Roman went back to Los Angeles from their honeymoon, there was another party given by friend Steve Brandt on February 18, 1968. Attendees included Patty Duke, columnist Rona Barrett, actress Lynn Loring and her husband, Roy Thinnes, actor and singer Michael Crawford, Noel Harrison, and apparently also Barbra Streisand and Elliott Gould. Sharon was on the rise.

A Brazilian magazine, *Capricho*, ran an article in its March 1968 issue titled "Hollywood Is Hell's Gate." It commenced with an all-caps breathlessness: "SHARON TATE, ONE OF THE MOST PROMISING AMERICAN STARS OF THE NEW GENERATION, ACCUSES HOLLYWOOD OF BEING FALSELY MORALIST AND SAYS THAT THE OLD CINEMA MECCA IS VERY DEPRAVED. SHE RESISTED A LOT OF PRESSURE TO GET HER STARDOM AND ENDURED ALL KINDS OF THREATS, EVEN FROM THE PRODUCER WHO DISCOVERED HER, JUST BECAUSE SHE DIDN'T WANT TO BREAK UP OR BETRAY HER GREAT LOVE."

Then it quotes Sharon at length: "I'm completely psychedelic. And not in Julie Christie's way, please! I know there are people who think that I imitate her! Can you believe that? I want much more freedom than she has. Julie became a slave of her ambition. I think she's frustrated. Now she says she's neurotic. I'm not inhibited at all. I just do what I want. If I feel like it, I flirt with a cab driver. I like new things, try new sensations. Why not?"

It also describes Sharon's troubles with her handler Martin Ransohoff when she fell in love with Roman: "I never promised Martin I would give up the right to live my own life the way I want. And then, it's funny when one falls in love. It happens suddenly. Contracts, plans, everything changes at that moment. The notion I was in love with Roman overwhelmed me. Nothing else mattered. It's wonderful and horrible at the same time. I stayed in London with Roman. I made *Fearless Vampire Killers* for him. Martin wouldn't accept it. He even threatened me. I told him to go to hell. And what annoyed him the most was that I was living with Roman. 'At least, get married,' he would shout. It's funny; Hollywood is a very depraved place, the hell's door, but knows how to be Victorian when it's about beginners like me. The pressure was such that Roman understood. He married me. He's an angel. He realized it was necessary. Hollywood offered me something wonderful through Martin Ransohoff: the role of

Jennifer, in *Valley of the Dolls*, America's number one best seller. The depraved and pill addicted vamp was coveted by people such as Candice Bergen, Anna Karina, Anouk Aimee, Anne Bancroft. They wanted to give me the role if I married Roman. And that happened. The worst, now, is that Martin doesn't know that when I love I don't give a damn to career and fame. When I love and get married, I want children, a home, a quiet life. He says *Valley of the Dolls* put Hollywood at my feet. And so what? Women who can handle marriage and career are very rare. When you want both things tragedy happens: the husband is jealous of his wife's success, the wife gets tired of the husband's jealousy, just because she wants the husband as much as her career. And what's more important? A magazine cover to look at for one whole day, or the love of a husband to have your whole life?" We're assuming the quote above is more or less accurate.

Roman in Early 1968

A filmmaker is always sketching new projects. And working maybe on a few scripts at the same time, even while completing a complicated creation such as *Rosemary's Baby*. Even before realizing that *Rosemary* would be a hit, Paramount started putting the brakes on Polanski's two additional Cadre-Paramount projects. They outright rejected the treatment of a "Western spoof" by Gérard Brach and started putting road-blocks into the Redford film, *Downhill Racer*.

Polanski wanted to film *Downhill Racer*: "I put a lot of work into it, developing a script with Jimmy Salter, and experimented with camera equipment and harnesses that could be mounted on skis." Polanski was eager to film in Europe, at major ski places, but Paramount wanted it done in the United States.

It was Robert Redford's project—he had conceived the idea of a movie about Alpine skiing, did research on the European ski tour, had talked Paramount into backing the film, then wound up producing and starring in the picture. Redford originally wanted Roman Polanski to direct the movie.

The details are lost in the time-mists, but after discussing budgets for several weeks, Paramount grew tired of the negotiations, and decided to hire a new director named Michael Ritchie for the Redford movie.

Polanski acquired an agent named Bill Tennant, connected with the Ziegler Ross Agency. They became friends. (Tennant, the following August, would be the one who had to make the fateful call to London to inform his client of the horrible events on Cielo Drive.) Tennant suggested that Polanski take some time off before trying to find a new movie to direct. That had important repercussions for Polanski, for had he been able to get a fully-funded big-studio Robert Redford project going, it would have allowed him to escape his past pattern of doing films in the occult/weirdo/violence warp. But such was not to be.

Polanski, whose film trajectory began with the two-minute film titled *Murder*, while at film school in Poland, and proceeded through *Knife in the Water*, *Repulsion, Cul-de-Sac*, and now *Rosemary's Baby*, seemed to be taken aback by the incoming flux of scripts dealing with "horror stories, exclusively concerned with madness and the occult," as he later described it in his autobiography. And he claimed "they didn't interest me in the least." Except that soon he began work on a screenplay featuring the cannibalism of the Donner Party!

The Chateau Marmont

Brian Aherne extended the lease on the *Rosemary's Baby*–era mansion in Santa Monica, but finally Polanski and Sharon moved. Polanski says they moved to an apartment-hotel called the Sunset Marquis. Their stay at the Marquis was brief, for they then soon rented a fourth floor apartment with a kitchenette at the far-famed Chateau Marmont. (They stayed in Suite 3F at the Chateau.) A bunch of other friends also took rooms at the Chateau, as Polanski noted, where there "evolved a daily routine that began when [Brian] Morris and [Simon] Hesera showed up in their bathrobes for Sharon to cook us a communal breakfast."

By 1968, the success of *Bonnie and Clyde* had caused Warren Beatty to become very powerful in the movie industry, and Beatty would visit the scene at the Chateau Marmont. As the book *Easy Riders, Raging Bulls—How the Sex-Drugs-and-Rock 'n' Roll Generation Saved Hollywood* describes it, "Beatty used to go to parties at the Chateau Marmont, where Roman Polanski and his girlfriend,

The Cheateau Marmount, from a lobby postcard

Sharon Tate, Dick Sylbert, and Paul, Dick's identical twin brother, also a production designer, and Paul's wife, Anthea, all had suites. Polanski, funny and elfin, loved to perform. He told stories that went on and on, twenty, thirty minutes. 'You couldn't get a word in edgewise,' recalls Dick, who designed *Rosemary's Baby*, which they had just finished. 'The guy was like those kids who get up at bar mitzvahs and dance and sing. Drive people crazy. And competitive. You told a joke, he told a joke. But he was a sweet-heart.'"

Tate and Polanski were one of the hottest of the hottest young couples in Hollywood. The newspapers and magazines paid constant attention to them. Now that money was bountifully inflowing, they could fly at will, or on whim, from London to New York to Paris to Los Angeles to wherever. They were invited to countless nights out with the wealthy and the famous. In the weeks prior to the release of *Rosemary's Baby*, while they were residing at the Chateau Marmont, they were completely swathed in renown.

One disturbing possibility regarding Sharon Tate's residency at the Chateau Marmont has to do with an investigation, in 1974 (six years later), conducted by an Immigration and Naturalization Service (INS) agent named Richard Smith. (The INS is a branch of the US Department of Justice.) Smith gathered information on the activities of an English occult group that had oozed to the United States in 1967 and 1968. John Phillips reportedly had befriended the group and donated oodles of money to it.

Smith prepared a report in October of 1974, in which he stated that information provided by the LA County sheriff's office stated that Sirhan Sirhan "was contacted by" the satanic English organization "and had attended some parties given by television personalities in behalf of the organization, where rites took place usually dealing with sexual deviations and heavy drug use. One of these parties took place at Sharon Tate's home."

The only two possibilities for such a party at Sharon Tate's home, during this time frame, would be either the mansion she and Roman had rented at 1038 Palisades Beach Road during the filming of *Rosemary's Baby* (which they had moved out of in early 1968), or the Chateau Marmont, where they dwelled during the winter and spring of 1968. (See the afterword to this book for further information.)

Mia to India with the Beatles

As for the star, Mia Farrow, just a few weeks after giving birth to the devil child in *Rosemary's Baby*, she set out in February of 1968 for a three-month retreat in what was called Transcendental Meditation led by a spiritual leader named Maharishi Mahesh Yogi and held in northern India, near the Ganges.

It was a very famous gathering, mainly because the Beatles along with their wives and mates joined the retreat, as did others, such as the folk singer Donovan, Beach Boy Mike Love, jazz musician Paul Horn, Mia's sister and her brother John, and maybe thirty others.

Soon there was discontent in the retreat. For instance, the Maharishi wanted the Beatles to tithe from 15 to 25 percent of their annual incomes to his Swiss bank account. Also the sacred leader made sexual advances to a California woman on hand, allegedly rubbing her crotch during private sessions of therapy aimed at promoting cosmic awareness therapy.

At last, John Lennon told the Maharishi he was leaving, and when he was asked why, Lennon replied, "You're the cosmic one, you should know."

The experience with the Maharishi led John Lennon in a few months to write the song that became "Sexy Sadie" on the *White Album*. It was a tune Charles Manson and his family felt was directly aimed at Susan Atkins (aka Sadie Glutz) under her Manson Family nickname, Sexy Sadie.

Perhaps it's too bad Manson couldn't have gone along on the spiritual journey to the Ganges. Perhaps he could have calmed down his turbulent psyche in the vibes of northern India. Or maybe he too, as Lennon, would have sniffed something lacking and scamful in the Maharishi's act.

Meanwhile, just a couple of weeks after the Beatles and Mia were hanging out with the Maharishi, there was a very upbeat article in *Newsweek* titled "The New American Beauties," with text such as: "Astoundingly photogenic, infinitely curvaceous, Sharon Tate is one of the most smashing young things to hit Hollywood in a long time. She began as the invention of wheeler-dealer Martin Ransohoff and in her five years on the Hollywood treadmill, she has, surprisingly, made progress. In fact, in her last film, *Valley of the Dolls*, she managed to be the only living doll. Now married to the brilliant and volatile Polish director Roman Polanski, perhaps she will begin to fulfill her tremendous potential.

"Remembering her husband's *Repulsion*, she dreams: 'I'd like to be an American Catherine Deneuve. She plays beautiful, sensitive, deep parts with a little bit of intelligence behind them.' [*Newsweek* borrowed the above two lines from the 1966 promo documentary, *All Eyes on Sharon Tate*.] And then about her past, 'They see me as a dolly on a trampoline.' Her gorgeous hazel eyes open wide at the thought of Faye Dunaway. 'Dunaway!' she sighs. 'Ooooooooohhhh! She's a woman. She's there, you know it, and there's no way around it.' But Sharon Tate is still looking for Sharon Tate.

"'Sometimes,' she sighs, 'I think it would be better to be a sex symbol, because at least I would know where I was. But,' she adds quickly, 'I'd lose my mind.'"

Also in March of 1968, columnist Sheilah Graham wrote: "It's a little bit awkward between Sharon Tate and her discoverer Marty Ransohoff, since her marriage to Roman Polanski. Roman and Ransohoff are in a bitter feud. Sharon is still under contract to Marty, but I'll bet that if she asked in a nice way for her release, she'd get it. The producer spent two years building Sharon to the point where she could act. One of the provisos was that she would not marry for several years. You can fight everyone except Cupid!"

In the spring of 1968, Mia Farrow had already begun work on a movie in London, *A Dandy in Aspic*, a spy movie with Laurence Harvey, but Polanski needed to do some last minute dubbing of Farrow, so he flew to London.

One of Sharon and Roman's good friends in London was Victor Lownes, head of Hugh Hefner's Playboy Club in England. It happened to be around the time of Lownes's birthday, so Sharon, Roman, and Gene Gutowski hatched up an idea for the "perfect gift"—a cock of gold. Sharon was acquainted with a Hollywood jeweler, and called him up. He did not have a life-sized penis of gold, but offered to make one, "if you supply the model."

Gene Gutowski created a version of his own, which Roman and Sharon brought to the jeweler. It was made and Roman brought it to London on a flight, stuffing it down his pants to get through Customs. The auric penis did not present any trouble, but Customs held up Mr. Polanski because of his can of film that needed dubbing, till Paramount sent someone to the airport to clear things up.

A Plane Trip to San Francisco to Show *Rosemary*

Living with Jay Sebring at the time, early 1968, was actress Sharmagne Leland-St. John. For this book she consulted her calendar for 1968, and reported: "Friday March the 19th we flew to San Francisco for *Rosemary's Baby*, and then under that it says party Sharon Tate and Roman."

About the trip, she further stated: "I do remember Jay and I dropping acid and going on a private plane with Roman and Sharon and I think Simon Hesera, Sharon's Mom and Dad, possibly Mia Farrow, and a few other's to somewhere up North for a sneak preview of *Rosemary's Baby*." LSD was more casually quaffed in the late 1960s than in any set of years since. It was everywhere.

There was that spring a further tad of glory for Sharon. The annual poll of the US movie theater owners, as tabulated by the industry trade paper *Independent Film Journal*, and reported in the *Los Angeles Times* for April 20, 1968, listed Sharon Tate as one of the best female "New Faces." She joined Faye Dunaway, Raquel Welch, Katharine Ross, Jean Shrimpton, Lesley Ann Warren, Judy Geeson, and Michele Lee.

The Beatles, Apple Records, and Terry Melcher

John Lennon and Paul McCartney flew to New York in May of 1968 to announce the formation of Apple Records. Both appeared on *The Tonight Show*, watched by twenty-five million people, and urged musicians and songwriters to send demo tapes to Apple for consideration of being offered a record deal. The word rocketed across the world, causing a total flood of tapes, ideas, proposals, and requests. The Beatles, because of the extraordinary success of their albums, *Rubber Soul* and *Sgt. Pepper* among them, plus their movies, were extraordinarily wealthy, and so the promise of Apple Records to provide a pay-off for demo tapes was believable.

Terry Melcher became a producer associated with Apple that summer, a fact with many karmic knots in the knotty future. Melcher was living at 10050 Cielo Drive with Candice Bergen.

Liberté Égalité Fraternité

In the United States the student takeover of Columbia University had just occurred, and then there was the great uprising in France which began in early May, during which the labor unions and students would form a successful coalition that brought about wage increases and nearly toppled the government of Charles De Gaulle.

The ghosts of 1789 danced into Paris with those three thrilling words, Liberté, Égalité, and Fraternité, as they do every few decades—for another great tossing it up for the Goddess of Grabs.

Back in March there had been attacks on US facilities in Paris over Vietnam. Several were arrested from the university in the Parisian suburb of Nanterre, a subsidiary of the Sorbonne. Then students had taken over the administrative building of the faculty.

Though there's no movement in world history with more splintery factions than the French Left, at that moment, March 22, seemingly led by Daniel Cohn-Bendit, a coalition of Guevarists, Anarchists, and Trotskyites from the Nanterre faculty formed a coalition to occupy the college. This was the movement known as Le 22 Mars. They were driven out of the buildings, and on May 3 they took refuge at the Sorbonne in Paris.

It was then the ghosts of 1789 began the "Whole World Is Watching" dance of 1968 and the well-organized cadres of various factions went into a rock-throwing, car-burning, poster-pasting, barricade-building war with the bourgeois State. Throughout the month of May there were riots and just about every university in the nation was closed. A million took to the streets in a spontaneous swell. "At last the spark has caught the wick," wrote artist/activist Jean-Jacques Lebel.

The radio kept people at barricades informed of what was happening—twenty thousand students occupied the Latin Quarter. Barge traffic was halted, the ports shut down. No trains. No planes. No mail.

When workers are well organized, that is, "know the new facts early," they can respond very quickly when industry tries to lower conditions, and so in France in 1968, farmers on their tractors came to the cities, joining the students while demanding full employment, fair taxation, higher income, and a larger voice in government.

As a result there was the Grenoble Protocol in which French industrialists had to give 10 percent wage increases in 1968 plus rises in both industrial and agricultural minimum wages, and a reduction of between one to two hours in the workweek. It was a thrill to follow in the newspapers of the spring of 1968. I could feel the ghosts of 1789 back in glory.

Meanwhile, Roman and Sharon drove down to Cannes on the French Riviera for the twenty-first Cannes Film Festival, scheduled for May 10–24. They pulled up to their hotel on May 12 in Roman's red Ferrari, with a great amount of luggage, and outfitted with a new-fangled tape deck that was blaring the unreleased Rolling Stones tune "Jumpin' Jack Flash." They were attired as if they were hot stuff in a cold universe—that is, in matching suede suits from Rodeo Drive, and various beaded necklaces and medallions. Hot stuff. Cold universe.

Roman Polanski was slated to be a judge, along with Louis Malle, Monica Vitti, and Terence Young, the British director of the early James Bond films. Among the twenty-six films selected for competition were Alain Resnais's *Je t'aime, je t'aime,* Milos Forman's *The Fireman's Ball,* Jan Nemec's *A Report on the Party and the Guests,* Richard Lester's *Petulia,* and Carlos Saura's *Peppermint Frappé.*

Summoned to a meeting about closing the festival, Polanski was applauded, but also booed and hissed, when he spoke against closing. Coming from Communist Poland, Polanski was very suspicious of left movements. "My own views were clear. I thought it utterly absurd to disrupt the festival on the ground that it was an elitist capitalist symbol."

Jean-Luc Godard, with whom Polanski had had friction in the past, announced that while he was willing for films to be shown, he wanted the festival totally reorganized, and no prizes awarded. Francois Truffaut, for his part, called for a complete cessation. "Everything that has a shred of dignity and importance is stopping in France," Truffaut said at the time. "I don't know how one must do it, but I know that this afternoon or tonight, at least through radio since there are no newspapers, it must be announced that the Cannes festival is stopped or at least substantially reformed."

In an interesting article, "Cannes 1968: Fighting on the Beaches," by Richard T. Kelly, it was noted: "One of the most striking features of newsreel footage of the festival is the onstage dynamic between the leading protesters, especially between Truffaut and Godard. Truffaut does a good job of communicating clearly, informing those assembled why Cannes should be closed down, even if he appears to entertain the possibility of continued screenings. Godard, on the other hand, comes across as grim-faced, hectoring and abusive, his legendary sardonic wit clearly having left the building." Godard claimed that everyone gathered in the Grande Salle, and the film industry itself, was failing to recognize the current time of revolution. "There's not a single film," said Godard, "that shows the problems that workers and students are going through. Not one. Whether made by Forman, by me, by Polanski, or Francois. We've missed the boat!'"

While some in the audience booed, Godard declared, "It's not a matter of continuing or not continuing to watch films. It's a matter of cinema showing solidarity with the student movement, and the only practical way of doing this is to stop all the projections immediately."

Polanski did reluctantly ultimately vote to close down the festival. One by one members of the Cannes jury started to resign—it began with Louis Malle, followed by Polanski, Italian actress Monica Vitti, and the British Terence Young.

"I was forced to resign," Polanski later reasoned. "It was not at all my feeling that we should have resigned. I came from Communist Poland, and I knew moments of elation like this where suddenly you just feel like you're doing something great, when in fact it's just an illusion."

"By this time the general strike was spreading throughout France," he wrote in his autobiography. "Train and plane services were grinding to a halt, gas stations running dry. Exhibitors began to pack up and go home and the festival ended in complete disarray."

Variety printed that Elizabeth Taylor and Richard Burton had chartered a private plane from London to get the stranded Universal Studios contingent out of Cannes. With the festival canceled, Roman drove Sharon to Rome with Michael Sarne following in another car, for an unplanned week of fun.

While in Rome, Sharon and Roman took part in a fifty-five-minute documentary made by Gideon Bachmann titled *Ciao Federico! Fellini Directs Satyricon*, in which the couple made a brief visit to the Cinecittà Studios during the filming of Fellini's film, *Satyricon*, set in the first century AD. Slender Sharon was wearing a miniskirt and a long-sleeved white pullover, plus dangling from her shoulders was a small dark purse on long thin straps. She was holding her sunglasses in her hand as they walked around the set. Sharon and Roman's brief walk-on at Cinecittà features a voice, apparently Polanski's, apparently inspired by the Roman-era set, urging Fellini to visit Disneyland, describing how on his first visit to Disneyland with Sharon they were high.

After the fun in Rome, the couple returned to London, then flew to Los Angeles. "Sharon's film career was progressing far better than mine," Polanski later wrote. "A funereal atmosphere reigned at Paramount. Expensive failures like *Darling Lili, Paint Your Wagon,* and *The Molly Maguires* had lost a fortune. [Paramount big wig] Bluhdorn responded by stripping Paramount of its saleable assets. He dismantled the studio, fired many of the skilled technicians who'd spent their whole lives on the lot, and transferred Paramount's headquarters to a small building in Beverly Hills."

Polanski arrived at the studio in the midst of this trouble. Even with *Rosemary's Baby* about to be a hit, the future looked, underneath the thrill of a success, a bit challenged and even bleak.

Sharon Tate, on the other hand, signed a deal to star in a Matt Helm spy-spoof with Dean Martin. Her fee was a nifty (for 1969) $125,000. ($1.00 in 1968 had about the same buying power as $6.37 in 2010, according to the website www. dollartimes.com. So that would make Sharon's fee for starring in the spy-spoof $796,250.) These were the months Tate was honored as a promising newcomer. She was nominated for a Golden Globe Award as "New Star of the Year—Actress" for her *Valley of the Dolls* performance, losing to Katharine Ross for *The Graduate.* She placed fourth behind Mia Farrow, Judy Geeson, and Katharine Houghton for a "Golden Laurel" award as the year's "Most Promising Newcomer," with the results published in the *Motion Picture Exhibitor* magazine. She was also runner-up to Lynn Redgrave in the *Motion Picture Herald*'s poll for "The Star of Tomorrow," in which box-office sales power was the main criterion for inclusion on the list. These sort of notices and laurels, while not the kind to get on the front page, combined to speed up her career, so that for her next film, her agent obtained an ever heftier fee.

Robert Kennedy's Campaign

Meanwhile the heroic and ever-burgeoning campaign of Senator Robert Kennedy (RFK) for the Democratic nomination to be president was blossoming forth. Patty Duke, Sharon's costar in *Valley of the Dolls,* was invited during the Oregon primary campaign, in late May, to fly up to speak at a rally for RFK at the University of Oregon.

According to John Phillips's autobiography, RFK's campaign, through Peter Lawford, asked Phillips to "write a Mamas and Papas song for his campaign in California. I never did write one, but we did meet Bobby and rode through L.A. on the back of a flatbed truck, singing songs for his rally that day just before the primary."

On the weekend before his final day, Robert Francis Kennedy made himself very tired in the struggle to win California (after losing in Oregon on May 28). Saturday evening, June 1, saw the debate with Eugene McCarthy in San Francisco. RFK prepared for it with briefing sessions at the Fairmont Hotel, and then did fairly well the histories say.

Sunday, June 2, Kennedy took six of his kids to Disneyland. Monday involved a long and exhausting series of plane rides, motorcades, and rallies up and down the state of California, covering the three main California "TV markets," till he ended that evening exhausted in San Diego almost unable to finish his speech at the El Cortez Hotel where friends, the singers Rosemary Clooney and Andy Williams, entertained the crowd, after which the entourage flew to Los Angeles.

During the flight RFK invited Rosemary Clooney to sit with Ethel and him. Then the Kennedys were driven to the house of Evans and John Frankenheimer at 101 Malibu Colony Road, for some privacy. Frankenheimer, the noted director of such films as *The Manchurian Candidate, Seven Days in May, Grand Prix,* and *Birdman of Alcatraz,* had been making a film of RFK and his campaign. Helping in the film project was movie art director Richard Sylbert, who lived in Malibu near the Frankenheimers. Evans and John spent the night somewhere else, giving Robert and Ethel some much-needed rest and privacy.

The Kennedys slept in the Frankenheimers' own bedroom. RFK at age forty-two had the wiriness of a coiled spring and the stamina of a star athlete in his rounds of campaigning. They said he slept only four hours a night but the non-stop weeks had sapped him. You know how it is—you boing awake, mind pulsing with stuff to do, calls to make, issues to jot down, and plans to polish.

Plus eating at the craw of his psyche, the death of his brother and the stomach-churning desire for vengeance on those who had done it.

Ethel was pregnant with their eleventh child. She too had bundles of energy, which she brought to the campaign with friend-rousing grace.

Richard Sylbert and Sarah Hudson

Living in a house on the beach near the Frankenheimers were set designer Richard Sylbert and actress Sarah Hudson, who had met Sylbert when both were living at the Chateau Marmont hotel in Los Angeles, in 1965. Sylbert was then busy designing *Who's Afraid of Virginia Woolf?,* starring Elizabeth Taylor and Richard Burton, which would win Sylbert an Academy Award. Not long after meeting, according to Sylbert's autobiography, he and Sarah, a stunning young woman striving for a career in acting, began living together.

They were still together in the late spring of 1968, and were staying at a beach house in Malibu near the beachfront house of John and Evans Frankenheimer.

Sylbert had just completed designing *Rosemary's Baby* for Roman Polanski, and was about to begin work on Mike Nichols's production of *Catch-22*. That spring, Sylbert had been assisting Frankenheimer in filming Robert Kennedy campaign events in California, and there was a dinner apparently in late May of 1968 at which Robert personally thanked Richard Sylbert for his work helping the campaign.

The morning of June 4, Robert Kennedy was up early after his tiring campaign trek of the previous days, and according to Sylbert's widow, took a walk in the company of Sarah Hudson along the Malibu beach. It was a vitally important morning for Kennedy, since voters in California were beginning to show up at election precincts to cast their ballots in the Democratic Primary.

Tate Family Website Maintains that Sharon Had Dinner with Kennedy on the Evening of June 3

Robert and Ethel would have arrived at Malibu late at night on June 3 after the exhausting day and evening campaigning. I would guess around 10 or 11 p.m., or maybe even at midnight. Could they have had a dinner at that time with Sharon Tate? The Sharon Tate website has it as follows: "Sharon had become very interested in the Presidential campaign of Robert Kennedy. She went to fund raising dinners in support of Kennedy and on June 3rd, 1968 attended a dinner at the home of John Frankenheimer. At the dinner was Robert Kennedy and his wife Ethel. Sharon was thrilled to be able to spend some time with Kennedy and felt even more convinced that he would make a wonderful president. However, the next day Kennedy was assassinated. Sharon was devastated not only over the death of an incredible man but also for the loss to the country." (The problem with June 3 was that RFK followed a super-busy almost nonstop final day of campaigning which did not stop till late in the evening in San Diego after which he and Ethel flew to Los Angeles, and then were driven to the Frankenheimer house in Malibu. They couldn't have arrived much before midnight, or perhaps even after.)

Robert Kaiser, in his book, *R.F.K. Must Die*, contends that Sharon and Roman, along with other guests, actually had dinner with Senator Kennedy in the early evening of June 4, California primary day. (I contacted Mr. Kaiser who was residing in Rome, and he replied that it was John Frankenheimer himself who claimed that the dinner on June 4 had actually occurred.)

Robert and Ethel Kennedy Spend Election Day in Malibu

First RFK, Ethel, and six of their ten children had lunch. Joining them was writer Theodore White in the midst of his research for a book on the 1968 race.

It was too cold to swim at Malibu, in the skin-chilling surf and a ten-mile-per-hour wind, but Robert Kennedy donned trunks and went with twelve-year-old David and three-year-old Max to the water's edge where he helped build a sand castle. He spotted David being pulled down by an undertow and dashed into the churn to save him, with father and son both a bit bruised from the saving.

After swimming in the ocean, there was more fun in the Frankenheimers' pool. RFK then changed, leaving his flashy pink and green Hawaiian trunks in the bedroom lavatory sink, where they remained till after the shooting, when some aides early in the morning arrived to retrieve his personal items.

That same day in London, at the studio on Abbey Road, John Lennon rere-corded the lead vocal for "Revolution" lying flat on his back. Also the same day Soviet tanks and troops shoved inward into Czechoslovakia ostensibly for maneuvers but excuses were found for leaving them there.

A couple of close RFK aides bought themselves bright-hued hippie attire to wear to the victory party that night at a discotheque called The Factory owned by Pierre Salinger and other well-known Democrats (such as Sammy Davis Jr.).

Senator Edward Kennedy, RFK speechwriter Richard Goodwin, and key RFK aide Fred Dutton arrived, and there was a bit of political talk, after which the candidate took a nap. Goodwin was getting some food from a buffet when he noticed RFK spread out across two chairs by the pool getting a restless shuteye.

Richard Goodwin Recalls June 4

Richard Goodwin had been a high official in the government of John F. Kennedy, and worked now as a speechwriter for his brother. In his memoir, *Remembering America*, (pp. 535–536), he recalled that after breakfast Bobby called him, telling him he was spending the day at the Frankenheimers' beach house in Malibu, and asking would Richard come out and join him.

When Richard arrived, he noted that there was a swimming pool and a broad patio separated by a glass wall from the living room and an adjoining dining room. He could see the "gentle-surfed" beach nearby. In the living room, Ethel Kennedy was talking with Theodore White and Evans Frankenheimer, but RFK was not on hand.

"Going into the next room for the buffet lunch," he writes, "I turned casually toward the pool. Robert Kennedy was stretched out across two chairs in the sunlight, he head hanging limply over the chair frame; his unshaven face was deeply lined, and his lips slightly parted. There was no movement. I felt a sudden spasm of fear. But it swiftly receded. He was sleeping, only sleeping."

Sometime later a telephone call had provided the first vote projections. By that time Robert and his assistant Fred Dutton were present in the living room. CBS television had surveyed voters in two hundred precincts as they left the polling places, and predicted RFK would win 49–41 over McCarthy. "They were pretty accurate in the other primaries," Kennedy remarked.

"But not in Oregon," replied Dutton.

Kennedy remarked how he had lost all the undecideds in Oregon, then also said, "Maybe they won't break away from us here. If only we can push up our percentage a point or two."

Goodwin commented how those in the room thought that, because of the Oregon defeat, Kennedy had to win big in California, "and that meant more than 50 percent of the vote, with 40 percent or less going to McCarthy. . . .

"We talked idly, reminisced, discussed future strategy, as if the big victory were already in—not because we were sure, but because that's the only way politicians can talk. But Kennedy was so tired that even the easily familiar shoptalk came haltingly, and he soon went back to the bedroom for a nap while I drove to my hotel to draft the victory statement."

RFK Restless in the Late Afternoon of June 4

RFK took a further nap (apparently in the bedroom) and then toward afternoon's end, around 6 p.m., was eager to head for the Ambassador Hotel in downtown Los Angeles. At around 6:30 p.m. John Frankenheimer himself drove RFK in his Rolls Royce to victory headquarters. Apparently Ethel was not quite ready, and went to the hotel a bit later. The children were to be transported to a bungalow at the Beverly Hills Hotel.

Problems of History: Figuring Out the Trip to the Ambassador

1. Evan Thomas, in his book *Robert Kennedy, His Life* (p. 387), wrote "At 6:30 it was finally time to head back into Los Angeles. . . . Frankenheimer daubed Kennedy's scraped and bruised forehead with some actor's makeup and Kennedy put on a blue pin-striped suit and a white shirt that made him look dashing." (There was no mention of Ethel on the trip.)

2. Jules Witcover, in *85 days* (p. 254), says RFK and key assistant Fred Dutton, but not Ethel, were driven to the Ambassador by "about 6:30." Kennedy was eager to get to the hotel, "but Ethel wasn't ready," so Frankenheimer wheeled them in the Rolls.

3. According to Lester David (*Ethel*, p. 196), "John Frankenheimer drove the Kennedys and the children down to town in his big car over back roads at speeds that made Ethel gasp. . . . At 7:15, they drew up before the Ambassador."

4. Robert Blair Kaiser, in *R.F.K. Must Die* (p. 15), mentions only RFK being driven by Frankenheimer to the Ambassador; but does not write that only RFK and Frankenheimer were in the Rolls.

The Dinner

Apparently John Frankenheimer had planned an early dinner and invited some guests over. According to *R.F.K. Must Die,* the guest list included director Roman Polanski, whose movie Rosemary's Baby was just about to open, and his wife, Sharon Tate.

Other guests, in Kaiser's recounting, were future head of Disney Pictures Frank Wells and his wife, Luanne, plus actress Anjanette Comer, nightclub owner Brian Morris, set designer Richard Sylbert, and Sarah Hudson. (I e-mailed Mr. Kaiser a few years ago, and he replied that Frankenheimer himself told him about the guest list and the early meal at his Malibu house.)

However, Evans Frankenheimer, widow of John Frankenheimer, informed me by e-mail during the writing of this book that there was no dinner served to Sharon Tate, Roman Polanski, Richard Sylbert, Sarah Hudson, and the others. She writes: "There was no dinner scheduled at our house in Malibu on the evening of the Democratic Primary, June 4th, 1968. The Kennedys wanted privacy during their stay at our house. There was, however, a large party scheduled at The Factory after the primary. The people you mentioned in your letter were on that guest list. It was not our private party and Sharon and Roman had been invited as guests of Dick Sylbert the set designer."

In preparation for this book, Richard Sylbert's widow, Sharmagne Leland-St. John (Richard Sylbert passed away in 2002), checked his day books, and reported the following entry by Sylbert: "On the afternoon of June 5th [actually the 4th], 1968 we all got into our respective Limousines outside the Frankenheimer's house and drove cautiously downtown to the Ambassador Hotel and walked into the Presidential Suites. One group disappeared with Bobby, while myself and Sarah (Hudson), along with several others went into a nearby suite. There were several old friends already ensconced there, Budd Schulberg, and as I remember, George Plimpton along with the mob of the faithful, chatting and watching the returns on the TV sets in each room." Sylbert does not mention Sharon and Roman.

(It may be that the invited guests appeared at the Frankenheimers' but then when RFK wanted to go early to the Ambassador, at least some of the guests in the "afternoon," as indicated by Sylbert's journal, piled into limousines and also drove to the hotel. It's murky.)

What is the answer? The past can be like quicksand.

Robert Kennedy's Drive to the Hotel

As we have noted, Kennedy was nervous and eager to get downtown, so John Frankenheimer wheeled his Rolls-Royce Silver Cloud rather rapidly on the Santa Monica Freeway toward the Ambassador Hotel. Since the last week of March, Frankenheimer had shot hours upon hours of film for a documentary on RFK to help him win in the fall. Frankenheimer missed the Vermont off ramp, and got mixed up in the Harbor Freeway interchange. He cursed angrily as he tried to get the Rolls headed back toward the hotel. "Take it easy, John," said Bob Kennedy. "Life is too short."

Kennedy's Suite at the Ambassador

The polls closed at 8 p.m., and it became certain that a huge Los Angeles pro-RFK vote was surging him to victory! Shortly after 9 p.m., Senator George McGovern called with good news from South Dakota, where Bobby had won the primary with more votes than Humphrey and McCarthy combined. A call came in from Richard Daley (mayor of Chicago and a Big Shaker in the party. He'd run the Democratic Convention in Chicago in August.) He was now an official RFK supporter. Pierre Salinger was standing next to RFK when Daley called: "Bobby & I exchanged a look that we both knew meant only one thing—he had the nomination."

Sirhan Sirhan That Day and Night

Three days previous, on Saturday, June 1, twenty-four-year-old Sirhan Sirhan had gone to the Corona Police Firing Range, where he later recalled that the range master showed him how to shoot at human targets and vital organs. Then, on the afternoon of June 4, while the polls were still open for the primary, Sirhan went target shooting in the company of a pretty young woman, quick-firing three hundred to four hundred rounds with a .22 at the San Gabriel Valley Gun Club in Duarte, outside Los Angeles.

In recent years, Sirhan has been examined and hypnotized for sixty hours over a three-year period, beginning in 2008, by a Harvard University memory expert, Dr. Daniel Brown. Half of the interviews involved hypnosis, and Dr. Brown has reported, in a court filing in 2011, the following about Sirhan Sirhan's memories of what he did on June 4, 1968:

"Mr. Sirhan freely recalled going to the gun range during the day of the assassination." Sirhan claimed he arrived at the Ambassador later that evening, looking for a party. Dr. Brown states that Sirhan recalled: "Now I'm going to another area . . . I don't know the name. . . . Later I heard it was the Embassy Room . . . it's like a huge hallway . . . tremendous lights . . . no tables . . . the

Sirhan's .22

brightness . . . a lot of people . . . I'm getting tired . . . I wasn't expecting this . . . It's getting hot . . . very hot . . . I want to get a drink. A make-shift bar area . . . I see a bartender . . . a white smock . . . he looked Latin . . . we just nodded . . . I told him what I wanted . . . it's like I have a relationship with this guy . . . Tom Collins . . . I drink it while I'm walking around . . . this bartender . . . he wasn't looking for a sale . . . he wasn't talkative . . . it is like he's communicating with gestures . . . a nod after I paid for it.

"I'm still looking around . . . he didn't make it (the drink) right in front of me . . . he made it and brought it over . . . after that I came back again . . . it was like a routine between us . . . like I'm more familiar . . . like I'm a regular customer of his . . . I don't remember seeing him before . . . it seemed like he was a professional . . . he never initiated a conversation but after a second time it was like there was a communication between us . . . he knew what I wanted . . . it's hard to figure out if he's targeting me or I'm targeting him . . . I don't remember him saying anything like 'shoot Kennedy' or anything like that . . . he's just very quiet . . . I begin to get tired . . . I sat down on one of the couches . . . I remember feeling that I had to go home . . . very bright lights . . . like under the sunlight . . . I want to go home . . . I've seen the party."

Dr. Brown: "It is notable that at this point in time Mr. Sirhan can only think about going home. Again, his expressed desire to leave the party and go home does not suggest the motivation of an assassin ready to kill a presidential candidate shortly thereafter."

Sirhan did attempt to go home: "I get in the car . . . I couldn't think about driving the car . . . it was late . . . I sit in the car . . . I couldn't make myself drive it. . . . There was no way I could drive the car . . . I don't want to chance it . . . I wanted to sleep . . . I wanted to sleep . . . sleep . . . sleep . . . sleep. Then I go back to the hotel to get some coffee."

According to Brown, "Mr. Sirhan recalled re-tracing his steps to the same bar. When Mr. Sirhan arrived at the bar he asked the same bartender for coffee. The bartender told him that there was no coffee at the bar. An attractive woman with a polka dot dress was sitting at the bar talking to the bartender. She overheard Sirhan asking for coffee and she said that she knew where coffee was."

Sirhan does not recall bringing his .22 from his DeSoto into the hotel. Dr. Brown: "Mr. Sirhan is adamant in his belief that he never brought the gun into the Ambassador Hotel. When asked to explain how he might have gotten a gun, he recalled being bumped up against and pushed around in the crowd on his way back to the bar to get coffee. He speculated, without specific recall, that the gun might have been placed in his waist band without his knowing it. It is also possible that the girl in the polka dot dress handed him the gun, but he does not remember so."

The Kennedy Suite Toward Midnight

The place was packed with favored friends and campaigners. Toward midnight, just before going down to the ballroom, RFK was talking with a close assistant and whispered that he thought they should tell Senator McCarthy that if he were to withdraw and support him, "I'll make him secretary of state."

In the final minutes in his suite Kennedy chatted with writer Budd Schulberg and some of his staff on what to say. Kennedy was speaking with civil rights hero John Lewis: "You let me down today," he joked. "More Mexican-Americans voted for me than Negroes." Those who heard laughed. "Wait for me," Kennedy said to Lewis, "I'll be back in fifteen or twenty minutes." To Lewis, RFK looked so happy "he could have floated out of the room."

He had a gulp of ginger ale, scanned himself in a mirror, then he was urged to go down. As he departed he asked that Al Lowenstein (organizer of the 1967 Dump Johnson movement) be telephoned in New York to say that RFK'd call him right after the victory speech.

RFK wanted to use the same path downward as back in Oregon a few days previous. There was a sort of gridlock in the hallway headed for the elevators. He encountered his eleven-year old daughter, Courtney, and paused a couple of minutes asking her about what her day had been like. They went down a freight elevator and through the kitchen, then up a ramp, then turning left, up through a curtain festooned with bunting with the candidate appearing on an utterly packed stage overlooking the ultrapacked Embassy Room.

He walked onto the stage with Dolores Huerta (cofounder with Cesar Chavez of the National Farm Workers Association) and escorted by Olympic decathlon champ Rafer Johnson and pro football star Roosevelt Grier, plus of course Ethel and some of their children.

The applause and excitement were enormous. There were jubilant young men in Kennedy straw hats and women in white blouses, red Kennedy sashes, and blue skirts. It was very, very hot in the ballroom. At first, there was trouble with the microphones on stage, but after about 20–30 seconds it was taken care of, and wow was the stage crowded! It was a time of playful joy. The winner first congratulated Don Drysdale of the Dodgers who'd just won a three-hit shutout. "He pitched his sixth straight shutout tonight, and I hope we have as good fortune in our campaign."

He thanked those who'd helped him, beginning a speech which would run around twelve and a half minutes.

A Plan to Talk with Pencil Press, Fred Dutton
Interrupts and Changes RFK's Stage Exit Plan

Uno Timanson, Ambassador vice president, was personally prepared, after the senator had completed his victory speech in the Embassy Room, to lead the senator down to the Ambassador Ballroom through the enclosed stairway. Just before the senator's speech was completed, Fred Dutton, one of the senator's aides, asked Timanson if there were television sets in the Ambassador Ballroom, and Timanson told him there were. It was then decided that the senator would visit the Press Room to make a press statement. Therefore, while Kennedy was standing at the dais to speak Dutton informed Uno Timanson that Kennedy would not be going down to the Ambassador Ballroom one floor beneath the Embassy where the overflow was watching RFK on television monitors. "The Senator will go to the Colonial Room," Fred Dutton told Timanson, "to have a session with the pencil press." Timanson escorted the senator and his party through the hallway behind the Embassy Room and into the pantry area, which was just a few feet away from the press.

Kennedy's security guys, nevertheless, were prepared to take him to the pencils by side steps off the stage. Thus, the Fates decided that Kennedy would be unguarded in his post-speech trip through the pantry.

Official with Suit and Clipboard Sends Sirhan and Polka
Dot from an Anteroom by the Stage to the Kitchen

Dr. Daniel Brown described in his 2011 court filing Sirhan's account of what happened during Kennedy's speech: "The woman in the polkadot dress then took

Sirhan by the hand and led him to the anteroom behind the stage where Senator Kennedy was speaking." There they found some coffee, at which point, Sirhan begins to feel attracted to her ("It was my job to woo her") when all of a sudden, according to Brown, "they are interrupted by an official with a suit and clip board. This official tells them that they cannot stay in the anteroom for security reasons, and the official then tells the girl in the polka dot dress to go to the kitchen."

Sirhan: "All of a sudden they tell us, we have to move. This guy comes by wearing a suit . . . darkish hair . . . a big full face . . . seems like he was in charge . . . he wasn't wearing any uniform . . . wearing a suit . . . she acknowledges his instruction . . . he motions towards the pantry. The man said, 'you guys can go back in this room.' I followed her. She led . . . I was a little like a puppy after her. I wanted to go back to the mariache band . . . but she went straight to the pantry area . . . with my being so attracted to her I was just glued to her."

Completing His Final Speech

The crowd was up to maybe 1,800 in the Embassy Room, way above fire code, and it was very very warm. There was jubilation in the packed throng. The overflow went down one floor to the Ambassador Ballroom.

After adjusting the microphones and going through the fairly lengthy list of those he thanked for their help, Kennedy spoke for approximately ten minutes. After congratulating pitcher Don Drysdale for his sixth straight no-hit shutout, the winner of California's 178 delegates congratulated his opponent Eugene McCarthy.

He pointed out, to great applause, that the "country wants to move in a different direction, we want to deal with our own problems within our country, and we want peace in Vietnam." He was looking forward to "a dialogue, or a debate," with Hubert Humphrey "on what direction we want to go in; what we are going to do in the rural areas of our country, what we are going to do with those who still suffer within the United States from hunger. . . . and whether we're going to continue the policies that have been so unsuccessful in Vietnam."

Then he finished, "We are a great country, an unselfish country, a compassionate country and I intend to make that my basis for running . . . so my thanks to all of you and now on to Chicago and let's win there."

The crowd chanted in a powerful rhythm, "We want Bobby, we want Bobby." His body guards, Olympic hero Rafer Johnson and huge Los Angeles Rams tackle Roosevelt Grier, started to help clear a path to Kennedy's left through the crowd and to the pencil press, but an assistant maître d' named Karl Uecker parted the gold curtain to the rear, "This way Mr. Kennedy," and reached for Kennedy's arm to lead him back through the curtain off the platform's back.

Uecker turned Kennedy to his right after passing through the curtain, and then down an incline toward the double door which led to a service pantry and the kitchen. It was hasty.

"Slow down!" someone cried. "You're getting ahead of everyone!" The bodyguards were not yet caught up. There were just two and one-half minutes between the senator leaving the stage and the arising of screams, shouts, and consternation from the audience in the ballroom, as knowledge of the shooting quickly spread.

Seventy-eight people were in the pantry when RFK came through the door from the hallway behind the stage. There was a sign, THE ONCE AND FUTURE KING taped to the wall near where Kennedy stopped by the ice machine to greet those lined and clustered there.

There were shots. Witnesses gave differing accounts of the number. There was an initial quick popping sound, then a rapid series pop-pop-pop-pop-pop-pop-pop pop-pop-pop pop-pop-pop, certainly more than the eight in Sirhan's Iver-Johnson.

According to Los Angeles coroner Thomas Noguchi, who did the autopsy on Robert Kennedy, all three bullets that struck Kennedy entered from the rear, in a bulletpath from down to up, right to left. "Moreover," he noted, "powder burns around the entry wound indicated that the fatal bullet was fired at less than one inch from the head and no more than two or three inches behind the right ear."

But Sirhan's weapon was never less than two to three feet from Kennedy, and certainly not near the back of his head. By the second shot, bystanders had slammed Sirhan's arm and gun to a table, though he kept on firing wildly, the bullets going nowhere near the senator.

Sirhan and the Woman on the Tray Holder

A man named Thomas Vincent Di Pierro, son of a maitre d' at the Ambassador, spoke to the FBI very soon after, in the time of fresh memory: "I observed a white male and a white female standing on a tray holder at the opposite end of the ice machine which is approximately 12–15 feet away.

"This white male turned toward the white female and appeared to converse with her very briefly. He then dismounted from the tray holder (and) went into the crowd and I did not observe him until shortly thereafter when I then saw him standing at the heating cabinet behind Mr. Karl Uecker, another hotel employee. I did not see this white female again after this time.

"As Senator Kennedy shook the hand of the hotel cook he then turned to his right in the direction of the heating cabinet and that time I saw the white male who was previously standing on the tray cabinet. I saw this individual reach his right arm around Mr. Uecker and in his hand he had a revolver which was pointed directly at Senator Kennedy's head." (Vincent Di Pierro to FBI, June 7, 1968.)

The woman with whom Sirhan talked on the tray table Di Pierro described: white female, twenty-one to twenty-five, wearing a form-fitting scoop neck dress. "The dress appeared to have black or dark violet polka dots."

Sirhan Claims He Thought He Was Shooting at Targets at a Gun Range

Sirhan has recalled to Harvard's Dr. Brown that when he fired his .22 in the pantry of the Ambassador Hotel kitchen he believed he was at a gun range and shooting at circular targets. Dr. Brown's statement, contained in an exhibit in a 2011 court case seeking a retrial of Sirhan Sirhan, stated: "Mr. Sirhan did not know and could not have known that Senator Kennedy was going to pass through the kitchen area. Mr. Sirhan was led to the kitchen area by a woman after that same woman had received directions from an official at the event. Mr. Sirhan did not go with the intent to shoot Senator Kennedy, but did respond to a specific hypnotic cue given to him by that woman to enter 'range mode,' during which Mr. Sirhan automatically and involuntarily responded with a 'flashback' that he was shooting at a firing range at circle targets. At the time Mr. Sirhan did not know that he was shooting at people nor did he know that he was shooting at Senator Kennedy."

Sirhan recounted: "I am trying to figure out how I'm going to have her. . . . All of a sudden she's looking over my head toward an area . . . Then she taps me or pinches me. . . . It is startling. . . . It was like when you're stuck with a pin or pinched . . . a very sharp pinch . . . I thought she did it with her fingernails . . . like a wake-up . . . it snapped me out of my doldrums . . . yet, I'm still sleepy. . . . She points back over my head. . . . She says, 'Look, look, look.' I turned around . . . I don't know what happened after that. . . . She spun me around and turned my body around. . . . She was directing my attention to the rear. . . . Way back. . . . There are people coming back through the doors . . . I am puzzled about what she is directing me to. . . . It didn't seem relevant to me. . . . Some people started streaming in. . . . She kept motioning toward the back . . . then all of a sudden she gets more animated. . . . She put her arm on my shoulder.

"I think she had her hand on me. . . . Then I was at the target range . . . a flashback to the shooting range . . . I didn't know that I had a gun . . . there was this target like a flashback to the target range . . . I thought that I was at the range more than I was actually shooting at any person, let alone Bobby Kennedy." Brown then asked Sirhan to recall his state of mind. "My mental state was like I was drunk and sleepy . . . maybe the girl had something to do with it . . . I was like at the range again." What did the targets look like? Dr. Brown asked. "Circles. Circles. . . . It was like I was at the range again . . . I think I shot one or two shots. . . . Then I snapped out of it and thought 'I'm not at the range.' . . . Then, 'What is going on?' Then they started grabbing me . . . I'm thinking, 'the range, the range, the range.' Then everything gets blurry . . . after that first or second shot . . . that was the end of it. . . . It was the wrong place for the gun to be there . . . I thought it was the range . . . they broke my finger." Then Sirhan was asked, "What happens next?" Sirhan: "Next thing I remember I was being choked and man-handled, I didn't know what was going on. I didn't realize until they got me in a car . . . later when I saw the female judge I knew that Bobby Kennedy was shot and I was the shooter, but it doesn't come into my memory."

Another Gun

Dr. Philip Melanson, a very reputable researcher, wrote "One witness asserts a man in a suit fired a weapon" (See *The Robert F. Kennedy Assassination: New Revelations on the Conspiracy and Cover-Up, 1968–1991*, chapter 6, p. 71.) Melanson also "found two witnesses who saw another gun in the pantry," whose assertions were "not recorded by official investigators." A bystander named Lisa Urso saw another person (not Sirhan, and not wearing a uniform), with a gun in hand. He was blond and wearing a gray suit. Another, "Martha Raines" (Melanson protected her name) saw a guy with dark wavy hair in a grey suit shoot his gun "once or twice" and run out of the pantry. He was seen with Sirhan earlier in the evening.

A Polish reporter named Stanislaw Pruszynski was covering the primary victory that night for the *Montreal Gazette*. He happened to have his tape recorder running during the shooting. He later gave the tape to the California State Archives, where it resided unexamined for a number of decades. The recording was not long ago reexamined and digitally remastered, and forensic examiners contend that at least fourteen shots were fired in the kitchen pantry during that burst of pop-pop-pop's (see recent book, *An Open and Shut Case*, by forensic scientists Robert Joling and Philip Van Praag.)

Juan Romero Kneels by Robert Kennedy

Working in the kitchen and pantry was young Juan Romero, who had several days before delivered a room service order to RFK in the Presidential Suite, and had shook his hand. Romero wanted once again to shake Kennedy's hand, and pressed through the packed pantry. Just as Kennedy clasped his hand there was a flash of heat, and suddenly RFK was on the floor.

"He was looking up at the ceiling," Romero later recalled "and I thought he'd banged his head. I asked, 'Are you Ok? Can you get up?' One eye, his left eye, was twitching, and one leg was shaking.' Romero slid his hand under the back of Kennedy's head to try to raise him and felt blood trickling through his fingers.

Ethel had rushed to the scene and then pushed Juan away. He asked if he could give Bobby his rosary beads. "I pressed them into his hand but they wouldn't stay . . . so I tried wrapping them around his thumb. When they were wheeling him away, I saw the rosary beads still hanging off his hand."

The writer Pete Hamill, who'd written a letter back in January urging RFK to run, was among the horrified seventy-eight people packed into the pantry. He glanced at his watch. It was 12:15 a.m. The senator was soon taken to the hospital, and he lingered till 1:44 a.m. on Thursday, June 6, when he passed from life.

Sharon and Roman on Assassination Night

It's not known where Sharon Tate and Roman Polanski were or what they did the night of June 4–5 when Robert Kennedy was assassinated just two or three minutes after concluding his victory speech at the Ambassador Hotel in Los Angeles, after winning the California Democratic Primary.

They might have gone to The Factory discotheque to await the celebration that night at which Sammy Davis Jr. was scheduled to perform. According to Evans Frankenheimer, both Sharon and Roman were on the invitation list. Tate and her husband were very likely at that time spending a few days at the Chateau Marmont hotel on Sunset Boulevard just prior to moving to Patty Duke's house at 1600 Summit Ridge Drive.

Renting Patty Duke's House

Patty Duke traveled to New York City by the summer of 1968 to star in a film called *Me, Natalie*. Her husband, Harry Falk, remained behind to rent out their house. As she described the house in her autobiography, "It was a colonial mansion off Benedict Canyon in Beverly Hills, jutting out on its own precipice at the top of the mountain with a twelve-car parking lot, a four car garage and a 360-degree view of Los Angeles.

"Its nine rooms were big, bright and airy, with bay windows and fireplaces everywhere. Everyone who sees the house loves it; Sharon Tate later rented it for a while when she first got pregnant; and she and Roman Polanski wanted to buy it."

By the week after RFK's assassination, Sharon and Roman had rented the house. Winifred Chapman had been the housekeeper and cook for Patty Duke, and stayed on for Sharon and Roman.

In celebration of their new house at 1600 Summit Ridge Drive, Roman and Sharon threw a party. Part of the rental deal was they would take care of Patty Duke's sheepdog, which escaped during the party and ran down the hill, where it encountered a vicious pack of Alsatian dogs owned by an English satanic cult called The Process Church of the Final Judgement. The dogs were housed at the Barrymore mansion located at 1301 Summit Ridge Drive, which featured a group of heated kennels. The dogs chased Polanski into a garage, where he was trapped till he broke a rear window and got back up the hill to the party at Patty Duke's house. Oo-ee-oo.

Filming *The Wrecking Crew*

Sharon's mother had trained her daughter well in what used to be called "Home Economics," in her case, southern-style cooking. Roman recalled it with relish: "After working all day on the set [of *The Wrecking Crew*] Sharon would return to our . . . house on Summit Ridge Drive and insist on cooking for me and the whole gang. Her repertoire included Virginia ham, upside-down cake, and all the great southern dishes she'd learned from her mother."

Polanski also noted with approval in his autobiography her attentiveness to his personal needs: "She was also a born housewife. Aside from cooking like a dream, she used to cut my hair—a skill acquired from Jay Sebring. She liked to pack my bag whenever I had to make a trip. She always knew exactly what to put in."

She was a kung fu expert in the film, and Bruce Lee was hired to be her instructor. The twenty-seven-year-old martial arts icon was several years away from the famous martial arts films that made him an international celebrity. Lee lived nearby and became a friend of the couple. Sharon invited him over to 1600 Summit Ridge, where he demonstrated his skills. Roman described how "before long we rigged up a training area on Patty Duke's driveway, and he was giving me lessons in—among other things—the celebrated Bruce Lee side kick." Lee was always urging Polanski to sneak-attack him. Once Polanski tried it, but Bruce quickly extended his guard-hand, and Polanski was tossed upside down on Patty Duke's lawn.

Distributed by Columbia Pictures, *The Wrecking Crew* was the fourth and final film in a series of American comedy-spy-fi theatrical releases featuring Dean Martin as secret agent Matt Helm. As with the previous three movies (*The Silencers, Murderers' Row,* and *The Ambushers*), the film was created as a spoof of the James Bond films.

Sharon Tate was given star billing, along with Dean Martin and Elke Sommer. Also appearing in the film were Nancy Kwan as Yu-Rang, Tina Louise as Lola Medina, and Nigel Green as the villainous Count Contini, who was trying to wreak havoc on the world economy through stealing oodles of gold aboard a train. It was a tad reminiscent of the James Bond film *Goldfinger*. Sharon appeared as Freya Carlson, a bungling British Intelligence agent who assisted playboy/skirtchasing/secret agent Dean Martin, working for a secret agency called ICE. She was Martin's sole support working to stop a team of gold hijackers. Tate of course was the romantic interest for Martin. As in the 1966 *Don't Make Waves*, she performed her own stunts.

In the early portions of the film, Tate is attired demurely, even unstylishly, in glasses, close-drawn hair; and a blue dress with orange sleeves, but toward the end of the film, as she helps to save Matt Helm/Martin's life, there are romantic sparks between the two. That is, Helm becomes impressed with Carlson/Tate's skills as an intelligence agent.

Dean and Sharon embrace and kiss after she wades into a too-deep creek and emerges enticingly wet. They construct the portable helicopter in which they escape, the parts having been stored in the trunk of Dean's automobile. It's the last possible minute to save the international monetary system, and Helm/Martin and Carlson/Tate appear above the gold-bearing chateau in the helicopter. Martin fires a machine gun to try to stop the gold transfer into a train headed for Luxembourg. After Dean and Sharon land the chopper on top of the train, they subdue the guards and make for the head of the train, where the gold-stealing count triggers the opening of a trapdoor leading down to the tracks. Tate is thrown down dangerously into the opening, but manages to keep hold enough to prevent falling to the tracks, as Dean subdues the count.

"Mr. Helm, is my hair a mess?" she asks after the count himself is tossed down onto the train tracks and crushed. At the end, Tate appears in a night-gown, "Hey, think we can have our little talk, now?" Carlson/Tate and Helm/Martin make out on a red bed, which Helm/Martin was able to cause to sink down into place in the diesel locomotive. The gold crisis is averted, after one hour, forty-four minutes of film.

The *Hollywood Reporter* weighed in with this assessment: "Sharon Tate reveals a pleasant affinity to scatterbrain comedy and comes as close to walking away with the picture as she did in a radically different role in *Valley of the Dolls*." In his *New York Times* review of the film, Vincent Canby noted "The only nice thing is Sharon Tate, a tall, really great-looking girl who, for most of the movie, wanders around wearing glasses, which, of course means that no one, including Martin . . . notices that she is beautiful." Sharon's father, Colonel Paul Tate, saw *The Wrecking Crew* in the cinema at his army base in San Francisco. He liked it very much.

Roman and Sharon at Their Apex

Polanski was rolling in the glory of success that summer of 1968, and Sharon was triumphant in light comedy. They were at their apex while dwelling in their rented house at 1600 Summit Ridge Drive.

Sharon wore a black lace, strapless Christian Dior gown to the premiere of *Rosemary's Baby* on June 12, 1968.

"*Rosemary's Baby* was the smash hit of the summer [of 1968]," noted Robert Evans in his autobiography. It was both a big hit at the box office and also with the critics, and, in the minds of critics, brought the modern-day horror film a new distance from the era of Alfred Hitchcock. Polanski earned his second Academy Award nomination, this one for Best Adapted Screenplay.

After moving to Summit Ridge Drive, Roman and Sharon began hanging out with both Peter Sellers and Mia Farrow, who soon became a couple of sorts. Peter was in Los Angeles filming *I Love You, Alice B. Toklas*. His current wife, Britt Ekland, was not in town, and Roman had introduced Peter to Mia during the filming of *Rosemary's Baby*.

Mia and Sellers shared an interest in what they called New Age spirituality. Joining the Beatles, Mia was one of the best-known followers, at least for a while, of Transcendental Meditation. Polanski described it: "It was through us that [Peter Sellers] met Mia Farrow—a true soulmate if ever there was one. Like her, Peter was heavily into the whole range of crackpot folklore that flourished in the 1960s, from UFOs through astrology to extrasensory perception. They both liked dressing up as rich hippies, complete with beads, chunky costume jewelry, and Indian cotton caftans."

Polanski wrote how Peter would walk off a movie set if anyone should show up wearing the "unlucky" color of purple, or how he would precipitously depart a restaurant if he detected any "bad vibes" in the establishment. Peter would mutter, "Ro, I can't stand it . . . bad vibes in here . . . let's go somewhere else."

Roman described a weekend the two couples—he and Sharon and Peter and Mia—spent at Joshua Tree, a famous area near Palm Springs, known for UFO sightings and superstitious vibes. "After smoking some grass one evening, Mia and Peter wandered off into the desert, hand in hand. I picked up a stick and tiptoed after them. They were deeply engrossed in a mystical dialogue about the stars, the infinite, and the likelihood of extraterrestrial life. I decided to enrich their experience and threw my stick high in the air so it landed at their feet—a real-life manifestation of the inexplicable.

'Did you hear that?' I heard Peter whisper in awe.

'What was it?' Mia whispered back.

'I don't know, but it was fantastic. Fantastic!'

'We've got to tell Roman and Sharon,' Peter said. 'They'll never believe this.'"
Polanski stealth-trotted through the darkness and back to the motel, where he
filled in Sharon about his ploy, so that, as he later wrote, "when they arrived,
panting, at our door, we both expressed suitable wonder."

Mia, in the video *Sharon Tate, Murdered Innocence*, recalled how eager Sharon
was to please her mate: "I remember we were in Mexico, and Roman had com-
plimented her on her dress, and she took it to a dressmaker, and she had nine
of those dresses made in different colors. She wanted so hard to please him, and
adored him, and clearly he adored her too."

In the words of one biography of Sellers: "Peter kept running with the
fast-living Polanski crowd, which, in addition to Roman and Sharon and Warren and Julie, included Yul Brynner, Peter Lawford, Gene Gutowski, the playboy Jay Sebring, and the screenwriter James Coe."

A Short Film, Featuring Sharon, at Jay Sebring's House

Sharon and Jay's friend, the photographer Shahrokh Hatami, made a four-
minute, forty-three-second home movie of Sharon, Sheilah Wells, Sheilah's husband Fred Beir, and others at a party at Jay Sebring's house on Easton Lane. The
time was sometime in late 1968, because Sheilah Wells recalls being pregnant.

During an interview, Wells urged me to view the video of "that party at Jay's,
have you ever seen that? It was at Jay's. We were laughing a lot. I had this head-
band on. I was pregnant at the time."

So, I located it on the Internet, and indeed among the eight or nine young
people gathered mainly out of doors in a patio area, there was a lot of jollity, laughing, and merriment, especially on the part of Sharon Tate and Sheilah Wells.

Sharon is attired in white pants, dark blue sweater, and a hooded, striped
mid-thigh jacket, talking and at one time passing a joint to someone on a porch
swing, by a table with a bowl of punch on a red-checked tablecloth. She looks
very happy, lifting her head back as she laughs, and appears to be wearing a
wedding ring. Sheilah Wells is in a porch swing. Sharon is sitting in front of her,
sometimes grasping the arms of Wells as they rock in laughter.

Wells: "We were always laughing, in those days." Since Wells gave birth
in March of 1969, the film would have to have been shot in, say, the fall of
1968. "Yeah, because you could kind of tell I was pregnant. Roman wasn't there.
There's a shot of Fred, Amanda's father, and he's on a swing." (Fred was her husband at the time.)

Wells told me she thought Shahrokh Hatami shot the film. I contacted Mr.
Hatami, and he confirmed he and Jay Sebring were good friends, and that in fact

he was continually shooting footage following his documentary on Mia Farrow and *Rosemary's Baby*, including this brief film at Jay's house on Easton Lane.

Sammy Davis Jr. Has an Experience Involving Jay Sebring

The extraordinarily popular singer and show-biz personality, Sammy Davis Jr., was a strong supporter of the candidacy of Robert Kennedy for president. In the spring of 1968 Davis was performing in Chicago at a theater, and in his free time he spoke at rallies and fundraisers for Kennedy. Davis did these events during the Indiana and Illinois primaries and was in telephone contact with the candidate.

For the upcoming California Democratic primaries, Davis had to be in London for a production of the musical *Golden Boy*, based on a play by Clifford Odets, which he had starred in on Broadway back in 1964. Davis was in London when Peter Lawford telephoned him that Robert Kennedy had been shot. Not long thereafter, still in shock over RFK, Davis had returned to Los Angeles, where he had a home. It was during that time when Davis had an experience involving Jay Sebring. In his *Why Me? The Sammy Davis, Jr. Story* he describes how he drove to the disco called The Factory, "that I had a piece of. I ran into a bunch of young actors I knew. One of them said to me, 'Hey, man, there's a party, you wanta go?' Each of them had one fingernail painted red, an inside thing among Satanists to identify themselves to each other. I was curious. Evil fascinated me. I felt it lying in wait for me. And I wanted to taste it. I was ready to accept the wildness, the rolling in the gutter, and having to get up the next morning and wash myself clean. . . . The party was in a large, old house up in the hills and they were all wearing hoods or masks. They had a naked girl stretched out and chained to a red-velvet-covered altar.

"I played it cool. 'Hey, what is this?'

'We're Satanists.'

'Oh, this is a coven . . . '

'Right. The chick's going to be sacrificed.'

"I'd read enough about it to know that they weren't Satanists, they were bullshit artists and they'd found an exotic way they could ball each other and have an orgy.

"And get stoned. It was all fun and games and dungeons and dragons and debauchery and as long as the chick was happy and wasn't really going to get any anything sharper than a dildo stuck into her, I wasn't going to walk away from it.

"One of the leaders of the group tilted his hood back to show me his face. It was a good friend of mine, Jay Sebring, my barber, who'd become famous in Hollywood. I'd always known Jay was a little weird. He had a dungeon in his house and he'd say, 'You've got to come over, man, see what I got downstairs. I've got some real antique pieces.' . . . I never went there, but we were friends and often went to the same parties."

Rosemary's Baby Opens in France, October 17, 1968

On November 9, 1968, *Paris Match* featured a photo of Sharon Tate in a leg cast, with the description: "Sharon, the anti Brigitte, has a plaster cast on her beautiful leg, now broken after an accident, and on which Metro-Goldwyn-Mayer placed a high bid last year. Sharon Tate, whom the Americans released against Brigitte Bardot, wife of the best-paid director in the world, fell down the stairs of her Paris hotel, where she came to for the preview of her husband's movie *Rosemary's Baby*."

Gene Gutowski recalled the *Rosemary's Baby* Paris premiere: "There was a fabulous happening, the premiere of *Rosemary's Baby* in Paris. Peter (Sellers) was very much in attendance. We took over a whole hotel—the little place where Oscar Wilde had lived and died. It had become a showpiece, boutique-type hotel. We had a magnificent three-day party, the whole place reeking of, uh, substances, controlled or uncontrolled, mostly un-. Peter liked to indulge." (Gene Gutowski's recollections from Ed Sikov's biography of Sellers, *Mr. Strangelove*, p. 286.)

The singer Regine threw a dinner party for Mia Farrow during the Paris festivities, as noted in *Paris Match* on November 9, 1968: "When the haunting film *Rosemary's Baby* made its Paris premiere Regine, French singing star, decided to throw an appropriate party. Among the celebrated guests at her party were the guest of honor Mia Farrow, who stars in *Baby*, Roman Polanski who did the film for her, Peter Sellers, and some of the most celebrated members of Europe's pop society. Regine decided that oysters and spaghetti would be the ideal main course. The guests seem to have enjoyed." There's a photo showing Roman signing Sharon's big white leg cast at the Regine party.

It had a dreamworld quality, all this rush of success, of triumph (however fleeting), all these expensive meals, limousines, fresh flowers in hotel suites, quick showers before assignations, shopping in expensive stores. Would it ever end? Never!

That December, Jay Sebring opened a hair salon in San Francisco, and rented a houseboat there to entertain clients. Colonel Tate took the opportunity to visit the boat every weekend to fish. "After a day of cold beers and watching the lure dip and swell," he later wrote. "I dropped my trash at the dumpsters. Each time, among the rubbish, I saw dozens of emptied bottles of rubbing alcohol, a necessary ingredient for making LSD." (This apparently became a clue he pursued during his personal investigation into the murders the next year.)

Sharon and Roman at the Paris premiere of *Rosemary's Baby*, October 1968—her left trouser leg covering the cast where she had broken her foot

Christmas at Cortina

Sharon, Roman, Peter Sellers, Roman's doctor friend, Tony Greenburgh, and others, including Joanna Pettet and her husband, Alex Cord, planned a group skiing vacation in Cortina d'Ampezzo, in the Dolomite Alps in northern Italy. Before Sharon, Peter, and Roman left Los Angeles, composer Krzysztof Komeda was walking with a friend in the Hollywood Hills, and somehow fell and injured his head (there are varying accounts). Komeda couldn't travel with his friends to London, and then to Cortina. He became increasingly ill, until a brain injury was diagnosed, and he went into the hospital in Los Angeles.

Komeda had composed scores for all of the major Polanski films up to then: *Rosemary's Baby*, *The Fearless Vampire Killers*, *Knife in the Water*, and *Cul-de-Sac*. He was a prominent jazz pianist, issuing an important European jazz album in 1965, *Astigmatic*.

Sharon was particularly distraught, and after she returned from vacation in early January 1969 she visited Komeda daily in the hospital. Eventually Komeda was flown back to his native Poland by his wife (because of the free health care available there), where he passed away on April 23, 1969. Sharon was grief-stricken by this, one of her first personal encounters with the death of a friend.

Chapter 6

1969: Cielo Drive and Pregnancy

In January of 1969, Sharon Tate was featured along with other celebrities in *Eye* magazine, a Hearst publication, responding to the question, "Who would you like to be in your next life?" Sharon's answer, "I'd like to be a fairy princess—a little golden doll with gossamer wings, in a voile dress, adorned with bright, shiny things. I see that as something totally pure and beautiful. Everything that's realistic has some sort of ugliness in it. Even a flower is ugly when it wilts, a bird when it seeks its prey, the ocean when it becomes violent. I'm very sensitive to ugly situations. I'm quick to read people, and I pick up if someone's reacting to me as just a sexy blonde. At times like that, I freeze. I can be very alone at a party, on the set, or in general, if I'm not in harmony with things around me."

As for Roman Polanski early in the year, "for want of anything better to do," as he later wrote in his autobiography, he began writing a screenplay based on a short story by Heere Heresma, a Dutch writer. It was another theme of defeat and disaster of the sort to which Mr. Polanski seemed drawn. The plot involved an alcoholic father who takes his daughter to a town on the sea, with a drunken binge ensuing and then, disaster. Peter Sellers agreed to take a part in the film, and Paramount's Robert Evans agreed to invest modestly, $600,000, in the low-budget project. Polanski's friend Simon Hesera would direct.

Meanwhile, on January 6, 1969, the trial of Sirhan Sirhan for the murder of Robert Kennedy opened in Los Angeles. There were a group of Sirhan's notebooks found in his room, which contained writing calling for the death of Senator Kennedy. Some have claimed the handwriting is at variance to Sirhan's. (In recent years, under hypnosis, Sirhan has alleged that the portions of his diaries about killing Kennedy were written during programming sessions conducted with a programmer over shortwave radio—Sirhan was a ham radio buff.) The prosecutor used them to show premeditated murder. Sirhan testified he didn't recall shooting RFK and didn't recall writing the notebooks, with hand-jotted entries such as "Kennedy must die/Kennedy must fall."

News About Sharon's Pregnancy

The doctor told Sharon she had conceived around December 15. Delivery date for the baby would therefore be sometime between late September to the first week of October. It has been asserted that Sharon secretly put a hole in her diaphragm; but her husband has written that it was an accident, since she used an IUD.

Sharon and Roman planed to London in January for the premiere of *Rosemary's Baby*. He'd had trouble with British censors. The longtime Hollywood reporter, Army Archerd (who had narrated the promotional film made of the pleasure liner trip from Italy to Los Angeles for *Valley of the Dolls*), wrote in *Variety*, January 15, 1969: "Roman Polanski, on the longhorn from London where *Rosemary's Baby* was scissored, sadly told us, 'This is the first country where I had a censor problem.' (They cut the dream sequence where Mia Farrow's legs are tied to the bed—and also snipped dialogue preceding) . . . Polanski said he'll show the original version at the London premiere, January 23, but afterwards 'What can I do besides protest?' . . . He said censor John Trevelyan also objected to black magic in the film. 'I was very upset,' Roman lamented. 'I didn't contemplate any problem like this in England. We've had none in Italy or even in South America. I told them I didn't see anything pornographic (as claimed) in the film.' . . . Polanski and wife Sharon Tate remain in England until the furor subsides then return here (to L.A) to prep Donner Pass."

In London, Sharon wondered whether or not to tell Roman. She called Jay from London to ask his advice. Jay's advice was to wait a month before letting him know, till it was too late to have an abortion.

Sharon returned alone in a few days to California, for more dubbing on *The Wrecking Crew*, and because they had given up Patty Duke's house, she stayed at the Chateau Marmont.

Because of Polanski's *curriculum vitae*, featuring films about satanic covens, mahemic murder, neck-slurp, and general weirdness, Polanski received a flow of scripts and book galleys from what could be termed the Poe Zone. He must have been comfortable with the P.Z. since he began creating, in early 1969, a project on the life of Paganini with Italian writer Ennio de Concini, a prolific screenwriter (and poet too) who had co-won an Academy Award in 1963 for *Divorce, Italian Style.* In addition, Polanski met English writer Ivan Moffat, who had an idea for a film on the Donner Party. And so the two, *Paganini* and *Donner Pass,* crept to life. Moffat had legs, having shared an Academy Award nomination for the screen adaptation of Edna Ferber's novel *Giant* in 1956. He had also served as associate producer of George Stevens's popular films *Shane,* in 1951, and *A Place in the Sun,* in 1953.

The Donner Party was a group of eighty-seven humans who trekked from Illinois in 1846 toward California along a dangerous and untested route through eastern Utah. They were trapped by snow, and a subgroup of seventeen set forth to try to bring help from California, while the remaining seventy stayed behind, starving and resorting to cannibalism to survive. A perfect flick for Polanski.

As for composer Niccolo Paganini, 1782–1840, he was reputed to have been the finest violinist in the history of Western civilization. He was a compulsive gambler, and would sometimes pawn his Stradivarius to pay off his debts. What was the hook for Polanski? Well, perhaps it was the belief, commonly held during Paganini's lifetime, that his music was so difficult to perform that he had entered upon a pact with the Devil to accomplish it.

His partner in Cadre Films, Gene Gutowski (in an interview in the 1990s) recalled the Paganini project: "We were going to do the story of Paganini. Roman was farting about instead of having a meeting; he was distracted in other directions. The writer finally delivered the screenplay which was to go to Paramount. It was way too long. Our lawyer Wally Wolfe was just afraid to take it to Paramount because it was just unprofessional. So we hired a writer to make it acceptable for delivery. So it was one of the pictures that never happened. But we did get paid."

A Possible Progression of Films

> *Murder*
>> *Knife in the Water*
>>> *Repulsion*
>>>> *Cul-de-Sac*
>>>>> *Rosemary's Baby*
>>>>>> *Paganini*
>>>>>>> *Donner Pass*

A. H. Weiler of the *New York Times* wrote an article published on February 9, 1969: "Having bewitched moviegoers with *Rosemary's Baby,* director Roman Polanski is now entranced by 'real, equally fascinating people of the 19th century.' Stopping over in New York last week en route from England to Holly-wood, the diminutive Pole said he is preparing both a biography of Paganini and a film called *Donner Pass*, the tragic story of Western pioneers who were forced into cannibalism when they became snowbound in the Sierras. Paramount will release both films."

Polanski noted that "Paganini has been an obsession with me for almost 15 years." Polanski looked shaggy-coifed and was dressed mod like a "King's Road hippie."

"We'll stress Paganini's amazing character," said Polanski, "so full of con-tradictions. There have been films about him before, but none of them caught the devilishness and virtuosity which guided the bow of the great violinist—his constant conflict with society, the church, kings, fellow artists, and the many women who fell in love with this physically ugly man."

Shooting was planned for Italy, France, and Austria for later in 1969. Mean-while, Polanski remarked that Ivan Moffat was finishing the script of *Donner Pass*, noting, "It will tell the story of a group of educated people facing the ulti-mate test of character. What interests me is showing how far such people can go before they break."

On February 19, 1969, Polanski sent a précis of *Donner Pass* to *Los Angeles Times* entertainment critic Charles Champlin. In it he described how in 1847, starving, members of the marooned Donner Party, "cut out the heart and liver, and severed the arms and legs of (Mrs. Fosdick's) husband. . . . She saw an immigrant thrust the heart through with a stick, and hold it in the fire to roast. . . . and the children were sitting upon a log, with their faces stained with blood, devouring the half-roasted liver of their father."

In early March he was still working with Ivan Moffat on the Donner project. In an interview with Joseph Gelmis around that time, Polanski described the *Donner Pass:* "The film is the story of people going from Illinois to Califor-nia. At that time, there were only seven hundred Americans in California. So these travelers were going to this paradise and they were stranded in the snow in the Sierras in very early winter. Most of them died. The few that survived were accused afterwards of cannibalism."

"Cannibalism?" the interviewer asked, as if in surprise.

"Yes, yes, I know, I know. But it has nothing to do with any of my earlier pictures. What makes you think I am obsessed by the bizarre?"

Another interview with Michel Delahaye and Jean Narboni in early 1969 hints at an additional project, based on a science fiction book:

Q: Do you have any projects in mind right now?

A: I have two projects with Paramount but I don't know which one I'll do first. One of them is a Western which Ivan Moffat is working on. It takes place in 1846 and is a slice of American history that hasn't ever been filmed but about which there's a lot of literature. The other is a science-fiction book that the author is writing at the moment and which I've read only half of. I'm waiting impatiently for the second half. I won't tell you the name of the author because I'm not committed yet."

An Allegation Regarding Films, Early 1969

Speaking of films, there are reports of strange home movies done at the Polanski residence, such as alleged in Thomas Kiernan's *The Roman Polanski Story* (a book much deprecated by Polanski as being full of untruths; Kiernan, a former editor of the Philosophical Library, also wrote biographies of John Steinbeck, Laurence Olivier, Rupert Murdoch, Jane Fonda, among others): "She (Sharon) went along with him in some of his more bizarre sexual practices—allowing him, for instance, to videotape the two of them making love and then sitting by quietly while he screened the tapes for friends at parties. But these were not the only tapes Polanski made. One of Sharon's closest friends recalls traveling to San Francisco with her early in 1969 to visit her family for a few days. Polanski remained behind at the Beverly Hills house. When they returned a day before having planned to, Polanski was not at the house. 'Sharon went into the bedroom to put her case away and found some tapes that she hadn't seen before. We put them on the machine, and they turned out to be of Roman making love to someone else on their bed. Sharon turned white, and then got madder than hell. The marriage almost ended there. It probably would have, except she had just found out she was pregnant.'" The friend recounted Sharon later having an affair in Rome, out of vengeance.

Sharon apparently confided much personal information to her friend, the photographer Shahrokh Hatami (who the reader will recall had filmed a documentary on the making of *Rosemary's Baby,* and who took pictures and films of Sharon in the new house on Cielo Drive in early 1969). In an interview with the author on March 11, 2010, Hatami said, "They did a documentary on the last days of Sharon Tate in Paris by a production company called Sunset Press; Sunset Press sent a reporter and producer-director to New York when I was living in New York in 2005. She interviewed me, and she took a lot of film footage of me, showing my photos of Sharon Tate in the back of the interview scene, and. . . . they censored a lot of what I said to her."

"Why?" I asked. He replied, "Because I think they didn't want to be too menacing to Roman Polanski. Because, Roman was—what I said that Sharon told me about Roman—about imposed sexual scenes on her."

I asked him to explain what he meant. Hatami answered, "He was bringing other girls to have threesomes with Sharon, and Sharon didn't like it that he was picking up girls on the Sunset and bringing them home to have sex with them." This was prior, Hatami said, to early 1969. It was something I heard talked about among reporters covering the Manson trial back in 1970. Mr. Hatami, of course was a prominent photographer, taking very early pictures of the Beatles, and would go on to photograph world events such as the Israel/Egypt peace talks of 1977–1978, and the Iranian revolution in 1979. A collection of photos by Hatami covering the Iranian revolution is owned by the US Library of Congress.

At a later occasion, the author had another opportunity to query Mr. Hatami about the above allegations. He was sure he heard about Roman picking up girls on the Strip from both Jay Sebring and longtime Polanski friend, Simon Hesera, whom Polanski had met while finishing *Repulsion,* and who was in Los Angeles, seeking to work in the film business, and staying at the Chateau Marmont at the same time as Roman and Sharon. (In 1969 Hesera directed a film, *Day at the Beach,* based on a screenplay by Polanski.) Hatami also claimed he was told about it by Sharon, saying, "I know about this because Sharon told me herself."

He further commented, "I wasn't fond of that, let's say, decadent Polanski's relationship with the woman I loved, I mean I cherished her, I really cared about her, I got to know her before she met Polanski. I almost launched her in Europe as an American movie star, before she got known in the United States. That's why I got the *Life* magazine assignment [in 1964]."

"Sharon didn't belong to any religion or anything?" I further queried.

"No. She was very much a flower child."

Finally, I asked, "She wasn't into the occult, let's put it that way."

Hatami: "No. I don't think so. I never knew anything in that picture of Sharon Tate."

Regarding threesomes and erotic filming, it *was* a revolutionary and experimental era, the 1960s, and a good number of young people—women as well as men—took part in activities that they later regretted or vowed not to repeat. Sharon Tate, raised a Catholic and imbued with monogamous values, would have been in those categories, and during her pregnancy, from all accounts, she lived a calm, pot-free, and normal life awaiting the birth of her baby.

After Sharon Became Pregnant

In a further interview with the author, Shahrokh Hatami brought up what Sharon had confided in him about her pregnancy. "Polanski didn't want to father that child," he recalled her confiding in him. I mentioned to Hatami what famous photographer and confidant of Sharon, Walter Chappell, had told me when I was researching the Manson group in 1971, about Roman not wanting to have the baby. (Chappell had told me back then that Hatami was making films of Barbara Bouchet, Ann Ford, and Sharon Tate. Ann Ford told Chappell that Roman Polanski had wanted Sharon Tate, when she became pregnant, late 1968-early 1969, to get an abortion.)

Hatami informed the author: "Sharon told me the reason he went back to live in London was a protest—Sharon was telling me all her secrets, what was going on in her life. 'I told him that I'm expecting his child, he's said that he doesn't want to father a child, and protested.' But Sharon told him, 'You can't do anything, it's my child. I'm going to keep it.'"

Even with his poor estimation of Polanski "as a person," Hatami told me he admires Polanski as a filmmaker. In fact, he stated in an interview with me, "Whenever I'm in Sacramento, I'd like to go see the governor, and to petition the governor to pardon him. If he does that, Roman could be free to come back to the United States, and being the great filmmaker that he is, to work in this country. Even though I don't like Roman as a person, I think he is a great filmmaker." (Polanski has been in exile from the United States since fleeing in 1978 a conviction for various charges involving the statutory rape of a thirteen-year-old girl.)

Meanwhile, *The Wrecking Crew* opened in New York City on February 5, 1969, and while it did not make an everlasting impression in the annals of time, it revealed Sharon's skills as a film comedienne. Dean Martin reportedly remarked that he wanted to make another "Matt Helm" flick, and he was eager to have Sharon Tate in her same role.

Whatever the reviews, Sharon had already signed on to do a lead role in a movie that also featured Orson Welles.

Melcher and Bergen Move from Cielo Drive: January 1969

Over the holidays, Candy Bergen and her mate, Terry Melcher, started to move their belongings from the house at 10050 Cielo Drive. In January they settled into his mother, Doris Day's beach house on Malibu Beach Road. Bergen wasn't sure why they moved, as she recounted in her autobiography: "He decided abruptly to leave the house on the hill, announcing on a Monday that we were moving that Friday to his mother's weekend house at the Beach. I was stunned; he gave no explanation, saying only that it was all arranged." She recalled that Terry Melcher was consumed in lengthy meetings attempting to sort out the messy finances left by his stepfather, Martin Melcher, who had passed away the previous year. Candice Bergen: "He never arrived at the beach house before ten o'clock at night after the debilitating days of meetings."

While the house on Cielo Drive was empty, Gregg Jakobson, a production assistant and talent scout for Melcher, arranged for Manson associate Dean Morehouse to stay there briefly. Morehouse was the father of a sixteen-year-old Manson follower nicknamed Ouish. Tex Watson visited Morehouse a number of times while he was at Cielo Drive.

Real Estate Agent Helps Find House on Cielo Drive

Real estate agent Elaine Young helped locate the property at 10050 Cielo Drive for Sharon and Roman. Young was also close to Jay Sebring. "I was his best friend!" she exclaimed years later to a writer of a piece on Sebring. She had been married to actor Gig Young, and would accompany him to Sebring's salon when Gig had his hair cut, for the chance to hang out with the stars and hear all the gossip. "Jay was very good-looking," Elaine Young recounted. "He was crazy about Sharon. The biggest mistake he ever made was not marrying her."

Sharon tossed a coin into the wishing well by the gate opening to the flagstone walkway leading to the house, and said, "We'll take it."

On February 12, Roman and Sharon signed a lease with Rudy Altobelli, the owner of the three-and-a-half acre estate at 10050 Cielo Drive. Altobelli was the well-known showbiz manager whom Melcher and Beach Boy Dennis Wilson had tried to interest in the project to make Charlie Manson a star. Altobelli had managed a number of stars over the years, including Henry Fonda and Katharine Hepburn, and at that time included the rising actor Christopher Jones, who had starred in the 1968 *Wild in the Streets*. In the future Mr. Altobelli would be coproducer of the hit CBS series *Rhoda*, starring his client Valerie Harper. Altobelli would live on the property in a smaller "caretaker's" house located about 150 feet away from the main residence.

On February 15, they moved into the house. The rent for the year's lease was $1,200 a month, which seemed to be a bit of a rip-off, especially since the house had only three bedrooms, although it was well lit by night and fully serviced by landscapers and groundskeepers.

There was an elegant loneliness of the location, high in Benedict Canyon, hidden in the wooded hillside. There was also a swimming pool and that huge two-story living room with an overhanging loft edged by a white railing. Roman Polanski was planning to put his offices in the apartment above the garage.

Sharon's friend Shahrokh Hatami has a somewhat variant memory of Sharon locating the house on Cielo Drive. In an interview Hatami told the author, "Sharon went to Europe for filming, and told me to find her a house. I was househunting for her and I found Cielo Drive."

"Through a real estate broker?" I asked. He replied, "The real estate broker was a woman, who showed me, and knows all about me being involved with the hunting of the house, and I got her to go see that villa. When Sharon got back and saw it, and said well, she was very happy, that's the house where I'll give birth to my baby. She was congratulating me; she was showing her happiness, by me finding that house, by just saying, Hatami, this is my dream house to give birth to my baby."

According to one account, Sharon's sister Patti recalled Sharon and Roman had moved into Cielo Drive on Valentine's Day. On February 28, they were still unpacking. Across the ravine was the back end of the Doris Duke estate, looking a bit like a castle. On the front side of it was a plaque reading "Falcon's Lair." Sharon had apparently mentioned Falcon's Lair when she described a nearby haunted house. (Looking at a map of Cielo Drive, I note that the property lines for 1436 Bella Drive, home of Doris Duke, and 10050 Cielo Drive are contiguous, to the north, so it is possible that Falcon's Lair, built in the 1920s for silent film star Rudolph Valentino, was accessible from Sharon's new house.)

Around the time of Sharon's move-in, her young sister, while visiting, wandered forth and somehow reached the driveway of Falcon's Lair, then slipped and scraped her knee. At that moment a limousine bearing the reclusive multi-multi-millionaire heiress Doris Duke came up the driveway, and Ms. Duke, spotting the child, invited her into the mansion for cookies and tea.

Sharon was called, and she arrived, saying "Miss Duke, I'm terribly sorry for the intrusion."

"Nonsense,' replied Duke, 'We're having tea. Please join us." Later Doris Duke sent baby clothes when Sharon returned from Europe to give birth to her child.

Once moved into Cielo Drive, Sharon was at last ready to tell Roman she was pregnant. Around the same time there was a fundraising party in San Francisco for Jay Sebring's hair salon, where Jay let slip to Colonel Tate that Sharon was pregnant.

Around February, 1969, Sharon called photographer Walter Chappell who had photographed her in Big Sur in 1964, for producer Martin Ransohoff. She asked him to take some more pictures of her, which he did. As a friend, Sharon also divulged personal information on her pregnancy to Chappell. During those years, 1968–1969, Walter Chappell shot pictures of Harrison Ford and Dennis Hopper (while Hopper was editing *Easy Rider*). Chappell was a follower of Gurdjieff. He would soon make a movie about the American Indian takeover of Alcatraz Island in San Francisco Bay beginning in 1969. (In an interview back in 1971, Chappell told the author that Roman, upon learning of her pregnancy, had urged Sharon to have an abortion.)

Sharon in early 1969, before the pregnancy began to show

Around the same time, Sharon also had additional photos taken, some in the nude, by another photographer in Los Angeles.

Polanski and Sharon hosted a house-warming party at their new house on March 15. There was a fight at the party involving uninvited friends of Wojtek Frykowski and Abigail Folger, friends whom they met through Cass Elliot, the well-known singer. Elliot lived near Folger and Frykowski on Woodstock Road.

Someone named Pic Dawson stepped on Roman's agent's foot and jostling occurred. Tom Harrigan, Ben Carruthers, and Billy Doyle sided with Pic Dawson in the hassle. Roman Polanski got angry and threw Dawson and friends out of the party.

The official homicide investigation report on the subsequent murders describes the party and altercation as follows: "In mid March of this year, the Polanskis had a large catered party which included over 100 invited guests. The persons invited included actors, actresses, film directors and producers, business agents for the above described people, and the Polanskis' attorneys. Most of the people invited came to the party along with several people who were uninvited. The list of uninvited guests included William Doyle, Thomas

Harrigan and Harrison Pickens Dawson. . . . During the party, a verbal altercation ensued involving William Tennant, Roman Polanski's business agent,
and William Doyle. Doyle apparently stepped on Tennant's foot during this
altercation. Dawson and Harrigan joined in the verbal altercation, siding with
Doyle. Roman Polanski became very irritated and ordered Doyle, Harrigan and
Dawson ejected from the property."

The homicide report continued: "The above-described party was held as a
bon voyage party for the Polanskis, who were leaving for a film festival in Rio de
Janeiro and then to Europe where Roman Polanski was to direct a film."

All through the following summer, however, the three mentioned above were
frequent house guests at the Polanski residence, while Mr. and Mrs. Polanski
were working in Europe.

(At Polanski's polygraph examination following the Manson murders, a
LAPD lieutenant showed him a picture of Billy Doyle. Polanski said, "That's
Billy Doyle. . . . I remember him because he crashed a party that we gave. He
came in, and he was trouble and I said, 'Gibby [Abigail Folger], who is that little
jerk?' And she said, 'Billy.' And I said, 'Get him out of the house.' And they got
him out of the house and he came back again because apparently his car broke,
and I said 'I want him out,' and he was drunk, and they said, 'He's crazy, he's an
idiot, something's wrong with his brain.' So I remember him.")

During the murder trial of Manson and his disciples, reporters exchanged
information. An NBC reporter told me an anecdote about the housewarming
party, supposedly emanating from the producer of *The Love Machine*. Nancy
Sinatra, the story went, grew incensed over the open dope-smoking at the party,
so she demanded that her escort take her away forthwith. As they were walking past a white wrought-iron settee on the elegant lawn, they noticed Warren
Beatty and Jane Fonda and Roger Vadim sitting together.

After Miss Sinatra and escort began walking to their car, they came across
a group of long-haired hippies who asked them, "Where's the party?" They
motioned back up the hill, and later wondered if the spores of Helter Skelter had
been pointed into the Cielo Drive estate.

John Phillips, the leader of the Mamas and the Papas, described a midsized
orgy (only five people) he says occurred after the Polanski housewarming party
(at another location) starring himself, his wife, a well-known movie director,
and his extremely famous movie star wife, plus another single male movie star.
(For the names see *Papa John: An Autobiography*, by John Phillips with Jim
Jerome, p. 291.)

In early 1969, Jane Fonda was making *They Shoot Horses, Don't They?* at a studio in Burbank. She and Vadim and daughter Vanessa were living in Malibu.

Years later, in A. E. Hotchner's *Doris Day: Her Own Story*, Terry Melcher presented a startling quote, based on what he claims Michelle Phillips had told him. "I knew they had been making a lot of homemade sadomasochistic-porno movies there with quite a few recognizable Hollywood faces in them. The reason I knew was that I had gone out with a girl named Michelle Phillips, one of the Mamas and the Papas. . . . Michelle told me she and John had dinner one night, to discuss maybe getting back together and afterward he had taken her up to visit the Polanskis in my old house. Michelle said that when they arrived there, everyone in the house was busy filming an orgy and that Sharon Tate was part of it. That was just one of the stories I had heard about what went on in my former house." Michelle later denied saying what Melcher alleged.

A New Film Project for Roman

The day after the housewarming party on Cielo Drive, March 16, Sharon's photographer Shahrokh Hatami and Sharon drove Roman to the airport for a flight to Rio de Janeiro (for the Second International Film Festival, March 23–31), where Mia Farrow was given an award for her role in *Rosemary's Baby*.

Various factors had hindered Polanski from acquiring a big-time film project, among them the reorganization and financial difficulties of Paramount Pictures, which had financed *Rosemary's Baby*. In early 1969 Simon and Schuster was about to publish a grim-toned, violent political thriller set in the Cold War by French author Robert Merle. The book, *The Day of the Dolphin* (Un animal doué de raison—A Sentient Animal), was translated by Helen Weaver. An executive for United Artists acquired the galleys before publication and sent them to Roman Polanski.

When I saw on the Internet that Helen Weaver had translated *The Day of the Dolphin*, I called her. She's a friend. Yes, she confirmed, she was the translator. She said she remembered, reciting it in French, when the dolphin finally understands what the military has in mind for him to do. The dolphin says, "Man is not good. He lies. He kills." She did not have anything to do with sale of the movie rights. She said that Michael Korda, editor-in-chief for publisher Simon and Schuster, being a gentleman, might tell me about it. She suggested I call him.

As for the offer to write and direct *The Day of the Dolphin* for United Artists, Polanski apparently was still miffed at Paramount for taking *Downhill Racer* from him, and he had no contract with Paramount, so he debated with himself what to do.

In a way, *The Day of the Dolphin* was an excellent project for Roman Polanski. It featured a nuclear explosion set off by a conspiracy involving a US intelligence or military agency, which was done to start a war with China. The book featured gentle dolphins who were trained to talk but who were then seized from their trainers and used to affix a nuclear weapon on the side of a US ship near Haiphong Harbor, Vietnam.

The book had plenty of dolphin slaughter and human slaughter; a presidential candidate who resembled Ronald Reagan; and it was set in the early months of 1973, just after a rancorous 1972 presidential struggle. When the bomb destroyed the ship, the new president prepared for a total war. The end of the book featured tension and fear galore, perfect for Polanski, who felt fear was very important in films, as elements of the military tried to kill the talking dolphins (who were supposed to die in the nuclear explosion but didn't) before they had a chance to tell the world what their handlers had gotten them to do. Researching, writing, and directing *The Day of the Dolphin* would bring Mr. Polanski into the dangerous darkness of the Vietnam era.

But, he wasn't sure if he should take it on. He discussed this question in the plane on the way to the Rio film festival, sitting next to producer Andy Braunsberg, who was set to show his movie *Wonderwall,* with a soundtrack by Beatle George Harrison and written by Gérard Brach, at the festival. Polanski outlined *The Day of the Dolphin,* and Braunsberg urged him to go ahead and do it. Roman agreed and decided right then it was a go.

The rule in Hollywood is that the Door Shuts Quickly, so the offer from United Artists was to be taken quickly, or blam! And so, after the Rio de Janeiro film festival, Roman Polanski was off to London to work on *The Day of the Dolphin,* which he was slated to produce as well as direct. Polanski later mentioned that his friend Wojtek Frykowski "wanted very much to work in movies and was devoting lots of time to research on dolphins for me."

Dissolution of Cadre Films

Cadre Films, the entity owned by Polanski and Gene Gutowski for the last four years, took a nosedive. Polanski's movie on the Donner Party was shelved by Easter of 1969. Cadre invested in a farce, *The Adventures of Gerard,* directed by Jerzy Skolimowski, who had cowritten *Knife in the Water.* The movie could not find a distributor to release it, so Gutowski and Polanski put a close to Cadre in April of 1969. Polanski: "With Cadre Films going nowhere fast, I felt it was time to wind up my partnership with Gene Gutowski. My worries would be fewer as a straightforward director."

Asked about why his partnership with Polanski had ended, Gene Gutowski, in an interview in the 1990s, said, "What happened was that there was a young and hungry associate of ours who consciously worked on Roman to convince him he would be better than I."

Quicksand.

Tate in a Positive Mood

Sharon's good friend Sheilah Wells had a baby in March of 1969, and Sharon visited in the hospital, giving her baby clothes she brought from Europe. Sharon was the godmother for baby Amanda Tate Beir, with her middle name for Sharon. At the baby shower Joanna Pettet and Sharon gave Sheilah a Victorian baby carriage.

Sheilah recalls Sharon telling her that she herself was pregnant.

Pregnant or not, Sharon was encouraged by positive reviews of her comedic performances, and chose the comedy *The Thirteen Chairs* (released as *12 + 1*) as her next project—as she later explained, largely for the opportunity to costar with Orson Welles.

Waiting for Melcher in a Miffed Mode

Charles Manson had spent a good part of the winter of 1968–1969 in the Panamint Mountains above Death Valley at a ranch house in a very remote place called Goler Wash.

Then, early in 1969, Manson returned to the Los Angeles area, renting a house and small guest house at 21019 Gresham in Canoga Park, California, in the San Fernando Valley, not too far from the Spahn Ranch. This house was dubbed the Yellow Submarine because of its color. Gresham had a red roof, and to the side were some horse stalls or stables behind a double garage. It was there that Manson lunged toward his bifurcated goals—becoming a star and putting together the proper equipment so that he could return with his followers to the desert. For this he needed things like electric generators, oodles of dune buggies, and money.

Money he decided to acquire through drugs, theft, and mooching. "Within three or four weeks of moving into the Yellow Submarine," he writes in his autobiography, "it had become a concert hall for musicians, a porno studio for kinky producers, a dope pad, a thieves lair, a place to dismantle stolen cars and just about everything but a whorehouse."

The thieves' lair/stolen dune buggy aspect of it he tried to keep from Terry Melcher and Beach Boy Dennis Wilson, from either or both of whom he was expecting a record deal.

Down the dirt road toward Devonshire Street were the Island Village apartments where various associates of Manson lived. Cutting down San Fernando Valley from the hills to the north is Brown Canyon wash, more like a huge paved storm sewer. This wash ran just to the west of the house on Gresham, and Manson used to drive his dune buggy down the wash to the Gresham house from the Devil's Canyon area, the future home of Manson's vision of Helter Skelter.

Because Manson allegedly was living in the Death Valley Hills, his federal parole supervision was shifted from Los Angeles to San Bernardino. On January 17, 1969, Manson's new federal parole officer attempted to pay him a visit in Death Valley. He got as far as the Ballarat General Store, and there he learned from an old miner that he would have to walk seven miles up the waterfalls if he wanted to visit the Family camp. No thanks.

After a week or so at the Canoga Park house on Gresham Street, Manson sent a squad up to the Barker Ranch to remove the rest of the Family. Three people were left behind at the Barker Ranch to take care of things: longtime follower Brooks Poston, a woman named Juanita, and Gypsy the violinist.

Specific information on the Manson Family is scant about this time period, but there is info on the famous "Death Mockup Party" that happened at the Yellow Submarine house on Gresham Street the day that a bunch of followers returned from living in the desert, dressed in leather, trim, and tanned. They gathered together, practicing what could be described as "mocking up snuff," each describing the details of their own deaths, for the purpose of *really* experiencing it.

Some were stoned, sitting together in the room. Charlie was there, and he commanded "Die," so they all lay down and pretended they were dead. A young woman named Bo started screaming "Charlie!!!"—and then groaned. Paul Watkins later recounted: "I was listening to Charlie say die." Watkins tried to think of a way to die but he couldn't, so he lay down and "acted like I was dead." So did the rest of them, as Charlie was twiddling his fingers, exclaiming how fine the confusion in the air was.

Brooks Poston was able to go into a trance on command, and when Charlie commanded him to die, he sank into a profound unconsciousness that lasted three or five days. As he wasted on a couch in the living room, the girls would cleanse him, and even Charlie couldn't pull him out of it. The fifth day, Charlie commanded that his very own sacred embroidered gray witchy vest be placed beneath Brooks as a symbolic diaper. Overwhelmed with the prospect of Jesus' very own vest being used as a diaper, Brooks flung himself from the trance and came awake.

During this time at the Gresham house the famous Manson fellatio-miracle also occurred. Manson was on acid and being blown by the disciple named Bo, a small masochistic girl with thyroid eyes and long black hair, one of Charlie's favorite pain-receivers.

Family legend has it that during the gobble Bo went bonkers and bit Manson's virility in two. Then, through his direct occult power, Manson was able to heal his tragic amputation and continued talking. Another miracle from M.

Manson follower Paul Watkins had come from the desert to the Yellow Submarine house to help with the music. Manson was eager to have Byrds producer Terry Melcher hear the Family singing, and Melcher had promised, sometime around the end of February or into March of 1969, to come one evening to the Submarine to listen. The Family, starring Manson, set up their instruments ready to sing, but Melcher didn't show up. Uh oh.

A Visit from Manson, Looking for Terry Melcher

Manson showed up at the front door of the Polanski residence at 10050 Cielo Drive on March 23 in the afternoon. Sharon's friend Shahrokh Hatami answered the door. Hatami was working that day filming Tate with an 16-millimeter camera as she packed for her trip to Rome the following day. Hatami told me he was filming for a documentary on what he described as "four rising-up actresses." They were Sharon Tate, Jacqueline Bisset, Ryan O'Neal's wife, Leigh Taylor-Young, and Mia Farrow.

The question is why was the short, hairy-chested man, Charles Manson, whose arms bore tattoos of women, knocking at Sharon Tate's front door.

Hatami testified at the trial that Manson wanted to know where "somebody" lived—referring to Terry Melcher. Hatami directed him to the caretaker's guest house on the other side of the pool, where Rudy Altobelli lived. While Manson was near the porch, Sharon Tate came to the door to ask who it was, and saw Manson.

(For his part, in an interview with Mr. Hatami while researching this book, Hatami told me he has no memory at all of Manson coming to the front door of Cielo Drive, but that the memory was suggested to him by an investigator named Reeve Whitson, who worked for both Colonel Paul Tate and the prosecutor Vincent Bugliosi. Under this pressure, recalled Hatami, he went ahead and testified at the trial that Manson had in fact come to the front door that March day—something he continues not to recall.)

Manson took the path back to the guest cottage, but Mr. Altobelli was not there. He returned that evening and knocked on Mr. Altobelli's door, while at that moment, in the big house, Sharon, Jay Sebring, Abigail Folger, and Wojtek Frykowski—were having dinner.

Rudy Altobelli was packing to fly to Rome the next day with Sharon Tate. Altobelli was in the shower when Manson came to the screened porch. He came to the door, clad in a towel. Altobelli testified that the purpose of Manson's visit was to find out where Terry Melcher was living, even though Melcher had been gone from Cielo Drive for almost four months.

Manson began to introduce himself, but Altobelli said to him, "I know who you are, Charlie." Altobelli supposedly told Manson that he did not know the whereabouts of Mr. Melcher.

Since Gregg Jakobson, a close friend of Melcher, testified at Manson's trial that they were recording Manson while the Family was still at the house on Gresham Street, it is difficult to believe that Manson didn't know that Melcher had moved out to his mother's beach house. The Manson Family was living at the house on Gresham, where Melcher had promised to come to a recording session, up till right around the time that Manson visited the Polanski residence March 23.

The visit of Manson to Cielo Drive is still mysterious.

The next day on the plane to Rome, Altobelli and Sharon had a conversation about Manson. According to prosecutor Vincent Bugliosi, Altobelli said that during the flight to Rome Sharon had asked, "Did that creepy-looking guy come back there yesterday?"

Warren Beatty Offered Cielo Drive

Around the time that Polanski and Tate were leaving for Europe, according to the book *Easy Riders, Raging Bulls* (p. 78), Roman had attempted to lure Warren Beatty, as Beatty later recalled, to "take over his lease—I went up to look at the house, and thought, Yeah, I'll stay here for a while, because I wanted to get out of the hotel, but then Abigail and Wojtek walked out from another part of the house, and said that Roman had told them to take the house. They said, 'There's plenty of room for everyone, but I thought, no, I don't want to be in a house with other people.'"

A young Englishman, Michael Sarne, the director of the motion pictures *Joanna* and *Myra Breckinridge,* was going to stay in the Polanski residence, but just prior to Roman Polanski's departure for Rio, he decided to rent a Malibu beach house instead.

Wojtek Frykowski volunteered then to stay at the Polanski residence for the spring and summer. Polanski agreed that Wojtek could move in, provided that Ms. Folger stay there also.

Rudy Altobelli, the owner of the Polanski residence, planned to spend the summer in Europe. Among Altobelli's clients had been Henry Fonda and Katharine Hepburn, and in 1969 he managed Christopher Lee and Christopher Jones, among others. One day Altobelli picked up an eighteen-year-old hitchhiker from Lancaster, Ohio, named William Garretson. Altobelli hired Garretson to serve as caretaker for the property while he was away in Europe. Garretson was given the "guest house" or caretaker's house on the property as his residence during employment. He was paid a whopping thirty-five dollars a week.

Garretson's duties included taking care of Terry Melcher's twenty-six cats, which Melcher evidently left behind for a while at the house. He also took care of Saperstein (Sharon's Yorkshire terrier) and, later, Abigail Folger's Dalmatian, plus Rudy Altobelli's hostile Weimaraner, Christopher, a dog that loved to bark and even to bite. Also on the care list was Altobelli's green singing finch. He was to keep an eye on the property, but not to fraternize, and he was to man the phone at the guest house.

Another Version of Roman Learning Sharon Was Pregnant

One biography of Sharon Tate claims Sharon kept the news about her pregnancy to herself for around three months. When she arrived in London on March 24, she was set to start on *The Thirteen Chairs* in April, working in both Italy and England. She settled in with Roman at their Eaton Place Mews house. That very week, John and Michelle Phillips flew in from the United States, and the two couples were invited by Alfred 'Cubby' Broccoli to stay with him at his country estate. Broccoli was the ultrasuccessful producer of a sequence of James Bond Films, beginning with *From Russia with Love* (1963) to *Goldfinger* (1964) and *You Only Live Twice* (1967) and the then forthcoming *On Her Majesty's Secret Service*.

Sharon's James Bond spy-spoof, *The Wrecking Crew*, had just opened. According to Michelle Phillips, on Saturday evening, March 28, when Roman and John Phillips were talking, Sharon asked Michelle to accompany her into a bathroom, where she puffed a cigarette. "Roman hated her smoking, and was always trying to get her to quit," said Michelle. "She used to sneak cigarettes behind his back." In the bathroom, Sharon announced that she was pregnant. "She said that she hadn't yet told Roman, and began to laugh about it. She seemed very happy, very giddy."

According to Michelle's memory, her pregnancy was so advanced Sharon could no longer hold off telling Polanski. She may have been fearful that he would try to get her to have an abortion. Anyway, she told him.

According to what Sharon's friend photographer Walter Chappell told the author, Roman had learned about the pregnancy while they were still in Los Angeles, and wanted her to go to Brazil for an abortion. Shahrokh Hatami, as the reader will recall, claims that Sharon told him a similar story.

Sometime around the weekend with Alfred Broccoli, Roman had a dalliance in London with Michelle Phillips. John Phillips subsequently learned about it and waxed jealous, as recounted in Phillips's autobiography. The soreness would surface in Polanski's personal investigation of his wife's murder later that fall. It will be recalled that Michelle and Warren Beatty also got after it in London in the same time period, and as he recalled in his autobiography, (p. 304), John Phillips, upon learning, called up Mr. Beatty to complain.

Chapter 7

Sharon's Final Film

For Sharon Tate, *The Thirteen Chairs* had a month of rehearsals, then the picture had a six-week shooting schedule in Rome, followed by a month of postproduction in London. The production ended in late May. Sharon was by then visibly pregnant.

The comedy *The Thirteen Chairs* (original title: *12 + 1*) is based on *The Twelve Chairs*, a 1928 satirical novel by the Soviet authors Ilf and Petrov. It was directed by Nicolas Gessner and Luciano Lucignani, and starred, besides Sharon Tate, Vittorio Gassman, Orson Welles, Vittorio De Sica, and Tim Brooke-Taylor. Most of it was filmed in Italy.

When Sharon Tate arrived in Rome for filming near the end of March 1969, she was about three months pregnant and beginning to show. Because the script called for several seminude scenes, the director arranged to film those scenes first. As evidence of her pregnancy increased, the director hid Tate's stomach with large purses and scarves.

In *The Thirteen Chairs,* Sharon played the part of Pat (no last name given), who works in an English antique shop. Vittorio Gassman, in the role of Mario Beretti, an American barber, flies to England to gather up an inheritance from an aunt. He has vast money on his mind, but discovers an empty and derelict old house and his inheritance: twelve old chairs. In order to pay for his travel expenses, he sells them to the local antiques dealer and Sharon Tate. This is a comedy, so Sharon conducts her part accordingly. Her first scene involves her selling a chamber pot to some American tourists, to whom she asserts the pot might have belonged to Queen Victoria, thus elevating the asking price.

Gassman peddles the chairs to Sharon's antique shop, only to discover his aunt has secreted a vast amount of valuable jewels in one of the chairs. But, by the time he rushes back to the store, the chairs have already been sold, and are on their way to London. Sharon assists Gassman in a journey to locate the chairs. She has the name of the purchaser on a strip of paper. In a hotel in London, Gassman grabs at Sharon, trying to seize the paper, which she eats. Struggling, he rips off her shirt, and bare-breasted she races through the corridors of the hotel to her room.

Sharon and Gassman track the chairs to Paris and then to Rome. They run into an assortment of unusual characters, among them a driver of a furniture moving van named Albert (Terry-Thomas), a prostitute named Judy (Mylène Demongeot), the head of a roaming theater company that stages a strange version of *Dr. Jekyll and Mr. Hyde* (Orson Welles), the Italian entrepreneur Carlo Di Seta (Vittorio De Sica), and his curvy daughter Stefanella (Ottavia Piccolo.)

The chase for the jewels concludes in Rome, where the chair containing the treasure finds its way into a truck, and is collected by nuns who auction it off for charity. With nothing much left to do as a result of the failure in his quest, Mario travels back to New York City by ship, as Pat/Sharon sees him off and waves goodbye to him.

Mario retreats to his barber shop, where he makes a discovery—not long before his departure for Europe, he had invented a way to make hair regrow miraculously. He now discovers that it works, and as the film ends, he laughs uproariously.

During the filming, Sharon continually called Roman, asking him over and over to join her in Rome, but he told her he was too busy in London.

Sharon Had an Affair in Rome?

Actor Christopher Jones was represented by Rudy Altobelli, owner of Cielo Drive, who had flown to Rome with Sharon Tate in March. Jones later claimed that he and Sharon had an affair in Rome that month while Jones was filming the movie *Brief Season* with his then lover, actress Pia Degermark.

"Sharon arrived in Rome with my manager," says Jones, "and so we all arranged to go out to dinner that night. We were on the patio, waiting for Sharon, when suddenly she appeared. She looked amazing. We sat next to each other and she was very nervous, almost like a deer, but she had this beautiful, perfect face. She had this little scar on the left of her face against all this perfection, and when I reached over to touch it, I could feel her react.

"She kept talking about off-the-wall spiritual things—she talked about reincarnation and how in a previous life she had died in a fire aged nine. The second she said that, the doors to the restaurant blew open even though there wasn't any wind, and she looked really shocked."

Did he put the make on her? Jones said he wasn't planning on trying, because "I knew she was married to Roman." Later that same evening, in any case, Christopher Jones said that he was in Sharon Tate's room: "We were sitting on the couch talking when I finally asked her where Roman was. She said he was stuck in London having trouble with his passport. We were talking and getting closer, and although her skirt was riding right up, she wasn't bothering to pull it down. . . . One minute she was looking at me and the next thing I knew, she was pulling me on top of her on to the bed.

"I hadn't even taken my clothes off but after we'd made love I told her I was going upstairs to sleep. She asked me to stay, but when I looked out the window I couldn't see a fire escape and my first thought then was: 'What if Polanski comes back?' I wasn't afraid of him, just worried about the repercussions, but she stopped asking me to stay and I left.

"The next day I ran into actress Nathalie Delon (wife of actor Alain Delon) who was a friend of Sharon's and whom I had also been seeing, and she said: 'Chris, what did you do to Sharon? She has never been so in love.'

Jones later told a newspaper reporter that he knew Sharon was pregnant, and felt guilty. "I've thought about this a lot since and the marriage vows say: 'What God joins together, let no man put asunder.' Well, God obviously separated them and put me there."

Another Jones memory: "One night we went to visit the Trevi Fountain, and I looked at her and had the strongest feeling she was going to die. Another time I was looking over at her and asking her what she was thinking about, and she suddenly came out with: 'The Devil is beautiful. Most people think he's ugly, but he's not.' I thought it weird at the time but Roman had just done the movie *Rosemary's Baby* so I related it to that.

"I told her she shouldn't say things like that because it made me nervous.

"I knew that she and Roman lived in quite an isolated place in LA, so I told her that for her own protection she should have a gun, but she said that she could never shoot anyone even if she had one."

Of the last night they spent together in Rome, Jones says: "I told her that we'd get back together when we were in America and she agreed, and when I said: 'What about Roman?,' she said: 'Don't worry about Roman.'

"I thought it was love. Whatever brief time we had together, we were very happy. I always expected to see her again."

Is it true? Did they really commingle during a busy spring in Rome?

Jones went from Rome to Dingle, a town in County Kerry in Ireland on the Atlantic coast, to begin shooting on *Ryan's Daughter*. (Loosely based on Gustave Flaubert's novel *Madame Bovary*, *Ryan's Daughter* starred Robert Mitchum,

Trevor Howard, Christopher Jones, Leo McKern, Sarah Miles, and others. Christopher Jones plays a shell-shocked World War I veteran engaging in an affair with the married Sarah Miles, in a drama set amidst the 1916 Irish uprising and Irish small-town life.) Filming went on for a number of months, during which his friend Sharon was murdered, and then after filming was concluded, Jones returned to Los Angeles where he lived for a while at the guest cottage owned by his agent Rudy Altobelli located just a few feet from the murder house. Jones was greatly stunned by the death of his friend, and was disturbed when Mr. Altobelli toured guests through the blood-spattered house.

On Easter weekend, Sharon flew to London from Rome. Roman met her at Heathrow Airport bearing a 1954 Rolls-Royce Silver Dawn, a gift. After the weekend, Sharon returned to the Grand Hotel de la Ville to do the remaining scenes of the movie.

Polanski on Top of the World in Spring-Summer of 1969

By April, Polanski at last settled in on *The Day of the Dolphin*. Gone were the cannibalism epic on the Donner Party, and Paganini's flirtation with the Devil. As he said goodbye to a composer and *Donner Pass*, and hello to kill-trained dolphins, Polanski was literally on top of the world in the late spring and early summer of 1969—about to be a father, with a fully funded thriller to create—living in adorable London while still young with a glorious ever-more famous and beautiful wife.

Happy, content, at his acme, succeeding, triumphant, energetic, creative, Polanski began work on *The Day of the Dolphin* in his London Mews house in fiscal security. "As usual in the case of a major new Hollywood project," he later noted, "no one quibbled about research and preproduction costs. Anything I needed I got and I was working with renewed relish."

The 1968 Academy Awards were presented April 14, 1969, at the Dorothy Chandler Pavilion, Los Angeles. Ruth Gordon won for Best Actress in a Supporting Role, for her work in *Rosemary's Baby*. Roman was nominated for "Screenplay Based on Material from Another Medium," against Vernon Harris for *Oliver* and Neil Simon for *The Odd Couple*, but all lost to James Goldman for *The Lion in Winter*. Roman did not attend, or at least there is no mention of it in any of the scads of books, interviews, Internet searches, and articles the author has studied.

There are always blizzards of scripts to read and storms of possible projects swirling around a scriptwriter/director, even in the middle of a fully financed project. One example for Polanski came in April when the original screenplay written by Polanski and produced by Cadre Productions titled *A Day at the Beach* had completed filming in Copenhagen. Adapted from a Dutch novel by Heer

Heresma, the film was directed by a Polanski friend, young Moroccan director Simon Hesera. Paramount Pictures had put up $600,000 after Peter Sellers had agreed to appear in the film. But there was trouble. In his autobiography, Paramount Pictures executive Robert Evans tells of not liking the finished product.

The movie is set in a beat-up Danish resort by the sea. It traces a day in the life of Bernie, an alcoholic (played by Mark Burns) who conducts Winnie (Beatie Edney), a young girl with a leg brace, in the rain to the resort. Winnie calls Bernie "uncle" but it is probable he is, in actuality, her father. Peter Sellers has a cameo as a gay shopkeeper who flirts with Bernie. In July, Evans flew to London to view a rough cut, and didn't like it. Polanski, wrote Evans, "wanted to stay on and reedit it." The film was not destined for heights, and in fact the movie may never have been released.

Never mind about the ill-fated *A Day at the Beach*, Polanski was busy with dolphins. *The Day of the Dolphin* is a book literary critics call "sprawling," that is, it covers a wide vista of concerns. It has plenty of Cold War analysis, criticism of the war in Vietnam, a parable on an agency such as the CIA duping a president, as at the Bay of Pigs, into carrying out a project planned by a previous administration, and an ultrasuspenseful plot line starring talking dolphins, which had to be done well, and definitely not in the chanting chipmunk mode, lest audiences think it was a satire and start chuckling. This gave Mr. Polanski plenty of trouble in coming up with a script.

Sirhan Sentenced to the Gas Chamber

Twenty-five-year-old Sirhan Sirhan was sentenced on April 23, 1969, to die in the gas chamber. A handwritten letter from Senator Edward Kennedy, asking for leniency, was read in open court. Judge Herbert Walker nevertheless sentenced Sirhan Bishara Sirhan to die. The next day, May 22, Sirhan was taken late at night by helicopter to the Van Nuys airport, where an Air National Guard pilot flew him to Hamilton Air Force Base, and then he traveled by caravan to San Quentin penitentiary north of San Francisco, arriving just at the arms of dawn.

Sharon Tate was in Rome working on her new movie at the time. Did she read about Sirhan's sentencing in the Italian newspapers?

Steve McQueen and the Occult

Around the spring of 1969, Sharon's friend Steve McQueen had finished filming his movie *The Reivers*, based on the novel by William Faulkner, in which he played the role of Boon Hogganbeck.

According to *Steve McQueen: Portrait of an American Rebel* by Marshall Terrill, evidence of McQueen's superstitions and belief in occult powers were adduced when, after completing *The Reivers*, he went for some rest to his Palm Springs home, and then took night walks in the desert. One night walking alone he spotted a campfire, and ventured close. McQueen spotted several young women sitting "Indian-style" while chanting, while nearby on the ground lay "Satanic paraphernalia." Apparently thereafter McQueen began to have headaches, and "an image of the devil in my mind."

After this event, McQueen reported that "every Friday night I would get these intolerable migraine headaches. My head would hurt so bad, and all the while there would be this image of the devil in my mind."

McQueen consulted a psychic. He was told that on Friday nights, "all the witches in England get together and circle" and pray for his death. They wanted it by his own hand. The psychic told him not to race in any auto with the satanic hues of red and black.

McQueen mentioned the occult in an interview, dated October 21, 1980, with a professor at UCLA named Brugh Joy, not long before McQueen passed away. Mr. Joy asked if at one time McQueen "went into the occult."

McQueen replied, "I was on the ring of it. Jay Sebring was my best friend. . . . I was sure taken care of; my name never got drawn into that mess. Jay was having an affair with the girlfriend of a warlock. It may be for the worse, but I was always against it. I was one of the ones who always felt that I was one of the good guys, but boy I tell you, they did a number on me. I'm against that whole thing."

The interviewer pointed out, and McQueen agreed "There's a subconscious area that was attracted into the circle. And it comes out of the power element of it." McQueen replied that it wasn't so for him. "It was the women, and the dope, and the running around. That's all that was."

It was pointed out that dope and women and running around were available on many scenes. There was something about the occult that attracted McQueen.

McQueen answered, "But I didn't know it was the occult. It's bullshit is what it is. No, I really didn't know what it was, and by the time I did, I had never gone to any of the meetings. Never knew anything about it, and was always against it. It was never for me."

What meetings? Or, meetings of what? A religious cult with members from the LA music and movie scene?

A Slice of London Life in June

After filming *The Thirteen Chairs*, Tate returned to her husband in London. She posed in their apartment for photographer Terry O'Neill in casual domestic scenes such as opening baby gifts, and also completed a series of glamour photographs for the British magazine *Queen*.

Sharon Tate was twenty-six years old, and seemed likely, in her film career, to escape her early trek through movies involving human sacrifice, vampirism, Malibu Barbieism, *Valley of the Dolls* suicide, and spy-spoofery. Her husband Roman Polanski was thirty-five and luxuriating in what many filmmakers desire, a fully funded Hollywood film which allowed him to spend well beyond the limitations of what his fee for *Rosemary's Baby* had allowed. With that kind of money, a jittery nouveau riche lifestyle could be conducted with a just-before-middle-age breeziness. It was a time of fame, largess, big money from United Artists, and the purchasing of fancy automobiles with the ease that Midwesterners purchased cherry phosphates after Sunday School.

Sharon meanwhile was enjoying her birthday present Rolls. In an article published on June 7, columnist Sheilah Graham wrote, "Sharon Tate, blonde, beautiful and pregnant, was at Margaret Gardner's party in London's Mayfair section." After the party they went away in Sharon's cream Rolls Royce, dropping Sheilah Graham off.

"It was Roman's birthday present to me," said Sharon. "We're taking it back to Hollywood to be with our 17 cats, three dogs and the new baby. I can't wait to get back to start on the nursery."

Sharon ran an ad in the *London Times* for an English nanny to come to Los Angeles and interviewed dozens of candidates, selecting one named Marie Lee.

Not everything was perfect. The normally randy Mr. Polanski, with his wife's increasing pregnancy, found that he had become impotent, at least with her. A biography of Roman by Thomas Kiernan paints how imperfect and uncertain it was: "'The summer did nothing to improve their relationship,' recalls a friend who was on the scene. 'God knows, Sharon tried, she tried almost too much. But he was bored with her being pregnant. He treated her like she was a piece of excess baggage. He was even pointedly cruel to her in front of others at times, calling her a dumb hag and criticizing her whenever she expressed an opinion.'"

However eager Sharon was to get back to Cielo Drive, as Robert Evans wrote in his autobiography, Polanski wanted to stay on in London and work on re-editing *A Day at the Beach*. More importantly, Polanski was having trouble finishing the script for *The Day of the Dolphin*. He decided that he had to remain in London to try to get it done. Sharon was too pregnant to fly, at least trans-oceanically, so she booked a room on the *Queen Elizabeth 2*.

Writer Peter Evans later wrote of a dinner with Sharon and Roman the evening before Sharon left to return to the United States to have the baby: "I had had dinner with him and Tate at Mario and Franco's Tiberio restaurant in London. The following day Tate was to sail to Los Angeles, where she was to have the baby, while Polanski headed for Paris to discuss a new movie. They were the Douglas Fairbanks and Mary Pickford of their time. Cool, nomadic, talented and nicely shocking. I had written a profile of them for *Goodbye Baby & Amen,* the book I had written on London in the Sixties, with pictures by David Bailey."

Sharon was eager to read what Evans had written about them. She was told she'd have to wait till the book came out. David Bailey had photographed them for the book, embracing, with both naked to the waist. Evans wrote that the photo was Polanski's idea. "'Anyone who is interested in the history of the Sixties and the permissive society must consider the Polanskis,' I had written. 'They knew very well the excitement, the miseries, the happiness and the fear of the times.'

"They helped to demolish the Hollywood image of what movie stardom was about. They had pursued the panaceas of the era from marijuana to LSD and knew the score. Polanski took three trips, two of them bad. Tate said that it had 'opened the world to me. I was like a very tight knot, too embarrassed to dance, to speak even. But I could never touch it again. Now I think it would destroy me.'

"There was an honesty that was almost naive about them," Evans wrote. "Together they believed they were challenging the citadels of censorship and cant. From Poland—his mother had died in Auschwitz—Polanski was especially sensitive about a person's right to freedom. Tate wanted to be like him. 'I wish I had the tolerance to let everybody have complete freedom,' she said. 'To be able to take a man home and make love and enjoy it without some lurking puritanical guilt interrupting the pleasure. . . . Mentally it's what I want, but emotionally it is more difficult to take.'"

Evans pointed out that if Sharon "was under her husband's spell, it was where she wanted to be. It was also plain that Polanski was totally in love with his wife. . . . Yet it was a happy marriage. 'We have a good arrangement,' Tate once told me solemnly. 'Roman lies to me and I pretend to believe him.'"

Just before returning to America, Sharon had read Thomas Hardy's *Tess of the d'Urbervilles,* which she left in their bedroom in London and told her husband would make a wonderful movie. Perhaps she was suggesting a path away from filmic weirdness, although the novel was a tragedy where the heroine, Tess, is captured at Stonehenge by the police after murdering a man who had tormented her, and Tess is hanged at novel's close. One account said Sharon's friend Julie Christie gave Sharon a copy of Thomas Hardy's novel, with the inscription, "For my Hardy heroine." (Julie had recently become a Hardy heroine in 1967's *Far from the Madding Crowd.*) When Polanski later made the film *Tess* (1979) he dedicated it "For Sharon."

Polanski's Version of Saying Goodbye on the Ocean Liner

He'd already shipped his Ferrari back to the States, and so borrowed Simon Hesera's Alfa Romeo to drive Sharon to the *QE2* where they had lunch aboard. Then it was time to part, and both, according to Polanski's account in his autobiography, had tears in their eyes. She accompanied him to the downward walkway, and pressed her round stomach firmly against him, "as if to remind me of the baby," he wrote. "As I held and kissed her, a grotesque thought flashed through my mind: you'll never see her again. . . . While walking off the ship and back to the car, I told myself to snap out of it—forget I'd ever had such a morbid feeling, call Victor Lownes, have a ball, see some girls."

Polanski's partner in Cadre Films, Gene Gutowski, has spoken of a fancy baby carriage he gave Sharon that she took with her on the *QE2*. Her Rolls Royce was shipped by separate vessel, and seems to have arrived in Los Angeles in August, right after the murders.

Chapter 8

The Summer of 1969

Jay Sebring met her plane in Los Angeles when she arrived on July 20, 1969. Apparently she had been too gravid to fly transoceanic, but not too gravid for a cross-US flight. Sharon and Jay arrived at 10050 Cielo Drive in time to view the epochal Moon Landing. In June the Tate family—Doris, Patti, and Debra—had moved from San Francisco to the Los Angeles area, to a home on Monero Drive in Palos Verdes. Colonel Tate remained stationed at Fort Baker (which borders Sausalito in Marin County, across the Golden Gate Bridge from San Francisco). The afternoon of the Moon Landing her parents had traveled from San Francisco to San Pedro to work on their house in Palos Verdes, then they drove to Cielo Drive to watch history being made. Sharon, Paul, Doris, Jay, Wojtek, and Abigail all viewed the marvel of Neil Armstrong's first descent onto the dusty surface. Mother Doris brought a wooden rocking chair as a gift—the very one in which she had rocked and nursed her three daughters, Sharon, Patti, and Debra.

Sebring would see Sharon often during the ensuing days. Kirk Douglas, in his autobiography, repeats the gossip: "Jay went with Sharon Tate before Roman Polanski did. There was talk that their romance still continued, even that the baby might have been Jay's. I knew Sharon Tate. Beautiful, naive young girl."

Joanna Pettet also recalls the intimacy between Jay and Sharon: "I knew Jay very, very well. I met Jay through my ex-husband Alex Cord. Jay was a great guy, and he was always in love with Sharon. They stayed friends even after Sharon married Roman. Jay would have done anything in the world for Sharon, he loved her so much. And Roman was not bothered by it, because I think he was secure with his relationship with Sharon."

Polanski watched the Moon Landing at his house on West Eaton Place Mews. The rest of his week was spent in "continual script meetings" with Michael Braun, who was contributing to the script, and set designer Richard Sylbert.

(Out at the Spahn Ranch, just at that moment, young Manson follower Snake Lake and a few others gathered in the building called the bunkhouse to listen to "That's one small step for a man, one giant leap for mankind" on Straight Satan biker Danny DeCarlo's radio.)

In the news that weekend was the tragedy at Chappaquiddick Island. Massachusetts Senator Edward Kennedy flew the afternoon of July 18 from Boston to Martha's Vineyard and took a ferry to Chappaquiddick Island, a spit of sand five hundred feet across from Edgartown, Massachusetts, for a quiet party that night for former campaign workers for Robert Kennedy. Later that night, he crashed his Oldsmobile off a bridge returning to the ferry, into a pond. He managed to rescue himself, but a young former campaign worker, Mary Jo Kopechne, also a passenger, drowned. It was in all the papers, including the *Los Angeles Times,* and on television. Sharon Tate must have watched or read of it.

Sharon Helping in the Marital Troubles of Sheilah Wells: July 1969

In an interview published in *Screenland,* November 1969, former roommate Sheilah Wells described how Sharon tried to save Wells's marriage after she returned that summer from London. Sharon had originally put Wells and her future husband together. Wells: "She had been working on a film called *Don't Make Waves* with Robert Webber. They'd had lunch together with an actor friend, Fred Beir. Suddenly Robert and Sharon decided that Fred and I would be perfect for each other. Fred and I fell in love on our first date. We were married in January, 1967. Sharon and Roman were married a year later, in January, 1968. My baby, Amanda Tate, was born March 16, 1969. And five weeks later, Fred and I started to have serious problems.

"Although Sharon was in Europe at the time, she heard about Freddie and me. So when she came home, just three weeks before she died, Sharon called Freddie and invited him to come up to her house. He went over and she talked to him. That was Sharon. She was always going out on a limb for everyone. Everyone but herself."

In an interview for this book, Sheilah confirmed that Sharon, upset over the possible breakup of Sheilah and Fred, had had lunch with Mr. Beir, and that the marriage was patched up, but only for several weeks. "There was an ethereal quality about her," Wells said to the author. "She had this thing I sometimes wished I'd had, even though I knew that eventually it might be bad for me. Do you understand? She had this kind of beauty and fragility, and you just knew she was bound to get hurt because of it. But still you couldn't help but admiring that quality in her. She was just such a special person."

In the *Screenland* interview, Wells continued: "I never really stopped to think about it until now, but for the past six years so many good things have happened to me because of my friendship with Sharon. She was always there. When I went to the hospital to have the baby, Sharon was the first person to come see me. She was so thrilled when I asked her to be the godmother and when she knew the baby's middle name was for her."

When Sheilah came home from the hospital, Sharon gave her many things for baby Amanda Tate Beir, including a stuffed dog and a tiny yellow-flowered outfit with jingling bells on it that Sharon had purchased in Europe. The same day that Sharon brought Sheilah the yellow-flowered baby outfit, she also carried swatches of fabrics for decorating the nursery on Cielo Drive. She asked Sheilah to check out the colors she had chosen, which Sheilah recalled as red, white, and blue.

In a German publication called *Constanze Magazine*, Wells commented, not long after the murders: "I remember an evening in July, about three weeks before the murder. I was with Sharon in the bedroom watching television. In the sitting room on the sofa lay Gibby and Frykowski. Sharon pointed at them both and said sighing: 'These people . . . I do not understand this, they are always stoned.'"

Jay Sebring in June–July of 1969

On again/off again Sebring companion Sharmagne Leland-St. John recalled moving out of Sebring's house on Easton Drive: "I am not certain of the exact date when I physically moved out of Easton Drive, but I had a burst appendix in early June and I remember attending Brian Morris's *Gone with the Wind Party* on June 7th at the Cielo Drive house; I had already moved out of Easton Drive. We had been burgled by a friend of Jay's. . . . A woman named Carol. Jay was in Vegas (I think cutting Frank's hair) and I was, with Jay's permission, out with Steve McQueen, who was Jay's best male friend. When we returned I found my belongings strewn all up and down the outside stairway. I got spooked and decided to get a place of my own. This woman stole enormous oil paintings, etc. I got one back which flew off the top of her car in Bel Air! I ran an ad in the *Free Press* and someone, an artist, saw it, luckily when he found the canvas, he re-stretched it. I remember the exact wording of the ad! 'Lost in the wee small hours of the morning, one original Massimo oil painting. Please return it because I love it. REWARD.' Peter Yarrow paid the guy the reward. I can't remember why. I guess because he took me to recover it. I moved out but we continued seeing each other, and I still spent nights at Easton."

Meanwhile, Sebring was ultrabusy running his ever-increasing hair styling mini-empire in June and July, and, when Sharon returned, he saw her regularly till the end.

The past—often like quicksand.

Abigail and Wojtek

Compared to the Spahn Ranch, the lifestyles of those living in the house on Cielo Drive to which Sharon Tate returned in July of 1969 were within the bounds of normality. Nevertheless, John Phillips, the songwriter, told a reporter that there were weirdos hanging out on Cielo Drive that summer of the type he had been studiously avoiding for years.

In April and May of 1969, Abigail Folger took an active part in the Tom Bradley mayoral campaign. According to a coworker, she worked at the youth headquarters on Wilshire Boulevard. She also worked for a few months as a volunteer helping children in Watts. During the mayoral campaign, Abigail Folger became interested in a black group called the Street Racers, who evidently served as security forces for the Bradley rallies and offices.

Sometime in June, after Mr. Bradley's defeat on May 26, Ms. Folger and her mother visited New York City. Abigail also traveled frequently from Los Angeles to San Francisco to see her family.

In the spring and summer of 1969, Mr. Frykowski made lengthy daily entries into notebooks in order to work on his grasp of the English language. He was hoping to become a movie scriptwriter, and as we have noted, he was also helping with research on dolphins for Roman's movie.

Around July 7 or 8, Frykowski learned that Sharon was coming back around July 20. He and Ms. Folger began to move clothing from Cielo Drive to their own home on Woodstock Road.

A Polish artist named Witold Kaczanowski, aka Witold K., had been brought to the United States through the kindness of Roman Polanski. He naturally came to live in Los Angeles where he cultivated the Polanskis' circle of friends. He was staying, during the summer of murder, at the Folger/Frykowski Woodstock Road home and was a frequent house guest at 10050 Cielo Drive during the spring and summer of 1969. An actor friend of Wojtek by the name of Mark Fine had also been staying at the Woodstock address but moved out the second week in July, having stayed one week.

Early in July, several friends of Frykowski from Canada promised Wojtek samples of a new drug called methlenedioxyl-amphetamine or MDA, a euphoric stimulant with overtones of aphrodisia that was coming into vogue. According to police reports, Frykowski was being set up to serve as a wholesaler of quantities of MDA manufactured in Toronto. (Both Mr. Frykowski and Ms. Folger were enjoying MDA on the night they died.)

In mid-July, Frykowski's friends from Canada went to Ocho Rios, Jamaica, allegedly to create some sort of movie about marijuana use there. This Jamaican movie project was a front for a large marijuana import operation involving private planes secretly winging the dope to the United States via Florida and Mexico. Investigation into the operation after the murders resulted in one of the biggest dope busts in Jamaican history.

They were making films on Cielo Drive. One day in July, William Garretson, the caretaker, saw Wojtek Frykowski taking pictures of a nude lady in the swimming pool. A cable-TV repairman named Villela came to the Polanski residence and encountered some sort of a nude love scene going on.

In the middle of July, Wojtek ran over Sharon's Yorkshire terrier, named after the doctor in *Rosemary's Baby* who prescribed weird herbal drinks during her satanic pregnancy. Wojtek called London with the news, and Roman then purchased another Yorkshire terrier, which was named Prudence.

Sometime perhaps in the middle of July, Brian Morris threw a catered party for 150 at the Cielo residence, apparently to round up members for a new private club, Bumbles, which Morris was set to open. Roman had apparently invested around $7,000 in the club. Morris had lived at the same time as Sharon and Roman at the Chateau Marmont in early 1968.

(Actress and Sebring girlfriend Sharmagne Leland-St. John recalls the large party put on by Morris at the Polanski residence as occurring "on or about June 7, 1969." It had the theme, *Gone with the Wind*. What did that mean? I asked. "It was a theme party," she answered. "We all dressed like Scarlet O'Hara and Rhett Butler!" For his part, Shahrokh Hatami recalls the *Gone with the Wind* party organized by Brian Morris as having occurred on August 1, which was the birthday of his then girlfriend, Ann Ford.)

The past is like quicksand.

Mrs. Polanski asked Abigail Folger and Wojtek Frykowski to stay on at 10050 Cielo Drive until her husband was to return from London.

In the early days of August, Sharon was spotted in local department stores purchasing baby supplies, books on child care, and supplies for the nursery, which was being outfitted in the north wing of the house. She was utterly delighted about the impending birth of the baby, and she was keeping in shape, watching her diet, preparing for the resumption of her film career.

Meanwhile, living at Falcon's Lair, a mansion on Angelo Drive (on a property contiguous to 10050 Cielo Drive), was ultrawealthy and eccentric heiress Doris Duke. According to a book called *Too Rich—The Family Secrets of Doris Duke,* "Doris (Duke) would take the young actress (Sharon Tate) on expensive shopping trips on Rodeo Drive in Beverly Hills where she would spend thousands of dollars buying mother-and-daughter designer ensembles."

Joanna Pettet also gave Sharon some maternity attire, as she told the author in a 2010 interview: "I gave off all my maternity clothes to Sharon, because I had some really sweet things from London. Another friend of mine, Sheilah Wells, and I bought her an old-fashioned wicker crib for the baby." Wells lived next door to Pettet and her husband on Woodrow Wilson Drive.

An Italian journalist named Enrico di Pompeo asked Tate in a late July interview (for the European release of *The Thirteen Chairs*) if she believed in fate, to which she replied, "Certainly. My whole life has been decided by fate. I think something more powerful than we are decides our fates for us. I know one thing—I've never planned anything that ever happened to me."

During those days Jay Sebring visited with Sharon often, whenever he wasn't overseeing his far-flung business interests. Paul Newman, according to the *San Francisco Chronicle,* said that Sebring's method prevented him from losing his hair. Actor George Peppard allegedly spent $2,500 to fly Sebring to a movie location to trim his locks. Frank Sinatra used to fly Sebring to Las Vegas to cut his hair. "He was a legendary name in hair styling," commented his friend, public relations executive Art Blum.

The corporate offices for Sebring International were located above the hair shop at 725 North Fairfax in Hollywood. In partnership with his friend Art Blum, Sebring opened another shop in the summer of 1969 in San Francisco at 629 Commercial Street. Shortly afterward Sebring rented a houseboat in Sausalito, California, just north of San Francisco. Throughout the summer, he frequently flew north to check on his new enterprises. On several occasions he visited Colonel Tate and family at Fort Barry. Mr. and Mrs. Tate would stay at Sebring's houseboat in Sausalito when they came to San Francisco. (Fort Barry lies in the coastal hills of Marin County. It was the home of very powerful Nike-Hercules missiles, capable of carrying nuclear warheads in order to destroy formations of approaching enemy planes. The Nike-Hercules missile batteries at Fort Barry joined more than three hundred identical missile batteries that once guarded US cities and military installations. Eleven missile sites ringed San Francisco Bay during those years. As we have noted, it is believed that Colonel

Paul Tate, as an intelligence officer, was involved in protecting these missile facilities.)

Toward the end of July or maybe August 1, Jay Sebring held an afternoon publicity party at his hair shop in San Francisco that was attended by Paul Newman, Abigail Folger, and many others. After that, during early August, Jay was back in Los Angeles spending much time with Sharon Tate.

He still owned, and possibly kept on his person, Sharon's high school class ring, which she had given him back in 1965. Twenty years later, in early 1989, Doris Tate told the author that Sebring's parents, who lived in Michigan, had recently sent her the ring.

The Question of *The Story of O*

Writing about what Sharon might do with her "troubled" marriage with Polanski, one biography of her states: "Sharon apparently decided to wait until the baby was born, perhaps to see if fatherhood altered her husband's extramarital activities. If there was no change, she would institute divorce proceedings" and begin a new path with her life.

Weighing against the theme that Sharon was prepared for a total focus on motherhood is the assertion that she was considering starring in a movie adaptation of the novel *The Story of O*. "Sharon was excited about plans to star for Just Jaecklin for his next project, *The Story of O*, dealing with erotic sex and sadism. An announcement from Allied Artists was planned after the birth of her baby." So writes Kirk Crivello in his 1988 book, *Fallen Angels: The Glamorous Lives and Tragic Deaths of Hollywood's Doomed Beauties*.

The Story of O is about a beauteous French fashion photographer, O, who is willingly blindfolded, whipped, branded, chained, and, wearing a mask, conditioned to be available for all kinds of intercourse. O gives permission in advance to those who desire her. O undergoes further training at a mansion dwelled in by women, where at novel's close, O appears enslaved, nude except for a bird-like mask, in front of a group of guests. Maybe it was enticing to Ms. Tate, who had long complained of being an object of physical attraction, and not admired for herself.

Founded in the 1940s, Allied Artists Picture Corporation, as it became known in the 1950s, was an established producer of fairly high-budget films, but then fell for a few years. Allied Artists ceased production in 1966 and became a distributor of foreign films, but restarted production with the 1972 release of *Cabaret* and followed it the next year with *Papillon*. Allied Artists in 1975 wound up distributing the French import film version of *The Story of O*.

I asked Sheilah Wells if she had heard that Sharon was thinking of appearing, after she gave birth, in a film version of *The Story of O*. "No," Wells replied.

"At that point, she was being offered a lot of different things, or at least had mentioned them."

"I think," Sheilah Wells added, "that Sharon was really on the brink. And I think that if she had had one more comedy role, I think that would have been an amazing thing for her career, because she was very funny."

Do you know anything about Sharon's putative intention to do *The Story of O*? I asked Sharmagne Leland-St. John. "No," she answered, "But it was the hot book around at the time with our circle. Richard (Sylbert) gave it to me to read in '68. I still have it here by the bed. In a way it mirrored her life. Jay liked to tie his lovers up and pretend to whip them. He liked to blindfold them. He liked to do all sorts of dominating things to make you sort of prove your love."

Quicksand.

Chapter 9

A Cult at the Spahn Ranch Kills

Out on the western edge of the San Fernando Valley was the Spahn Ranch, which was the site for Western-themed TV and low-budget films. People also could rent horses for rides along nearby trails. The ranch, located at 12000 Santa Susanna Pass Road, had once belonged to silent movie actor William S. Hart, but a man named George Spahn had purchased it in 1948. Over the years, George Spahn became blind. He had a longtime partner named Ruby Pearl who managed the ranch. Ruby was a former animal trainer and dancer and was in her late forties during the Manson era when she tended to ranch business, attired in a cowboy hat and riding clothes. She had an up and down relationship with the Family. Ruby was constantly reporting to blind George what Manson's group was doing, except at night when she went home.

The Family desperately sought to keep on George's good side, so Manson took care that a nubile female was on hand to take care of the blind Mr. Spahn, who was very fond of friendly physical communication with the young women. Lynnette Fromme, who seven years later would try to assassinate President Gerald Ford, was responsible for much of the taking care of George Spahn. Family member Paul Watkins recalled that Fromme had picked up the name Squeaky from the "eeks" she made when George Spahn ran his hand up her leg and pinch/caressed the inside of her thigh. During the murder trial of 1970, a defense attorney told me that Squeaky claimed she had performed fellatio on Mr. Spahn.

The Spahn Ranch was located about halfway between the wilderness and the city; it was just a thirty-five-minute ride to Sharon Tate's house in Benedict

Canyon, but also it was a fairly quick dune-buggy ride up Devil Canyon into the Santa Susanna Mountains.

The ranch was situated just in front of a creek that cuts down from the northwest and oozes and trickles down along Santa Susanna Pass Road, which is behind the ranch. There are waterfalls in the creek, which were the bathing spas of Helter Skelter. The Spahn Ranch is backed up by bouldery hills that climb sharply north and south. It is grade B Western movie turf from the 1950s. The ghosts of Tim Holt and the Durango Kid yodel in the mountain crags.

The Western set, where movies were made, was located just off Santa Susanna Pass Road. It was a ramshackle collection of buildings in a straight row. A boardwalk extended the length of the set. Sleazy awnings held up by crooked posts ran the length of the mockup cowboy main street. There was a mockup restaurant called the Rock City Café; a jailhouse with a wooden-barred cell; the Longhorn Saloon, complete with mirrors and room-length bar and juke box; a carriagehouse full of old carriages; an undertaking parlor; and several other buildings, including George Spahn's small house, which lay perpendicular to the right of the movie set. All these were built in the manner of a Kansas town of early America. A dirt driveway connected the movie set with the reality of Santa Susanna Pass Road. Painted movie props often were strewn about, leaning against the haystack or corral.

Spahn Ranch, "Longhorn Saloon," and "Rock City Café," August 1969

Aerial photo of Spahn Ranch, with Santa Susanna Pass Road on left

The ranch was a bit of a fantasy land, though the era of the formula Western was over, and George and Ruby needed horse rentals to keep it afloat. On holiday weekends the ranch sometimes earned up to $1,000. In addition, the coffers were enhanced by an occasional TV commercial (one or more of the famous Marlboro Man ads reportedly was filmed there), plus an occasional beaver, sci-fi, or monster movie.

Salary for the ranch hands was a place to sleep, some food, and a pack of cigarettes a day. A few of the ranch hands, such as the one known as Randy Starr, worked as movie stunt men. Starr's stunts involved horse falls and neck drags, and he considered himself a high-quality performer. Other hands worked in rodeos. One hand, Shorty Shea, whom the Family would later murder, was an actor who avidly pursued a career in the movies in addition to doing stunt work. The stunt men utilized the ranch as a business address.

The Death of Gary Hinman

Thirty-two-year-old Gary Hinman, who lived in Topanga Canyon, was close to getting his PhD in sociology from UCLA. For several years Hinman had befriended the Manson Family. His house was known in Topanga Canyon as a place where people could crash for a night or two. For the previous year, Gary had been devoted to Nichiren Shoshu Buddhism, a sect with Los Angeles headquarters located on the Coast Highway by the beach in Santa Monica.

Sheriff's detectives told me that Hinman made quantities of synthetic mescaline at his house on Old Topanga Canyon Road. A young couple, who had lived with Gary up to several days before his death, partnered with him in the manufacture of the mescaline. The husband told me in an interview, "We were making mescaline. It was a really long, long process but the advantage was that it was really cheap. You bought things and no one would ever connect the things you bought with what you were going to do. You could order zillions of them from the chemical supply houses and they'd never get hip, not unless somebody really did some thinking. Gary had a degree in chemistry."

Eric, the mescaline partner, visited Hinman's house about four days before Gary was murdered. He told me later that when he entered the small hillside house he found Hinman hassling on the phone with Manson: "When I came into the house they were arguing. Like, Gary was really into Nichiren Shoshu and the concept of leadership and the concept that people needed to be directed, which was something that Charlie was very opposed to, and so they were in a heated discussion about that and then it was like there was a response: it was pretty together and I talked to Gary afterwards to verify what Charlie said—He said, you know, like it's your last chance, Gary. And Gary responded to that: 'I'm sorry, Charlie. I'm not going to sell all my things and come and follow you.' Those were his exact words.

"And so Charlie said, in response to that, that he couldn't be responsible then for the karma that Gary was going to incur. He then reiterated that it was his last chance. And Gary said, 'I'll decide . . . I'll take care of my own karma.'"

On July 24, Manson sent disciple Ella Bailey, aka Ella Sinder, formerly a close friend of Hinman, from the Spahn Ranch to Hinman's house to obtain Hinman's money and then to kill him. Although Ella was a longtime Manson devotee, she was not willing to kill for him. Another Family associate named Bill Vance loved Ella and tried to argue with Charlie, but Charlie was very angry. The result was that Ella and Bill split for Texas. The Mansonites talked among themselves how they were going to kill Bill and Ella if the two should dare to return.

Formed in the year of Flowers, 1967, now everything, just two years later, was murder. Murder and control. Around this time, another Manson disciple, Cathy Gillies Myers, went off by herself without telling anyone. Upon return, Tex Watson threatened her. "Don't you ever leave here without telling someone where you're going, next time I'll kill you, your life means nothing to me."

The next day, July 25, pregnant Kitty Lutesinger asked her boyfriend, Robert Beausoleil, if she could depart. She was very tired of the constant hassles, the raids, and the general atmosphere of apocalypse and impending race war. So Bobby said that he would ask Charlie for her, and his reply was that she absolutely could not leave the ranch.

Because Charlie felt that Kitty looked too much like his mother, also a thin, short redhead, he and Kitty never got along. Manson accused her of trying to cajole Bobby into leaving the Family, threatening to torture and kill her. That afternoon Manson paced up and down the Spahn Ranch boardwalk, jabbing his sword at bales of hay, very angry.

Also that afternoon, Bobby rode with Charlie in his "command" dune buggy up Devil Canyon. They looked at an abandoned mine, whereupon Manson noted that it would be a good place to hide a body. Manson was well armed; his magic sword was sheathed in a metal tube on the steering column, a pistol was in a holster between Charlie's legs, and a knife was strapped to his ankle.

Several weeks previous, M had ordered all female followers to shear their hair, leaving only a thin dangle of hair down their backs. Apparently the long hair swatches from the girls were tied together and were attached to his dune-buggy roll bar. There was an ocelot fur canopy stretched across the buggy's rear deck by the machine-gun mounts. Manson shifted in his seat toward Beausoleil and asked if Bobby was thinking of leaving. Bob said yes, and Charlie replied, "Maybe I ought to slit your motherfuckin' throat."

Beausoleil was a rival to Manson. He composed his own songs, and recorded them. He had attracted his own female followers. He was well-known in certain parts of the American counterculture for his relationship with the filmmaker Kenneth Anger. Back in 1967, Beausoleil had dwelled with Anger in an old house in San Francisco called the Russian Embassy, where Anger introduced him to the universe of magic, not to mention the cruelty-tinged world of Aleister Crowley. Beausoleil has said that at that time he was on an all-meat diet and believed himself to be the devil. Anger was involved in making an occult movie called *Lucifer Rising,* in which Beausoleil played the role of Lucifer. Beausoleil was also the lead guitarist and sitarist for The Magick Power-house of Oz, an eleven-piece rock ensemble formed by Anger to perform the music for *Lucifer Rising.*

In 1967, around the time that Beausoleil met Manson, The Magick Power-house of Oz played at a gathering at the Straight Theater on Haight Street to celebrate the so-called "Equinox of the Gods." The film *Lucifer Rising* was supposed to be nearly completed so the night was one of celebration. Anger filmed the event that night but Beausoleil remembered later that Mr. Anger flipped out during the proceedings and smashed a priceless caduceus-headed cane that had once belonged the king of sex-magic himself, Aleister Crowley.

Things went awry between Beausoleil and his mentor Kenneth Anger shortly after the Equinox of the Gods gathering at the Straight Theater. Beausoleil seems to have ripped off Anger's car, some camera equipment and, more importantly, some of the footage of *Lucifer Rising*. Then he split. When he discovered that Beausoleil had ripped him off, Anger thereupon fashioned a locket, the face of which bore the likeness of Bob Beausoleil. The obverse contained the likeness of a toad, with the inscription "Bob Beausoleil—who was turned into a toad by Kenneth Anger."

Beausoleil moved down to Topanga Canyon in the fall of 1967 following his break with Anger, where he became friends with Gary Hinman. When he met Manson, Beausoleil and a girlfriend were living at Hinman's small hillside house on Old Topanga Canyon Road.

In July of 1969, after Manson threatened Beausoleil against trying to leave, Manson quickly changed the subject to Hinman and asked Bobby if he would be willing to go over to Gary's house and try to get some money out of him.

Beausoleil later testified that the main reason for asking Hinman for money was to assist the Family to move to the desert. "I was supposed to tell Gary about the idea of making the desert a place for a lot of people. Gary is the type of person who would be interested in something like that, making a place for people where they could express themselves in music."

M disciple Linda Kasabian recounted that one early evening she was standing by the ranch boardwalk while Bobby and Charlie were chatting in the bunkhouse. Sadie Glutz (Susan Atkins) and Mary Brunner were standing obediently outside the bunkhouse, waiting for Bobby to come out so that they could go someplace. Sadie told Linda Kasabian that they were off to get some money, plus that she and Mary had been selected for the chore in order to work out a "personality conflict."

Manson later admitted several times that the Hinman murder was about a botched dope deal. Sixteen years later, in his autobiography, he told what may possibly be the truth. He reaffirmed that Hinman was making mescaline, slowly, in his home lab. "For several weeks," he states, "Bobby had been moving Gary's stuff off on a group of bikers, without any problems. But one morning three of the bikers came riding into the ranch and wanted to see Bobby. The bikers said the latest batch of stuff he had sold them was bad, laced with poison. Some of their own group had gotten deathly ill and some of the people they sold to were also sick. They wanted their money back."

True or meadow muffins?

Manson wrote that the amount was $2,000. Manson claimed that Hinman sought to examine the alleged poisoned mescaline, then refused to give over the $2,000. Manson stated he requested Hinman give him enough mescaline to earn back the $2,000. "Can't do that," Hinman supposedly said. "I'm getting things together so that I can go overseas for a few weeks. Besides, you guys still owe me some on the last stuff you got."

Ace Manson disciple Bruce Davis drove Bobby, Sadie, and Mary to Hinman's house in the same beat-up Ford that would soon be driven to the murder of Sharon Tate and the others.

Mary Brunner was silent as the grim trio mounted the steep steps to Hinman's house. "Bobby seemed nervous but his natural arrogance compensated for it, and he was as cocky and confident as ever. I thought of his competitiveness, especially with Charlie. He was gripped with the need to prove that he could do anything Charlie could do. He seemed to need to prove it to himself, to Charlie, and to all of us."

Gary Hinman had gone down that afternoon to Los Angeles to apply for a passport; he intended to go on a religious pilgrimage to Japan in two weeks. He returned from Los Angeles, stopping to visit with a friend who owned a music school where Hinman taught piano, bagpipes, trombone, and the drums. Hinman stayed there until about 7:10 p.m., when he said he was going to a meeting somewhere.

Hinman delivered a warm and friendly "Hi!" as he welcomed Sadie, Mary, and Bobby. Friendliness ceased to exist, though, after he was asked for money and his autos, and he told them to leave.

Beausoleil had brought a 9-millimeter Radon pistol. After the trio spoke with Hinman for several hours with no result, Beausoleil drew the gun on Hinman and informed him that the situation was serious. Bobby then punched Gary, who spat out a piece of tooth. Bobby fired the pistol, then handed it to Sadie, whereupon he and Hinman fought furiously, rolling on the floor. When Sadie placed the pistol on a table, Gary Hinman grabbed it, then held it on Mary, Bobby, and Sadie.

Instead of calling the Malibu sheriff's office, the nonviolent musician did something that probably cost him his life. Sadie Glutz recalled, "With tears in his eyes, he handed the gun back to Bobby. 'I just don't believe in violence,' he said. 'Here, you take the gun. I don't want it. Why don't you just go? Just leave me alone.'"

Hinman then went into the living room, and lay on the couch while Beausoleil continued to try to talk Gary out of the money.

They called Manson at the ranch and told Charlie there had been a fight, and gunfire, and Hinman wouldn't give in. Around midnight, Bruce Davis and Manson, waving his sword, arrived at Hinman's. Right away an angry Charlie said that he wanted "to talk about that money." Hinman started to shout, ordering him to get out and take the others with him, at which Manson raised up his sword and whacked Hinman's ear, leaving a five-inch wound deep into the jawbone and extending up through the ear.

After this, Manson and Davis split, with M telling Hinman he'd better fork over the money or else. The trio left behind tied Hinman up and placed him on the rug on the living room floor, where he lay, cursing Manson and vowing vengeance. They agreed to guard him all night to prevent his escape. They gave him a drink of wine or beer, and Sadie went down to the Topanga store to purchase bandages and some dental floss with which to sew up his gaping wound. Bobby and Mary turned Hinman's house upside down, even tearing open a cash box, but failed to locate any cash.

For several days, Hinman refused to tell them where the pink slips for his two autos were. When Beausoleil fell asleep, Hinman tried to escape and was beaten. Finally he signed over the VW microbus and the souped-up Fiat.

On July 26, two friends of Hinman, associates of the Manson Family, tried to contact Gary while he was held by the trio. One called Hinman's house in the afternoon, supposedly to ask Gary to rent him the lower apartment in his house. A girl answered the phone, apparently Sadie Glutz, who spoke with an English accent. The English voice announced Gary was in Colorado, where his parents had been involved in an automobile accident. Another person from Santa Barbara named Dave showed up at Hinman's house in person. A woman, not one of the Family according to Dave, answered the door and refused him entrance.

Sometime early on July 27, they called the Spahn Ranch. Manson told them to kill Hinman. "He knows too much," biker Danny De Carlo claimed Charlie said.

Another scenario has Manson saying that they were all set to take Hinman out to the ranch to let him heal his wounds but that Beausoleil panicked, evidently when Hinman started screaming out the window. Gary Hinman was stabbed twice in the chest by Beausoleil, with one of the thrusts cutting the pericardial sac and causing death by bleeding.

While Hinman passed away, they placed him on the floor of the living room. Above him they created a makeshift Buddhist shrine. They gave him his prayer beads and he chanted "Nam Myo Ho Renge Kyo—Nam Myo Ho Renge Kyo," until he lapsed into thanatos.

Mary and Sadie took away the bloody bandages from Hinman's thread-sewn face, and the bloody towels and clothing, for disposal outside. There was somebody's bloody black cape that was also brought out of Hinman's house.

They laid a green bedspread over him. On the wall just above Hinman's head, someone scrawled, in Hinman's blood, "Political *Piggy*," next to which someone fingerpainted in blood the paw of a cat, intended to be a panther. Using a narrow brush, he or she painted the claws of the paw, hoping the police, and the press, would think that black militants had committed the murder.

They wiped the house down for fingerprints and burnt some documents, evidently those linking the Family with Hinman, in the living room fireplace. They locked all the doors and crawled out the side window. As they were leaving, they began to hear Hinman making a lot of heavy rasping sounds, so Beausoleil climbed in the rear window and went over to Hinman's body and started smothering him, and Sadie came in and grabbed a pillow and put it over his face until he lay still. Mary pulled Hinman's wallet out and removed twenty dollars, then thrust the wallet halfway into his back pocket.

Then they tripped down the steep, wooden staircase to the street, where they hot-wired Hinman's VW van painted with a thunderbird. They were hungry, so they drove over to the restaurant at the Topanga shopping center and had some cherry cake and coffee. They then headed for the ranch where, when Hinman's microbus was spotted and others of the Family joined them, some of the girls noticed that there were paints in the back, which they used to paint some pictures. Then Mary Brunner, Linda Kasabian, and Kitty Lutesinger used Hinman's Fiat to go on a garbage run for preparing the evening meal.

Troubled Times

In the afternoon of July 30, someone at the Polanski residence called the Esalen Institute at Big Sur, California. Three days later Charles Manson visited the Institute. That same day, Robert Beausoleil went back to the Hinman house, now full of flies, to wipe down the place more thoroughly for fingerprints. Beausoleil failed to wipe away a fingerprint from the kitchen door with twenty-six points of identification, helping send him to death.

While Bobby was at Hinman's house, his girlfriend, the pregnant Kitty Lutesinger, took that moment to flee.

Frank Retz, the agent for the Transcontinental Development Corporation (which was attempting to purchase the Spahn Ranch), was visiting a property near the Spahn Ranch at the very moment that Kitty made her escape. She fled along the underbrush to find a stretch of road away from the main ranch complex where she might hitchhike safely away.

Just minutes previous, Retz had stormed in on the Spahn Ranch's so-called "back ranch," which lay on the property line, and insisted that Manson and the others leave the premises. When Mr. Retz returned to his car, Lutesinger dashed from the brush and asked for protection from Manson.

Retz took Kitty Lutesinger to a police station, and then she was brought by police officers to her parents' horse ranch in the San Fernando Valley. This served to dissolve Helter Skelter even before the murders were committed. The sheriff's office began visiting her home to acquire insight into the Spahn Ranch, which they by now considered an illegal haven for runaways and an assembly line for converting stolen vehicles into dune buggies.

A Dire Warning from Psychic Maria Graciette: Did This Actually Happen?

Ordinarily one wouldn't pay much attention to articles in the *National Enquirer,* but nevertheless there was an article "Psychic Warned Sharon Tate & Three Others of Bloody Tragedy—Just Before They Were Slain by Manson Clan."

The article stated that "only days" before August 8, 1969, "At a public reading in a chapel near her Hollywood home, Maria Graciette (age 37) was handed a scarf and a set of questions by Sharon Tate." With Sharon were Jay Sebring, Abigail Folger, and Wojtek Frykowski, or so the article alleges. Her scarf was to give the psychic some connection with the questioner's personality. "'I closed my eyes and concentrated. Then it was horrible. Everything in front of my eyes went red, red like blood. I saw pain, suffering. I saw a lot of blood, people screaming, people running. . . .

"'I dropped the scarf and yelled out: 'This is terrible, horrible. I can't go on with the reading. Run, run—you must go away.'"

What's most interesting to the author is that the article states that later Graciette was questioned under hypnosis by a Los Angeles doctor long connected with CIA mind control experiments named William Kroger. "Maria's examination under hypnosis was conducted by psychiatrist William S. Kroger, MD, and psychologist Ernest Rossi, PhD. Dr. Kroger, an authority on hypnosis for 50 years, said: 'I would say that she is telling the truth about that night.'" (Dr. Rossi was a board member of the American Society of Clinical Hypnosis. In addition, Dr. William Kroger, with a practice in Los Angeles, was thought to be a high official in the CIA's brainwashing program, including the programming of former model Candy Jones, which extended into 1968 and 1969.) "In addition," the article contended, "Maria's statements were analyzed by Charles McQuiston, co-developer of the Psychological Stress Evaluator . . . and he confirmed that 'there is no trace of deception.'"

Of course, Maria Graciette was wrong on some of her prognostications. Apparently she years later predicted that the largest earthquake ever recorded would strike the sea bed near New York City, sending in a tidal wave that would flood Manhattan.

Chapter 10
Sharon Tate's Final Few Days

AS WaS previously noted, on Wednesday, July 30, 1969, at 3:07 in the after-noon, someone at 10050 Cielo Drive, using a number listed to Roman Polanski, telephoned the Esalen Institute in Big Sur, California. Esalen was a popular place to visit, with the stupendous beauty of that part of the coastline, the hot springs and steam baths at the Institute, and its many workshops and therapy conferences in the field of humanistic psychology.

On Friday, August 1, according to an interview I conducted in 1970, a hair-stylist named Carol Solomon and a girl named Linda, a Beverly Hills doctor's daughter, attended a small party thrown by Wojtek Frykowski at 10050 Cielo Drive. Chicken and champagne were served at the pool. Sharon Tate and Abigail Folger were not there. Linda was Wojtek's date and was known to have "hung out" at the home during the summer. It was a nonboisterous gathering of about ten people, some of whom spent time in the bedroom watching TV. The two girls, according to Solomon, were invited over again for the following weekend.

(Sharon's friend the photographer Hatami told me that he was living with an actress named Ann Ford in August of 1969, and that for her twenty-second birthday, August 1, there was a party for her at 10050 Cielo Drive.)

According to the vice president of Sebring International, Jay Sebring had visited the Polanski residence on Sunday, Tuesday, and Thursday during the week before the murders.

The foggy veils and vales of the past.

In early August, Sharon and her younger sister Patti had gotten into Sharon's red Ferrari to go to the market. Sharon backed by accident into her mother's Corvair, so that Sharon's car was taken to a garage to be repaired. (This incident caused Doris Tate to be carless the morning of August 9, and thus she couldn't rush to Cielo Drive.) On Monday, August 4, 1969, Sharon rented a 1969 Chevrolet Camaro from Airways Rent-a-Car "to be leased from August 4, 1969 till August 8, 1969," as the contract reads.

On August 4, Wojtek's actor friend Mark Fine called and reminded him that Frykowski had a meeting with a movie producer on the sixth regarding the sale of a story. Frykowski told Fine that on August 6 he would have to pick up some friends at the airport coming in from Canada.

Sometime during that week, perhaps Tuesday or Wednesday, a dope dealer from Canada, according to an LA homicide officer who helped break the Manson case, was whipped and video-buggered, apparently not at 10050 Cielo Drive, but at Cass Elliot's house on Woodrow Wilson Drive. In the days before his death, Sebring had complained to a receptionist at his hair shop that someone had burned him for $2,000 worth of cocaine, and he wanted vengeance. The dealer from Canada was involved in a large-scale dope-import operation involving private planes from Jamaica. There seem to have been a good many dope-burns, perhaps like the falling of a line of dominoes, during the days around the Tate-LaBianca murders.

Dennis Hopper, in an interview with the *Los Angeles Free Press,* said, about the video-bugger and the circumstances there: "They had fallen into sadism and masochism and bestiality—and they recorded it all on videotape too. The L.A. police told me this. I know that three days before they were killed, twenty-five people were invited to that house to a mass whipping of a dealer from Sunset Strip who'd given them bad dope." (Mr. Hopper was at the time living with Michelle Phillips, singer with the Mamas and the Papas. Phillips, a close friend of Cass Elliot, was apparently also a source for Hopper's account.)

Easy Rider had opened July 14, 1969, in New York City. It had cost something like $500,000, but sold $19.1 million in tickets. Hopper was nominated for an Academy Award for the Best Screenplay (with Peter Fonda and Terry Southern). He was hot hot hot. *Life* magazine named him "Hollywood's hottest director."

As for Michelle Phillips, she had visited Cielo Drive on one of the days preceding the fatal Friday, August 8. Sometime during her final days, Sharon had learned about Michelle's one-time fling with Roman, which had occurred in London the previous spring, perhaps while Sharon was in Italy filming *The Thirteen Chairs.*

On Tuesday or Wednesday, August 5 or 6, according to an interview with someone who said she was there, there was a gathering at Cielo Drive to celebrate French director Roger Vadim's newly released movie and his imminent return to Europe. Indeed, at the end of July there had been the American premiere of *Spirits of the Dead,* based on stories by Edgar Allan Poe. It was a three-part movie, and Vadim had directed one part, which starred his wife, Jane Fonda, and others. (According to the biography, *Jane Fonda,* by Fred Lawrence Guiles, Vadim was in Malibu and Jane in France on August 8, 1969.)

Sharon, Wojtek, and Abigail on August 6 were at Michael Sarne's house in Malibu for dinner. Sharon was tired and got up to leave shortly after dessert. Her life revolved around the baby. She floated during the day in a rubber ring in her swimming pool—to take the weight off her stomach.

Sarne was heavily involved at the time directing the film, based on a novel by Gore Vidal, called *Myra Breckinridge,* which received an X rating when released by Twentieth Century Fox in 1970. It starred such luminaries as Mae West, John Huston, Raquel Welch, Rex Reed, and Farrah Fawcett. Nevertheless, upon its release, *Time* magazine opined that "*Myra Breckinridge* is about as funny as a child molester. It is an insult to intelligence, an affront to sensibility and an abomination to the eye." The film is also cited in the book *The Fifty Worst Films of All Time.* Since its release, it has achieved something of a cult following, just like *Valley of the Dolls.*

John Phillips had been hired to write music for *Myra Breckinridge.* He had been living in a guesthouse at Sarne's rented house in Malibu Colony.

On August 6, 1969, Abigail Folger had an appointment with her psychiatrist Dr. Marvin Flicker, as she did each afternoon at 4:30, five days a week. According to what Dr. Flicker told the LAPD, Folger wanted to break off with Frykowski. "She discussed her use of drugs," the *First Homicide Investigation Progress Report* (p. 27) reported, "and her disappointment with Frykowski. Doctor Flicker states that he thought she was almost ready to leave Frykowski. She was building up enough nerve in her own mind to go it alone."

Sebring Drops Off Film to Be Copied: August 6, 1969

In the probate records for Jay Sebring in the Superior Court in Los Angeles is a "creditors claim" from General Film Laboratories, 1546 North Argyle Avenue, dated August 6, for the amount of $736.85, for two separate films, one of them a 16-millimeter reel of Kodak film, 3,835 feet in length; and for the same film electro-printing a copy, $65.00. What sort of film or films was Jay Sebring dropping off?

Prolegomenon on Cielo Drive

Two or three days prior to his death, Wojtek Frykowski received a new shipment of MDA. One of Wojtek's dope-dealer friends from Canada later claimed to reporters that Frykowski was in the fifth day of a "ten-day mescaline experiment." In fact, the dealer claimed that both Jay Sebring and Mr. Frykowski were

Sharon and Jay, loyal friends all the way

stoned on mescaline. The dealer spoke to Frykowski about an additional shipment of MDA. The same dealer said he showed up in the afternoon on August
7 and shared a bottle of wine with Frykowski. He met Sharon Tate that day,
indicating that he was a recent friend of Frykowski.

Novelist Jerzy Kosinski told me that he and his wife were set to fly to Los
Angeles on August 7 to visit at the Polanski residence and wait for Roman to
return for his birthday on August 18. The Kosinskis' luggage was misplaced on
the way to New York from Europe so, instead of traveling immediately to Los
Angeles, they waited in New York for the luggage. This may have saved their
lives, because they were not able to arrive in Los Angeles by August 8th.

Over in London that morning, the four Beatles walked across Abbey Road
while a policeman held up traffic as a photographer (Iain MacMillan) on a step-
ladder took a few pictures. Not long later Paul McCartney made some sketches
for the design of the album called *Abbey Road*, an album a bit more peaceful
than the *White Album*, but too late to impact the locusts of the Spahn Ranch.

That same morning, August 8, 1969, the housekeeper, Winifred Chapman,
arrived at the Polanski residence at 8 a.m. At around 8:30 a.m., a Mr. Guerrero
arrived to paint the nursery. He worked until midafternoon, completing the first

coat. He was scheduled to return on Monday to finish the second coat of paint. Before lunch, Winifred washed down the front Dutch door because the dogs had dirtied it. "PIG" and a fingerprint would dirty it later.

Mrs. Chapman testified that on Tuesday, August 4, she had washed the French doors in Sharon's bedroom, where Friday midnight would find a murderer's fingerprint. Wednesday and Thursday were Mrs. Chapman's days off.

At about 11 a.m. Roman Polanski called from London. Mrs. Chapman answered the phone. Then Sharon talked. Sharon hinted she might throw a birthday party for him on August 18, when he returned. There was a heavy heat wave in Los Angeles, and there was an edge to the conversation. She was anxious for him to arrive soon, so that he might attend a course for expectant fathers. Mrs. Polanski planned to have natural childbirth. She told her husband that a little kitten had wandered onto the property, and she was feeding it with an eyedropper. She was edgy. She didn't want houseguests any longer. She was due in two to three weeks. One of the prime reasons for her edginess was obvious—she wanted her husband, and the father of her child, home.

Polanski was having trouble finishing the script and planning the production of *The Day of the Dolphin*, so he had hired an American writer named Michael Braun to help him with the final sequences and had postponed returning to Los Angeles a number of times. "It dawned on me, as we talked," he recalls in his autobiography, "that I was getting nowhere with the ending . . . and that the sequence I'd been working on could probably be cut altogether. 'That's it,' I said, 'I'm coming. I'll finish the script over there. I'll leave tomorrow.' I couldn't hop a plane the next day, a Saturday, because I needed a US visa and the consulate was closed, but I made up my mind to do so the following Monday or Tuesday (August 11 or 12), as soon as the visa was granted."

In the afternoon, the gardeners and groundskeepers of the estate, Joe Vargas and Dave Martinez, arrived.

Lunch on a Hot Friday Afternoon

Joanna Pettet and her friend from London, Barbara Lewis, arrived about 12:30 for lunch. Pettet recalls "We went together. I think I called Barbara, and said 'I'm going over to Sharon's,' and we went together." Abigail and Wojtek showed up, too, after which Mrs. Chapman served a late lunch for Pettet, Lewis, Sharon, Abigail, Wojtek, and herself.

Joanna Pettet was twenty-six when she had lunch with Sharon. She got her big break appearing in a film based on Mary McCarthy's novel, *The Group,* in 1966. That triumph triggered appearances in *Night of the Generals,* the James Bond spoof *Casino Royale,* and Peter Yates's *Robbery* with Sir Stanley Baker, all three of which opened in 1967. There was a nude layout of Pettet in *Playboy* in 1968. She'd married actor Alex Cord in 1968, the same year she gave birth to their son, Damien. She starred in the movie *Blue,* which opened in May of 1968. *Blue* was a Western set in the Texas-Mexico border country of 1850, and starring Terence Stamp and Karl Malden, in addition to Pettet. *The Best House in London,* described as a "Victorian period comedy," was also released in June of 1969. Pettet went on to a successful acting career into the 1990s.

Joanna Pettet recalls the luncheon that hot August day: "I saw Sharon all the time. That very last day I went up to the house with my friend Barbara Lewis." Barbara Lewis had been in a low-budget horror movie, *The Ghosts of Hanley House,* the previous year under the name Barbara Chase, and later had a part in the well-received film *Nine to Five.* Lewis, under her birth name, Blum, was later married to psychedelic writer and teacher Timothy Leary from 1978 to 1992.

Pettet further remembered the lunch: "We had a great day. The most memorable moment of that day—after this horrible thing happened, I kept replaying this in my mind—we were at the swimming pool and all of us were out there—there was Wojtek, Abigail Folger, Sharon, myself, Barbara Lewis, and my son.

"Wojtek was in the pool teaching my son to swim, who was ten months old. And Sharon was absolutely gorgeous. She had no top on, but just the bottoms with her beautiful baby belly. She was just so happy.

"The housekeeper made us lunch. And Sharon said, 'I'm not eating the rest of my sandwich.' She only ate half of her sandwich. And this is the main thing I remember, that she only ate half of her sandwich, because she was watching her weight. Pettet commented on how lean and svelte Sharon's figure was, even though she was about to give birth. "You wouldn't even know she was pregnant if you took the belly off."

I asked if Sharon was going to continue her career after the baby, and Pettet replied, "She was. She intended to work." I asked also about Sharon appearing in *The Story of O.* Pettet: "*The Story of O,* if she did mention it, I don't remember." Regarding that, Pettet commented, "Sharon would never have done anything that Roman said not to do. She was completely under his spell."

Sharon Very Much Had Wanted to Have Her Baby in London

"Sharon did not want to come back to the United States alone," Pettet told the author. "She was really lonely. She did not want to come back here to have her baby, and he just filled that house with friends, basically friends of his, not friends of Sharon's, because he didn't want her to be lonely, but he wanted her here. He must have tremendous guilt, because she wanted to have her baby in London."

Sharon Tate, August 8, 1969

At the luncheon, Sharon brought up her suspicion that Roman had sent her back to the United States because he was having an affair. "That's what she thought," said Pettet.

I mentioned I had read that during this final luncheon Sharon mentioned that she had found out recently about a fling that Roman had had with Michelle Phillips. Joanna replied, "That's true. She actually didn't tell me that it was Michelle, but she did mention she had heard that Roman was having a fling with someone. I tried to reassure her, 'No, no, don't be silly.'

"She wasn't devastated—she had just said she had heard that he was fooling around, she wasn't surprised about it—you know, Roman and Sharon they had, not an open relationship, but I know it was a very, uh, 1960s marriage, where you could maybe fool around with somebody and it wasn't going to be the end of the world. But, she was not happy about the report she had heard. She didn't mention Michelle."

Joanna Pettet and Barbara Lewis departed at 3:30 p.m. At around 3:45, Dave Martinez, one of the gardeners, left the property. He asked Bill Garretson to be sure to water the grounds during the weekend.

Jay Sebring called at 3:45, and Wojtek left at 4 p.m. in Sharon's rented yellow Camaro. At 4:30, Abigail Folger went to her usual daily appointment with her psychiatrist.

Frykowski drove to Sebring's house on Easton Drive and picked up a woman named Susan, with whom Sebring, according to a police report, had spent the previous night. Frykowski drove with Susan to artist Witold K.'s gallery-boutique at the Beverly Wilshire Hotel to get the keys to Wojtek and Abigail's house on Woodstock Road (where Witold K. was staying.) Mr. K. did not have the keys to the house because they were over at Mr. K.'s girlfriend's house. Mr. Frykowski finally located the keys and then went with the woman to the Woodstock Road house. There they spent time listening to records.

At 4:30 a gardener at Cielo signed for Roman's two steamer trunks, just arrived from London. He didn't want to awaken Sharon, who was napping in her room.

As it was extremely hot, Sharon had asked Winifred Chapman if she wanted to stay over. Chapman had declined. At around 4:45, the gardener left, giving the housekeeper a ride down to the bus stop. When they departed, Sharon was alone in the house, asleep.

At around 5:30 p.m., Sebring was seen on Easton Drive by a neighbor, zooming past in his black Porsche, followed closely by another sports car.

Between 6:30 and 7 p.m., a lightweight bicycle was delivered to the residence. Abigail Folger had purchased it that afternoon. Jay Sebring answered the door, wine bottle in hand.

Sharon was supposed to stay overnight with Sheilah Wells at Wells's house. Something, probably the heat and tiredness, caused her to change her mind. (According to an LAPD interrogation report, Wells lived at 7419 Woodrow Wilson Drive, not far from Cass Elliot's place at 7708.)

Joanna Pettet, along with her husband and their baby, went to Sheilah's house that night. Pettet remembers it well: "I said, 'Where's Sharon?' and Sheilah said, 'I just called, she's not coming. Jay's coming over.' It was just a couple of hours after I left Cielo."

I asked Sheilah Wells during a conversation while researching this book, "She was going to come over?" Wells replied, "Yes, she was, and then I phoned her back, and I said don't park in this certain driveway, because the other neighbors had been complaining about it, that people were parking in their part of the driveway. And then she said, 'You know, Sheilah, Jay is going to come over,'— and it was really hot, August 8—and she said, 'I don't know, maybe we'll just go for a hamburger, or do something, I just don't feel . . . ' I knew how she felt, because of just having had a baby, and being hot and all of that. And I didn't push it, and that stayed with me for a long time. I should have just pushed it, and acted that I was hurt by it, because I had other people coming over."

Something to think about during the next flow of decades.

In an interview in the November 1969 issue of *Screenland*, Wells spoke of Sharon's final evening: "Early on the night she was murdered, my phone rang. It was Sharon. She asked me to come over. I told her I couldn't, that I was having a few people in for dinner. Then she said, 'Can I come over to your house?' I said, sure, of course, come on over. But a little while later she called and said she wasn't coming. She was too tired, she said. She'd decided just to go over to a local drive-in and get a hamburger. I told her that was silly. In the time it took her to drive to the restaurant she could come over to my place. And I asked her to spend the night. But Sharon said no. She had to do her hair. She thought she'd better stay home. She was so lonely, she said, she missed Roman and she was so tired. She decided not to come."

During Jay Sebring's Final Day

Sebring's friend Sharmagne Leland-St. John described that final day: "I had spoken to Jay that afternoon; I invited him to join me at a Peter, Paul and Mary concert. Peter [Yarrow] was my first serious boyfriend and Jay used to cut his hair. Peter had given me a front row center box for the concert at the Hollywood Bowl. At the last possible moment Alex Cord and Joanna Pettet Cord cancelled on me as did one other person. I was trying to fill the box. Jay said he was tired from traveling. [He had come in from San Francisco a day or so earlier.] He said he was just going to hang loose, and suggested I call him after the concert and maybe come hang out. He also invited me to come for a swim the next day either at Easton Drive or at Sharon's. (I had moved out of his house prior to the murders.)"

According to a Mrs. McCaffrey, a receptionist at Sebring's hair shop, her boyfriend Joel Rostau delivered cocaine and mescaline to the house on Cielo the night of the murders. She said that Frykowski and Sebring wanted more, but Rostau, unable to score, didn't return. (Rostau was discovered in a car trunk in New York a few months later.)

Frykowski called his friend the artist Witold K. in the evening sometime and invited him over, but Witold K. was busy laying down a rug in his new art gallery at 9406 Wilshire Boulevard.

The photographer Shahrokh Hatami told me that he also had been invited to Sharon's house that night. Hatami was residing at the Chateau Marmont. He said that he was then living with Ann Ford, an aspiring 22-year old actress from Texas. Hatami: "Ann Ford was living with me. And that night Sharon told me,

'Come to dinner, but not with Stevie.' Stevie was the [five-year-old then rambunctious] son of Ann Ford, who was living with us. We couldn't find a babysitter for Stevie, and I was not driving, and my driver was Ann Ford, to take me to the villa (on Cielo Drive). So we couldn't find a babysitter. I called Sharon, and said 'Sorry, darling, I can't make it tonight. I'll see you later, I'll see you tomorrow.' I was there always. And the boy always said to me later, 'I saved your life, I saved your life.' Then I went to a motion picture festival, of Orson Welles. Bobby Lipton also joined us, and said after the movie was finished, 'Let's go to Sharon's place.' I said, 'It's too late.'"

Hatami also recalled that, as she had for a number of her friends (such as Joanna Pettet and Sheilah Wells), Sharon had given him relationship advice, telling him that Ann Ford "is not the girl for you."

Director Michael Sarne also was considering going to Sharon's on Friday night. Ditto for Dino Martin Jr. and a host of others, including John Phillips. One popular folk singer, according to Leonard Lyons, claimed that he was supposed to go to the murder house that night to get a haircut from Jay Sebring.

If the number of people who claim to have been invited to 10050 Cielo Drive the night of August 8 had shown up, perhaps such a large crowd would have scared away the murderers.

The foursome—Jay, Wojtek, Abigail, and Sharon—had a late dinner at a Spanish restaurant, El Coyote, on Beverly Boulevard, about the same time as the coyote-worshiping Charles Manson was plotting his evil.

Ms. Folger's mother called from San Francisco. Ms. Folger was scheduled to fly the 10 a.m. United Airlines shuttle the next morning to Frisco in order to be with her mother for her birthday.

Around midnight, they were quietly settled. Wojtek was asleep upon the flag-draped living-room sofa. Abigail was in the northeast bedroom reading a book. And Sharon Tate and Jay Sebring were chatting in Sharon's bedroom when the knife stabbed into the gray screen, slicing an entrance into the empty nursery at the far end of the house.

Chapter 11
Death on Cielo Drive

Beausoleil later testified at his April 1970 trial that after Charlie departed in the bakery truck for parts unknown, he felt that people were watching him as if to prevent his leaving. Throughout the history of the Family, whenever Charlie took a bit of time off, that provided the opportunity for people to escape. Tex Watson and Bruce Davis seemed to be keeping their eyes on him. Bobby waited. "I smiled a lot, tried to be myself. It seemed that they were trusting me, so I left." He testified that he told the girls to clean up Gary Hinman's customized Fiat station wagon which "was full of junk."

Why did Robert Beausoleil leave for San Francisco driving the car of the very man in whose murder he had participated? Perhaps it was pure arrogance and the inability to think multiple motions ahead that caused Beausoleil, around Tuesday, August 5, to surge forth in Hinman's grille-less Fiat, with Toyota motor and a radiator set at a 45-degree angle, toward San Francisco, unaware that Hinman's body had been discovered.

He passed through Santa Barbara and stopped at a restaurant, where he was told by a policeman to take his Mexican sheath knife off. He put it in the car trunk. He continued driving north, and sometime in the night the Fiat broke down on Highway 101 near San Luis Obispo. At 10:50 a.m. a California Highway Patrol car stopped behind the parked car and, as it halted, Beausoleil raised up in the back from a sleeping bag. Beausoleil had no driver's license to show the officer but had identification for Jason Lee Daniels and a credit card plus a business card for the Lutesinger Ranch.

Officer Humphrey of the Highway Patrol called in Hinman's license number to the computer and he learned that the car was reported stolen from Los Angeles. He drew his revolver and arrested Beausoleil. When he arrived at the station, there was an LA sheriff's office "All Points Bulletin" that requested the car be impounded and the occupants be held in regard to Hinman's death.

As part of a prearranged scheme, Beausoleil said that he had bought the car in the week previous from a black man. The Fiat was locked up, to preserve fingerprints, and Jim's Tow Service hauled it into custody in San Luis Obispo.

That same day at around 8:30 p.m., homicide officers Paul Whiteley and Charles Guenther and a fingerprint expert named Jake Jordan arrived in San Luis Obispo to interrogate Beausoleil. They brought with them the card bearing Beausoleil's thumbprint lifted from the kitchen door jamb of Hinman's house. They had the man.

Beausoleil remained pretty quiet during interrogation, though he finally admitted going to Hinman's house with two female caucasians. He claimed he did not reveal their names but only said that Hinman was injured when they got there, and that they came to his aid, sewed his face, and so on, and then left. He said that Hinman rewarded them for suturing his face with dental floss by signing over his automobile to them. Hinman, he said, told them he got involved in some political hassle with blacks and that one of them had knifed his face.

The next day, on August 7, Robert Beausoleil was brought to Los Angeles and booked for homicide. As per California law, he was allowed to call the Spahn Ranch. New Manson follower Linda Kasabian was responsible for incoming calls that day and Beausoleil gave her the bad news but said that everything was okay and that he was staying quiet.

Beausoleil himself has said that Linda was upset and that she asked what could be done to help him and that a discussion was held regarding possible plans of action. According to Beausoleil the discussion involved copy-cat murders or murders removing those who might have known about the Hinman matter. Such discussions of possible murder to get Beausoleil out may have served to rev up the Family for more carnage, another example of the self-fulfilling prophecy.

Sadie Glutz, aka Susan Atkins, testified at the Tate-LaBianca trial that soon after Bobby called, Leslie, Sadie, Linda Kasabian, Katie (aka Patricia Krenwinkel), and others had a homicide-klatch to discuss and to determine how to get Bobby, their brother, out of jail. According to the Glutz-Atkins testimony, one of the girls had seen a movie where copy-cat murders were committed over a period of time, enabling a killer to get out of jail.

A Spate of Arrests

A dejected and rejected Charles Manson arrived at the Spahn Ranch in the early afternoon of August 8. With him was the pregnant runaway graduate of Anaheim High School, Stephanie, whom he had picked up near Esalen. Charlie was quickly apprised of Robert Beausoleil's arrest. The whole trip up north had been a bummer for Charlie, who hated rejection, and now, with Beausoleil's arrest for murder, Manson's very freedom was up for grabs.

As soon as he got back, driving the 1952 Continental Bakery Hostess Twinkie truck, Charlie sent Mary Brunner and Sandy Good off to run a credit-card caper at the Sears store. Before they left they took Stephanie's credit cards and identification away from her, naturally, and filed them with the master credit-card hoard in George Spahn's house.

Around 4 p.m., Mary Brunner and Sandy Pugh—for Sandy was using the name of her former husband, borrowed Manson's bakery truck, and soon were making purchases at a Sears store. They used a stolen credit card, recently stolen from a Manson follower's brother-in-law in Bothell, Washington. Mary Brunner forged the name Mary Vitasek on the credit card. The two young ladies then split. If they had gone away immediately, they probably would not have been arrested.

But instead they decided to make some more purchases at a different check-out counter and again presented the same stolen credit card. An alert cashier saw that the card was on the "warning sheet," and also became suspicious when the pregnant Sandy kept looking over her shoulder.

The store manager approached and the girls fled. He followed the two in his automobile, trying to get them to pull the truck off to the side of the road. Sandy and Mary cut through a service station in a ditch-maneuver. The chase led to the Chatsworth entrance to the San Diego Freeway, where the girls were stopped. Sandy had managed to toss the credit cards out the window, but the act was spotted by those pursuing.

Captured with the two young ladies, therefore, was a stash of various credit cards. Mary and Sandy were charged with several violations of the California Penal Code. Mary Brunner admitted that she, in fact, forged the credit card, but Sandy Good/Pugh denied guilt.

The two were booked at the police station just as, thirty miles away, Abigail Folger was ending her appointment with her psychiatrist. Brunner and Good/Pugh were taken to a police station and later that evening to downtown Los Angeles where, at 10:21 p.m., they were booked into the Sybil Brand Institute Inmate Reception Center.

Meanwhile, back at the Spahn Ranch, murder was on their minds. Mary Brunner arrested. Sandy Good arrested. Bobby Beausoleil arrested. Charlie Manson rejected in Big Sur. It was time for drastic action.

First, some went on a garbage run for the evening meal. Then, at the back ranch, they cooked dinner on a Coleman camp stove. People were excited that Charlie had returned. Charlie said that the people "up north" were not that together, they were just off on their own little trips. According to Tex Watson's book, *Will You Die for Me?*, Manson said, during the meal, "Now is the time for Helter Skelter."

During the communal dinner, Charlie instructed that all people under eighteen were to sleep in the wickiup by the back ranch. Then the obedient girls washed the dishes and Tex Watson and Charlie plotted what to do about Beausoleil's arrest.

When Mary and Sandy were booked into Sybil Brand jail at 10:21, they likely called the ranch and told them the news. About an hour later, the killers were on their way.

After dinner Charlie brought fresh love Stephanie to a trailer. "He told me he'd be back in a little while," she testified at the murder trial. Manson would not return till dawn.

Manson pulled Sadie aside about an hour after the meal, and told her to get a knife and clothes to change in. Sadie called the back ranch over the field

Charles Manson holding the broken Straight Satans sword at the Spahn Ranch, early August 1969. To the left is the 1959 Ford the killers drove to Cielo Drive.

phone and told a young follower named Barbara Hoyt to gather three sets of dark clothing and bring them to the front of the ranch.

Linda Kasabian had helped with dinner and the cleanup, then had gone to stand by the Rock City Café when Charlie came up and pulled her off to the end of the boardwalk and told her to get a knife, a change of clothing, and her driver's license. Linda was the only person at the ranch with a valid driver's license. She walked across the dusty driveway from the Spahn Ranch movie set and into George Spahn's saddle-lined house to look for creepy-crawly equipment. She rummaged through a box and found a blue denim miniskirt made from chopped-off blue jeans and a lavender knitted top. She asked Squeaky Fromme, the Family quartermaster, where her driver's license was.

Squeaky suggested some chests of drawers. No. Next, a box on the fireplace mantel. No. Then she went into the saloon to look for a Buck knife she had brought with her when she had come to the ranch in July. She couldn't find it. She walked down the boardwalk to the Rock City Café kitchen, where a ranch hand gave her a kitchen knife with a handle wrapped in dark electrical tape. It turned out that Sadie was packing Linda's Buck knife.

Patricia Krenwinkel was coming down from an LSD trip and was asleep when she was nudged and told to get a knife and a change of clothes. She really didn't want to get up, but she did, under the summons of someone claiming to be both Jesus and the Devil.

Someone may have called in advance to the Polanski residence to see who was going to be there, or at least that there was no party going on. Vern Plumlee, for instance, has claimed that they thought Sharon Tate was not going to be there.

In the hot August evening, people were sitting and chatting on the boulders and rocks and chairs that were situated in front of the Spahn Ranch, unaware of what was going on. In the presence of Manson, Brenda (aka Nancy Pitman) came up and handed Linda her driver's license. All was ready.

Manson prepared Watson for the event by blaming him for the "killing" of drug dealer Bernard Crowe back in July. It was Tex's fault M had to shoot him; therefore Watson owed him plenty. Manson laid out a fairly comprehensive set of instructions, and he wanted severe gore. Watson claims M told him, "Pull out their eyes and hang them on the mirrors."

There may have been a tinge of amphetamine psychosis in the air, because, in violation of family rules, Tex Watson had a secret supply of powdered amphetamine in a Gerber baby food jar. He and Sadie had been snorting it constantly for three or four days. When Manson gave the kill instructions, Sadie was already stoned on amphetamine, and Watson went to where the Gerber jar was hidden on the porch. "I took a couple of deep snorts of speed," he writes, "and went to get the clothes and rope and bolt cutters as Charlie had ordered."

The automobile, an old yellow and white 1959 Ford with another car's license plate on it, was parked and ready in the space between the end of the Rock City Café and George Spahn's house. George Spahn was not at home. It was his custom to dine about this hour at the International House of Pancakes in Chatsworth. Or perhaps he was visiting his relatives, following his meal.

Linda Kasabian got into the car, in the right front passenger seat. Sadie and Katie were in the back of the car. Also in the back of the car were a pair of red-handled bolt cutters and a long, coiled, three-quarter-inch nylon rope. Tex got into the car and the car backed away and then headed out down the dirt driveway toward the exit to the west, by the corral. About halfway down the drive, Manson stopped them. He came over and stuck his head into the window on Linda's side and said, according to Linda, "Leave a sign. You girls know what to do. Something witchy." Then Manson stood alone, watching the car drive off.

Tex Watson's memory was that Manson told him to get money for Mary to get out of jail. "If you don't get enough money at the Melcher house, then go on to the house next door and then the house after that until you get six hundred dollars."

The car belonged to Johnny Swartz, a horse wrangler at the Spahn Ranch. He was sitting in his trailer near George Spahn's house when he recognized the sound of his engine and walked to the window of his trailer just in time to see the taillights of his automobile fade away down the road.

Tex told Linda that the gun was in the glove compartment. Three knives were on the front right floor of the automobile. Tex told her to bundle up the knives and gun and then to throw them out the window if the police attempted to pick them up. This Linda did, bundling them with her very own shirt. Linda Kasabian testified that she believed she was merely going on a second-story caper in Beverly Hills. A second-story caper with forty-three feet of rope, a gun, changes of clothing, and three sharp knives.

After the 1959 Ford, license plate GYY435, had pulled away toward its desolate goal, Barbara Hoyt came trundling to the front ranch from the back ranch, bearing the three sets of dark clothing that Susan Atkins had ordered over the field phone. Charlie was angry at her and snapped, "What are you doing here?" Because it was a rule that all those who didn't have a reason, particularly soulless females, were to stay in back out of sight and not appear in the public part of the ranch. Miss Hoyt told him what Sadie had asked her to do, and Manson said that they had already left.

In the speeding car, the girls seemed to be barefoot. Sadie had on blue denim genuine Sears Roebuck jeans and a baggy blue T-shirt. Linda was barefoot and

The 1959 Ford in which the murderers drove to Cielo Drive. Photo taken exactly one week later.

in her lavender top and dark blue denim skirt. Tex wore moccasins, jeans, and a black velour turtleneck sweater. Katie wore a black T-shirt and jeans.

Tex told the girls that they were going to Terry Melcher's former place, but that Melcher no longer lived there. He described the setup of the house, including the rooms inside, and evidently noted that there was a smaller guesthouse on the property, and to make sure that the guesthouse was creepy-crawled also.

According to Sadie, Tex said that they were going to kill whoever was in the house and then get all their money.

They drove there straightaway, leaving around eleven o'clock in the evening. They got lost and ended up going all the way into Hollywood, then back west on Santa Monica Boulevard past the Tropicana Motel and the Troubadour Bar, through West Hollywood and the edges of Beverly Hills. Then they cut up past the perfect mansions with their tall elegant palms, to Sunset Boulevard, then to Benedict Canyon, then finally turned left onto Cielo Drive and proceeded to the house on the hill.

Why Were They Killed? It's a Mystery

Was it to help trigger the Black Uprising known in Mansonland as Helter Skelter? Or, perhaps to blame the murders on the "Black Panthers" through writing in blood, with the word "PIG" on the front door of Cielo Drive repeating the "Political Piggy" written above Mr. Hinman's body in Topanga Canyon, thus possibly to help free Robert Beausoleil? Or was Sharon Tate the real target? (See the afterword to this book.) Or, did they think she was not going to be there? How could they have believed she was not going to be in the house? Who could have told them?

Manson had said several times that, if the true story were known about the Tate-LaBianca murders, there would be a "big stink" of a scandal. He has said that he has chosen silence because of the age-old code of criminal behavior that makes telling the names of people involved in a crime equal to the crime itself. Manson has, naturally, also said that the Polanski murders were the idea of his followers. "I don't care. I have one law I live by and I learned it when I was a kid in reform school, it's don't snitch and I have never snitched, and I told them that anything they do for their brothers and sisters is good, if they do it with a good thought," Manson testified on page 18123 of his trial.

A dope burn has been proposed as one possible motive. One former family associate stated that he was told by Gypsy that the burn involved "63 keys [kilos] of grass, something like fifty dollars' worth of smack and some speed." One of Manson's closest friends outside the Family told this writer on December 1, 1970, that an $11,000 LSD burn was involved and that involved also was a "real millionaire" friend of Manson whose car Manson wrecked around the time of the murders. Vern Plumlee also claimed that the motive involved LSD. Plumlee, certainly a trusted Family member during the time of the murders, worked closely with Bill Vance in committing various robberies and forgeries during those days of murder. Plumlee, in a taped interview, said that Bill Vance told him that the Tate and LaBianca murders were both committed as a result of an acid burn. This is what Plumlee said about Vance's explanation of the motive: "You see, I worked with him for quite a while, you know, burglaries and things like that. . . . And during the time I was doing it I was, you know, we got to be pretty able to talk with each other.

"I heard things about something to the effect the LaBiancas were supposed to have sold to 'the Tates,' the Tates were supposed to have sold to the Family, and some people got uptight about it, 'cause it was a burn. . . . Like, I was told by him, he says, 'don't worry about it though because they'll never find out who did it.' So I just let it slide."

On another occasion Plumlee told a reporter that the Family went there to get Frykowski and anyone else present. According to Plumlee, the Family had received information that Sharon Tate was not going to be at Cielo Drive. But how could that be? How could anyone associated with Manson know that? I asked Sharon's close friend Sheilah Wells, "Who else knew that Sharon might be staying over at your place?" (I told her the rumor I had heard that the "family" had thought Sharon was not going to be there. Wells replied, "No, huh unh, because that whole conversation (with Sharon) was that Friday. It was a last minute kind of thing."

Even while the Manson murder trials were under way, in the fall of 1970, several private investigators, working for the district attorney, were looking into the possibility that the murders were contracted. It was believed that a wealthy individual in Kansas City, Missouri, issued the contracts. They checked banks in Kansas City, Kansas, to see if money had been deposited for Manson, Watson, Susan Atkins, Bill Vance, and three others. They also checked possible bank deposits in a coastal town of Texas, perhaps Corpus Christi, to no avail.

A reporter covering the Tate-LaBianca trial got ahold of Tex Watson's address book and found the phone number of a former Polanski residence in it. A private investigator who worked on the case for the family of one of the decedents for months after the murders told this writer that the motive for the crimes was that "they knew too much about what was going on."

Sadie Glutz, aka Susan Atkins, said the impetus for the murders was two-fold: to get Beausoleil off and because Linda Kasabian was burned on a purchase of MDA. On Volume 180, page 23049 of the trial transcript, she testified that Linda Kasabian came to her and complained about being burned at the Polanski residence: "'You remember the thousand dollars I had?' I told her yeah—and she said, 'Well, I went up to some people in Beverly Hills for some MDA'—some new kind of drug . . . MDA. Oh anyway, she went up there to buy something and they burnt her for the bread."

Robert Beausoleil claimed that Tex Watson and Linda were operating together during those weeks prior to the murders and that the key lies there. There remains the possibility that Manson wanted to raise a large amount of money in an attempt to pay off someone for the purpose of freeing Beausoleil. Danny DeCarlo said this in a police interview: "Mary [Brunner] and Bobby got busted. It was all—the main objective was to get money to get them out of jail so they could all get in the wind which was to the desert. Mary's bail was $500 and they were going to get out—they needed some fantastic amount of money to get Bobby out. Hell, I didn't understand. There was no bail on him."

So perhaps the Family went into a flurry of quick dope deals or Manson took a murder contract to raise large amounts of fast cash.

DeCarlo, after his testimony at the Tate-LaBianca trial, told a CBS-TV reporter that the true motive had not been told, but he would not elaborate.

Sharon's mother, Doris, was eager to find out the real reason. She was not willing to accept any of the motives discussed in public. Years later, when I went to the home of Doris and Paul Tate in Palos Verdes, Doris, who knew I was corresponding with Manson, urged me to ask him for the actual reason he dispatched his marauders to Cielo Drive. (In the course of a few difficult-to-decipher letters to me, however, Manson kept the reasons to his chest.)

A husband-and-wife team of informants surfaced in 1974 claiming that Manson had been hired by an English Satanist to kill Sharon Tate because of something she had learned about Sirhan Sirhan. This issue is discussed in the afterword of this book.

Over four decades later, well into a new century, the reason or reasons are still a lingering mystery.

Sharon's Father Watches *The Wrecking Crew* That Fatal Night

Meanwhile at Fort Baker in San Francisco that night, Colonel Paul Tate attended an eleven o'clock showing of *The Wrecking Crew* at the base movie house. In the ultimate of ironies, he enjoyed the film during just about the same hours as Sharon's house was invaded by the spores of evil. "Sharon had enjoyed working on the picture and it was apparent in every moment of her performance. I left the theater immensely proud, with a plan to call Sharon in the morning."

Cielo Drive

The caretaker of the cottage at the Polanski residence, Bill Garretson, consumed a dexedrine, two marijuana cigarettes, and four cans of beer on Thursday night, August 7, which made him ill, so he stayed home all day Friday until the evening.

It was near the close of Garretson's employment at the Polanski property. Rudy Altobelli, the owner, was about to return after spending the summer in Europe. In addition to his salary of $35 a week, Garretson was to get a free airplane ticket back to his hometown, Lancaster, Ohio.

Garretson tended to go to bed late and get up early in the afternoon and go check on his mail. The guesthouse lay up against a steep hill, at an angle to the main house. The swimming pool was between the two houses. The cottage had a back door, a door to the dogs' room, a door to the backyard, and a front door, plus numerous windows, which made the guesthouse very easy to creepy-crawl.

Garretson, in the company of unknown others, drove down the Canyon to the Sunset Strip around 8:30 in the evening. Garretson purchased a TV dinner, a Coca-Cola, and a pack of cigarettes at a drugstore, and then he strolled up and down the Strip. After the stroll, he hitchhiked back to Benedict Canyon Drive, then up Benedict to Cielo Drive. He walked up Cielo and up the hill to the back house, arriving around 10 p.m. He watched a movie, then put the TV dinner in the oven. While his dinner cooked, he ate potato chips and drank Coca-Cola. At around 11:45 p.m., a friend named Steven Parent arrived unannounced, with an AM/FM clock radio to sell. Parent asked Garretson who the two pretty young ladies were who were inside the main house.

Garretson mistakenly thought that Wojtek Frykowski was Roman Polanski's younger brother, so Garretson said that Abigail Folger was the "younger Polanski's" girlfriend and the other one was Polanski's wife, to which Parent replied, "You mean Polanski has a girlfriend and a wife?" Garretson answered, "No, the younger Polanski has a girlfriend and the other one was the older Polanski's wife."

Around 11:45 or 11:55 Parent phoned a man in Hollywood, and Parent told him that he was at the home of a movie star, "somebody big." Parent was asked if there was a party going on, and Parent said there was not. Parent was going to help the man build a stereo, so they made a date for Parent to come to his house in about forty minutes, which would have located Parent at his pal's house around 12:30 a.m.

As Garretson walked Parent to the door, Christopher the Weimaraner began barking and Steve asked, "What's the matter with Christopher?" Garretson replied, "Oh, I don't know. He usually barks." According to Rudy Altobelli's testimony at the trial, Christopher gave forth two types of barks, a generalized bark and something called a people bark when anyone approached the house. Probably Garretson was not able to distinguish between the two types of barks. The Weimaraner was not known for its gentleness. In fact, it had once taken a bite out of Rudy.

Around 12:15 a.m., when Garretson said good-bye to his young friend, the dog was yipping and barking. Garretson stated that he only walked Parent to the door, and he never heard any shots or shrieks during the upcoming slaughter on the lawn, less than 150 feet from the house. He claimed that he enjoyed the rest of the night writing letters to a friend of his named Darryl Kistler and listening to the record player, which was turned up to medium volume. At one point, the Weimaraner began to bark and Garretson looked up from the couch in the living room and noticed that the bar-shaped door handle had been turned down by somebody. He walked to the bathroom and glanced out the window to see if anybody was trying to force the door. Garretson also noted that someone had cut loose the screen to one of the windows near the guesthouse kitchen.

(Garretson was given a lie detector test on Sunday, August 10, and admitted that he may have gone out to the backyard at some point during the night. Patricia Krenwinkel told her attorney, Paul Fitzgerald, during the subsequent trial that they creepy-crawled the back house and found no one there. So maybe Garretson, hearing the shrieks and bullets, hid out back, then slinked back into the house at dawn, either fearing for his own life or that he would be charged with murder.

Before Parent departed, just after midnight, he unplugged his unsold Sony AM-FM clock radio, taking it with him. When the police found it the next morning on the front seat of the Rambler Ambassador, the clock showed 12:15.

Steven Parent walked away, past the redwood picnic table, past the small swimming pool set against the steep hillside, then along the walkway by the white split rail fence, then down the paved driveway past Sebring's Porsche, Abigail's yellow Firebird, and also the Camaro that Sharon had rented, then got into his car.

Something may have startled him because he backed his car out of the driveway so quickly that he broke the split rail fence that borders the parking lot. The paint from the fence was found on the underside of his car the next morning by the police. He may been alarmed by the killers coming across the paved entranceway or cutting the communication wires. Or he may have heard the splat of the severed telephone cables. Parent never got as far as the button that activated the main gate. He never touched it. Bullets burst.

The Arrival of Evil

The backseatless white and yellow 1959 Ford arrived up the cliffside driveway to the top, facing a rattan fence, whereupon it turned around with its lights off. Tex parked facing downhill, away from the main gate and next to the telephone pole that jutted around eighteen feet up. Tex requested the bolt cutters from the back seat, then shimmied up the pole and cut two wires—one a telephone wire which did not fall and the other an old communications line from the days when musician Mark Lindsay and Terry Melcher first rented the property in 1966. That line fell and draped over the iron-framed wire electric gate.

Watson slid back down to the road, got into the car, and coasted down the hill, lights off. At the bottom of the driveway, he twisted to the right and parked on Cielo Drive. All emerged from the Ford—Linda Kasabian, Tex Watson, Sadie Glutz/Susan Atkins, and Patricia Krenwinkel.

The entrance to 10050 Cielo Drive consisted of a wrought-iron fence and a gate. The gate was six feet high and twelve feet wide. On either side of the iron gate, rattan facing had been placed. To the left, a cliff fell away. On the right was a steep hillside.

The electronic button opening the gate was never locked, so that a person could push the button and the gate would swing inward, with the gate automatically closing behind them.

Tex wasn't sure just what sort of line he had cut that had splatted across the electric-eye gate. It had fallen over the gate, and he was afraid it was some sort of utility cable, charged with electricity. They had nothing to fear, since the

Tex climbs the telephone pole outside 10050 Cielo Drive to cut the wires. Other marauders are still in the car.

wire, which had once been connected to communication speakers, hadn't been used since the Polanskis moved into the estate.

The four invaders scrambled up the hill, carrying their extra clothes, their weapons, and a rope. About ten feet up the embankment they climbed over the fence. Then, as they crept toward the driveway, they spotted the lights of a car that was moving down the driveway. Tex said, "Lie down and be still," then he ran toward the vehicle, after setting aside the coils of rope from his shoulder, holding his revolver in his right hand.

Parent spotted the four and said, "Hey, what are you doing here?" Luckily for Garretson, Watson thought that Parent was the caretaker. Tex ran up in front of the white, 1966 Ambassador sedan and yelled, "Stop! Halt!" Tex jammed his weapon up against Parent's head—a weapon right out of the spirit of the American West, a .22-caliber, nine-shot, walnut-handled, blue steel, long-barreled, Buntline Special fifteen-inch revolver, loaded with .22 long rifle bullets. Parent reportedly said, "Please don't hurt me. I won't say anything." Then bang bang bang bang.

Parent's Lucerne wristwatch was torn off, indicating Tex was jabbing him while he was shooting him. It was found in the back seat with a severed watchband. There was a defensive deep wound in Parent's left hand cutting the tendons between his ring and little finger.

The young man from El Monte, California, was wearing a white and blue plaid shirt, blue denim pants, black shoes, and white socks. His body slumped over toward the passenger's seat when he was shot, his head leaning back and to the right, and his blood, bone chips, and bullet frags were spattered on the dashboard, on the rubber floormat, and on the front door.

Tex switched off the lights and the engine, shoved the gear selector in neutral, pushed the car back out of the way. He picked up the coils of rope, and said, "Come on." Why was Watson carrying about seven or eight coils of white, three-quarter-inch, three-ply nylon line, a total of forty-three feet, eight inches? The marauders' plan, later abandoned in their haste, was to tie the victims up to the ceiling beams in the living room, then draw and quarter them (thus proving that at least Watson knew the inside of the house.)

Watson had instructed the girls to hide their changes of clothing in the bushes. They walked by the trees that hovered over the edge of the front lawn, and up the walkway, where they paused near the house. Linda Kasabian was told to go around to the back of the house to check for any open windows or doors. Linda checked the back porch door, looked into the kitchen windows and through the back door into the living room, but there was nothing open. On her way back, evidently she spotted the bouquet of flowers on the table in the dining room. Returning, she found Tex standing by the fresh-painted window of the nursery room on the house's far north end, where he was slitting the lower part of the screen with his bayonet.

Tex ordered Linda to go down by the walkway and maintain a lookout, so she headed to the end of the parking lot, by the fence, and she knelt down, not far from where Steven Parent slumped in the Ambassador. Sadie and Katie crept along the elliptical sidewalk, which curved along to where it hooked into the covered flagstone-floored front porch.

The temperature was hot, and the house and grounds were well lit. The poolside light was on. The two front porch lights were on.

After Tex had removed the slashed window, he slithered into the house, encountering the smell of fresh paint in the nursery being prepared for the baby. The first coat of paint had been finished that very afternoon. Tex entered the kitchen walking south, through the dining room, into the entrance hall where he opened the front door and let the two slashomorphs in. They grabbed a left out of the entrance hall into the large, white-walled, cream-carpeted living room.

Bordering the west side of the living room was a loft, carpeted and furnished with chairs and a telephone, reached by a redwood ladder, located adjacent to the left side of the large stone fireplace on the west wall of the living room. In the southeast corner of the living room, facing out into the room at a triangular position, was a baby grand piano with a metronome on the left side. On the music holder of the piano were two compositions, a song called "Straight Shooter" by John Phillips of the Mamas and the Papas, a song off their first album, and on the other side of the stand was Edward Elgar's "Pomp and Circumstance."

The stereo, located inside the front hall closet beneath the shelves of film and videotapes, was blaring, which may have prevented the shooting of Steven Parent from being noticed. In the center of the wall was a large desk, which stretched into the living room. On the desk were a candelabra and flowers, plus a white push-button phone and various scripts.

Jay's blue leather jacket was hung up on the high-backed chair next to the desk, containing his wallet, with a hundred dollars, plus a tube of coke. Jay's briefcase was nearby, with hair dryer, mirror, electric clippers, an address book, a pilot's map, and various haircutting tools.

The part of the living room that was to be the scene of the murders was a kind of enclosed section near the large stone fireplace on the west wall. In front of it was a large zebra-skin rug. Books and movie scripts lined the hearth. A large, three-cushioned, beige velvet sofa faced the fireplace, a few feet from the zebra skin.

Left of the sofa was an end table and two cream-colored, stuffed chairs were set at angles on each side. A floor lamp and a brown, wide-reed basket for holding magazines sat near the chair on the right.

Running the entire length of the living room, east to west, above the sofa, was an apparently solid, four-inch by twelve-inch beam, painted white, over which the killer Watson was soon to toss his nylon rope.

A large American flag was draped over the back cushions of the beige sofa, turned upside down. In spite of the mutterings of the police about "ritual murders" a few hours later, the flag was about the only unusual element in the decor of the room. The flag had only been in the house about two weeks, according to the testimony of the housekeeper, Winifred Chapman.

Sharon's close friend, Sheilah Wells was asked about it not long after, replying, "Yes, it's true, there was a flag draped over the back of the sofa. It had been there ever since Wojtek and Gibby (Abigail Folger) moved in. It belonged to them. Whenever I went over to Sharon's and I'd see the flag there, I'd tell her it wasn't right. She'd nod and say she knew, but that Gibby and Wojtek thought it was funny.

"That was Sharon. She knew that the others were making fun of the flag, of the establishment. She didn't go along with it, but felt she might hurt them if she took it away."

There's a famous scene in Jack Kerouac's *On the Road*, where the novel's narrator, Sal Paradise, accidentally puts an American flag upside down on a sixty-foot pole. One of his duties working as a guard in a military barracks was to raise the flag in the morning, and after a drunken night, he raises it incorrectly. "Do you know you can go to jail for putting the American flag upside down on a government pole?" a colleague comments. 'Upside down?' I was horrified; of course I hadn't realized it." (*On the Road*, p. 66)

In nautical terms, flying a flag upside down was a distress sign—and by the late 1960s was commonly used as an anti-Vietnam war statement. History is silent on whether the flag was draped upon the living room couch when Colonel Paul Tate and Doris Tate visited during the July Moon Landing.

How I Learned the Details of the Murders

How did I put together the course of the killings? First of all, I sent questions to two defendants during the subsequent murder trial through an attorney for one of the defendants, and I received very useful responses. I also sent detailed question lists to Manson, which is how I learned that he went to the murder scene, "to see what my children had done." In addition, I obtained a copy of a large blueprint of the house, six feet wide by forty inches high, that listed each blood spot on the floor, the doorway, the door, the walkway, and so on. I got ahold of the official police reports listing the locations of all the blood found, plus both the lengthy first and second homicide investigation progress reports. I obtained a photocopy of Linda Kasabian's handwritten description of the murders. Plus, I watched the trial as it unfolded for a number of months, taking notes—all of which enabled me to re-create, with fair accuracy, what happened on that horrible, hot night in Benedict Canyon.

My description of the murders may be too shocking for some readers. I originally decided to write all its horrid details because there had been some favorable publicity for the Manson group in a few underground publications, so I was determined to describe for all time what these marauders had done. It stands as a testimony to the potential for evil among humans. Accordingly, the hesitant reader might well consider skipping the next few pages.

Horror on Cielo Drive

Wojtek Frykowski lay on the sofa, in front of the fireplace, dozing off, zonked under the apparently pleasant influence, MDA. The devil-minded Tex Watson stalked past the desk toward the back of the couch. Evidently he took position on the zebra skin, with his back to the fireplace, and aimed the long revolver at Wojtek's head. He indicated with his knife hand where Katie and Sadie were to line up behind the sofa. Wojtek awakened, stretched and asked, "What time is it?"

"Don't move or you're dead," said Watson.

"Who are you?" replied Frykowski.

"I'm the Devil. I'm here to do the Devil's business. Give me all your money," replied Tex Watson. Watson, a former high school track star in Texas, would later, in Death Valley, tell a young Manson follower, "it was fun" to kill those in Sharon's residence.

Attractive and elegant Abigail Folger was alone reading on the antique bed in her bedroom, wearing a full-length white nightgown. She was slightly stoned on the euphoric MDA. Though most of her and Wojtek's belongings had been taken back to their house, she and Wojtek were staying with Sharon until Roman should return.

In the living room, Wojtek Frykowski kept asking, over and over who the invaders were, what they wanted, saying "My money is in the wallet, on the desk."

Sadie went over to the desk and reported she couldn't find it. Tex ordered Sadie to go get a towel in the bathroom to tie up Frykowski. Sadie brought a towel back to the couch by the fireplace and tied Wojtek's hands behind his back with a loose knot.

Frykowski was then forced to lie down on his back, thus trapping his hands behind him. Tex then told Sadie to scout the house looking for others. She climbed up the redwood ladder to search the loft, and then she walked toward the hallway off which were the two main bedrooms of the house. When she reached the one the left, Abigail Folger lay reading. When she saw Sadie, she waved! and smiled! and Sadie smiled back then walked away.

Sadie crossed the hallway, and peeked into Sharon's bedroom. A very tanned and very gravid Sharon was lying in bed, propped up on pillows, with her blonde hair over her shoulders, wearing matching blue-yellow, floral-patterned panties and bra. She was also adorned with her wedding ring and gold earpins. Lime green and orange sheets were pulled down. It was around 12:25 a.m. On the edge of the bed where the beautiful Sharon Tate was stretched out on pillows sat Jay Sebring in a blue shirt, black high-top boots, and white pants with black vertical stripes. On his wrist was an opulent Cartier watch. They were chatting and did not see Sadie.

On each side of the bed were marble-topped tables, one holding an oval-framed wedding portrait and a princess phone. A bottle of Heineken's beer, Jay Sebring's favorite drink, rested upon the other.

There was a large closet in the bedroom, as well as a bathroom and a dressing room. A tall armoire with drawers near the bottom rested against a wall. One drawer was packed with photos of Sharon. On top of the wardrobe lay a new white bassinet for the baby, wrapped in clear plastic. To the right, an ornate hookah.

A Sony videotape viewer and a television lay to the left of the armoire.

Sadie returned to the living room and informed Watson that there were people in the bedrooms. He was angry. He told Sadie to go into the bedrooms and bring them to the living room. Sadie opened her Buck clasp knife and walked into Abigail Folger's bedroom, and said "Go out into the living room. Don't ask any questions." She went to Sharon's bedroom and did the same thing.

Jay Sebring said, "What's going on?" when he arrived in the living room. "Sit down!" shouted Tex, but Jay refused.

Sebring, a cool, experienced businessman, and Frykowski, survivor of Hitler, probably tended not, at first, to fight. But then when Tex commanded all of them to lie down on the floor on their stomachs atop some pillows, Sebring said, "Let her sit down, can't you see she's pregnant?" Then he grabbed for the gun and Tex shot him in the armpit. Jay fell, and Tex kicked him in the bridge of his nose. Abigail then screamed.

Christopher, the Weimaraner, somehow escaped the back patio porch of the guesthouse, barking excitedly. The dog trotted into the front door of the main house about this time. Sadie said later that a "hunting dog" came around. Sadie even thought that somehow the dog got hold of her knife, which several minutes later she accidentally dropped down the side of a cushion during a scuffle. "We looked all over for it. I really think the dog got it."

Next Tex Watson snarled, "All right, where's the money?" Abigail replied that her purse was in the bedroom. Sadie jabbed her Buck knife up against Folger's back and conducted her to the bedroom. Abigail there opened up her black canvas shoulder bag and gave out seventy-two or seventy-three dollars. Sadie turned down Abigail's credit cards, and they walked back into the living room.

Tex then tied Sharon and Abigail around and around their necks with the nylon rope and threw the end of it over the white ceiling beam, telling Sadie to choke the rope so that the two had to stand up or else choke. Jay's unconscious body acted as a weight on the other end of the rope knotted around his neck.

Concerned about Wojtek Frykowski, Tex instructed Sadie to retie his hands with a bigger towel. She returned with a large Martex bath towel, and tied his hands behind him more securely, then she shoved Wojtek back onto the couch, and then stood guard over him.

Tex told Katie to turn out all the lights. The next morning the only lights the police discovered turned on were the hall light leading into the back bedrooms and the desk lamp in the living room.

As Katie was hauling on the end of the rope, one of the victims asked, "What are you going to do to us?"

Tex Watson replied, "You are all going to die." And once again he announced he was the Devil. Right away a thick blast of moans, begging, and shrieks arose as the victims struggled to free themselves.

Wojtek Frykowski was bouncing up and down, trying to loosen the knot behind his back, and Tex ordered Sadie to kill him. Sadie raised her knife then paused. Frykowski tore his hands free, reaching up from the sofa to grab her hair and pulled her down, gripping her knife arm. He hit her on her head and both rolled onto the stuffed chair.

Sadie freed her arm, and started wildly stabbing, first four times down his left leg. He tried to flee toward the hall to the entrance, while she stabbed him in the back, hitting bone, but then she got him in the right lung. Sadie lost her knife, which the police later found lodged, blade up, between the cushion and the back of the chair. Without a weapon, Sadie yelled for help, clinging to his back.

Still Frykowski pushed onward. Then Tex twisted him around and shot him in the middle of his back and again in his right thigh, but still Wojtek walked. Then when the .22 misfired, Tex began to club his face and scalp with the gun, breaking one of its walnut grips into pieces. When Tex ran to get Wojtek, Sharon and Abigail were struggling to free themselves from the knots on their necks. Abigail broke loose and headed for the back bedroom, toward the French doors to the swimming pool that led to freedom. Abigail clawed at the shuttered door, smearing blood, to open it up. Krenwinkel raced after her, and the taller and stronger Abigail fought fiercely. Katie put herself on Death Row when she tried to prevent the door from being opened, leaving a fingerprint above the knob on the right French door.

Meanwhile, Tex stabbed the struggling Sebring four times, and kicked his face, then, his black velour turtleneck beginning to get bloody, his eyes shiny with the thrill of kill, he raced to Abigail, wounded only defensively at this point, having fled out the bedroom door. Abigail surrendered. "I give up. Take me." He did, smashing her head with the gun butt, and stabbing her chest and abdomen till she fell on the lawn.

Watson then heard Wojtek screaming near the front lawn; he ran toward him, and saw him rise up from the bush into which he had fallen and then stagger across the grass. Sadie/Susan Atkins later told a cellmate, "He got to the lawn and was standing there hollering, 'Help! Help!' and nobody even heard him."

The young mother Linda Kasabian was kneeling in the dark by the electric gate. She heard screams, and ran up the walkway onto the grass. As she later wrote, "Then I saw Frykowski staggering out the door—drenched in blood—I looked in his eyes—he looked in mine—I saw the image of Christ in him, I cried and I prayed with all my heart." It was then, she recounted, that she began to feel Charles Manson no longer to be Jesus Christ. Instead, he was the Devil.

Sadie left the house upset that she had lost her knife. She spoke with Linda Kasabian, and then when Wojtek got to his feet and began to scream into the hot night, Tex sprinted out the front door and rode poor Frykowski to the ground, while stabbing.

At that moment, all the killers were out of the house, leaving Sharon as yet unharmed. Sharon started toward the front door just as Krenwinkel reentered the back door by the pool and entered the living room.

Sharon was crying for her unborn child's life. Sadie caught her in a headlock. Tex said it looked like Sharon wanted to sit down, so, as Sadie later reported, "I took her over and sat her down on the couch."

"All I want to do is have my baby," said Sharon. Sadie spoke with her to calm her down, but also mentioned how she had no mercy for her. A Manson Family member, about a month later, overheard Sadie say that Sharon was the last to die because she "had to watch the others die."

Sharon sat quietly, and the killers waited for a few minutes. Finally it came. Sadie later told a cellmate that she held Sharon's arms back behind her. And Sharon turned her head around and looked back at Sadie, "Please don't kill me, please don't kill me. I don't want to die." She was crying. "Please, I'm going to have a baby."

Sadie answered, "Look, bitch! I don't care if you're going to have a baby. You'd better be ready. You're going to die." Sharon begged her killers to take her with them and let her have the baby before they killed her. It seemed like a good idea to Tex at first—after all, the Family adored children. Then someone said, "Kill her."

Tex told Sadie to kill. Sadie said she couldn't do it. Katie? No, Tex you do it. So Tex stabbed her several times in the left breast through the brassiere. Then they all stabbed her, sixteen times, with both knives. Sadie said she was thrilled. "It felt so good, the first time I stabbed her."

All of a sudden, Tex said: "Get out." The girls left, and then Tex came out and proceeded to evilly conduct a final circuit. He ran counterclockwise: first to Abigail to stab her, then over to the lifeless Frykowski, where Tex kicked him.

Then the man who had called himself the Devil ran inside the house to arrange the tableau.

While Tex was inside the house, Sadie and Katie walked around looking for Linda, but couldn't find her. Tex came out of the house and ordered Sadie to go in the house and write something on the door—something witchy.

Tex and Katie walked down the walkway, and Sadie went back through the front door. Sadie walked into the haunted room. Evidently Tex (or Manson himself when he visited the house a few hours later) had looped the nylon rope twice around Sharon's neck. There was a double loop around Sebring's neck, with an overhand knot formed by the second loop. The rope led from one end, which was under Jay's body, around his neck twice over to Sharon, who was lying in front of the couch beneath the flag, around her neck twice, then back along the couch and over the ceiling beam.

Sadie went over to Sharon Tate and put her head on her stomach to listen, kneeling on the floor by the velvet couch. Finally Sadie went to the yellow towel used to tie Wojtek's hands, came back, and obtained some blood from Sharon's breast, then licked some blood from her fingers.

She knelt down by the front door to print "PIG" in blood type O-M. Then she went back into the living room, tossed the towel toward the hearth, and departed. She left the door wide open, and as she moved off the porch, left behind two barefoot prints in blood. Sharon's black kitten walked mewing amidst the carnage.

She found them waiting for her when she reached the electric gate. Tex forgot life imprisonment and left a smear of red on the gate button. The blood was Sebring's. The gate opened, and the stabbers scooped up their spare clothes and huffed down the hill as the gate closed.

Linda Kasabian had already started the Ford, and Tex yelled at her, and pushed her to the passenger's side. Then he low-voice yelled at Sadie for losing the Buck knife. He turned right onto Benedict Canyon Drive switching the lights on. Then the four drove up Benedict Canyon while changing their clothes. They talked excitedly in the hot a.m.

Linda gathered the bloody attire into a ball, and Tex told her to wipe the prints off the gun and the two knives. Linda threw the bundle down a ravine, which bounced down intact, lodging against a bush. Then she hurled down the knives. Tex said they needed to wash up, so they pulled left off Benedict onto a street just a block north of the street where Jay Sebring lived.

Tex spotted a garden hose hooked up to a house, so he turned the Ford around, parking toward the Canyon road in case they needed to escape quickly. Then they walked a few feet to the hose. The owner of the house heard splashing water, so he took a flashlight and went into his basement to look for leaks. Then there were voices from the street, so he flashed the light on them, saying, "Just what do you think you're doing?"

Tall Tex replied, "Hi, we're just getting a drink of water, and we're sorry to have disturbed you."

"Is that your car?" asked the owner. "No, it's not. We're walking."

Tex opened the door for the girls and then flooded the engine. Finally the engine caught and Tex peeled out, wrenching the owner's clutching hand. As the car sped away, he memorized the number and later wrote it down, GYY 435.

Tex didn't turn on his lights until he reached the Valley, where they stopped for gas. The three killers went to the john to wash, and Sadie noticed there was blood on the car. Tex told Linda to drive the rest of the way to the ranch. Somewhere Tex evidently threw the Longhorn revolver out the right window down a ravine at a location about one and a half miles from Sharon's house.

During the rest of the drive, the foursome seemed to relax, becoming even semi-jovial. The weapons, the blood, the clothes, they were safely tossed, weren't they? And they began to trade anecdotes.

Tex groaned that he had hurt his foot and it was painful. Sadie's scalp was awfully sore where Wojtek had grabbed her hair. Katie's contribution was how the knife handle hurt her hand each time she stabbed. The knives were inadequate, all agreed. Sadie complained about the toughness of Wojtek's legs when she hacked at them. They had vivid memories of the moans, and how Sharon kept calling out to God and Abigail kept crying out to her mother.

Manson was dancing naked with key disciple Brenda, aka Nancy Pitman, by the Longhorn Saloon at 2 a.m. when the quartet returned. "What're you doing home so early?," he wanted to know.

When Tex traced the events, Manson was distressed at the low body count. He had ordered additional killings in other houses near Cielo Drive. Watson remembered later, "When he asked why we didn't go to any other houses, I just shrugged."

Sadie announced that she had seen blood on the vehicle, so Charlie instructed her, Linda, and Katie to wash it with a sponge and water. After the three washed the Ford, he told them to go into the bunkhouse while Sadie wiped the exterior.

Several chuckled when Tex told how he had said to people in the house, "I'm the Devil, I'm here to do the Devil's business, where's your money?" Next, Manson polled the hackers to see if any felt remorse for what they had done, and all replied, "No."

Not long thereafter, Tex and Charlie entered the bunkhouse together for a further colloquy on what had occurred. Manson was pleased when Tex recounted that everything had been messy; bodies were lying around, but all were certainly dead.

The killers were sleepy. Kasabian went to the back ranch to rest. Sadie made love with a man—she thinks it might have been Clem—then went to sleep. Katie and Tex slept in the Saloon.

There is a considerable difference between the scene of the murders, as left by Atkins, Krenwinkel, Watson, and Kasabian, and the one found by the police the next morning. For instance, none of them had tucked any face towel over the head of Jay Sebring, yet the police found a towel over his head.

There was not enough slack in the rope that extended from Sharon Tate to Jay Sebring for Sharon to have stood and moved around, yet she moved around the room, the killers recounted. So the rope perhaps was affixed sometime after her death. The murderers, particularly Sadie/Susan Atkins, did not mention fixing the rope, although the ever-babbling Atkins gave lengthy confessional torrents about every aspect of the crimes to anybody who would listen. Nor did she mention the brown-framed glasses found by the bloody steamer trunks.

Also Roman's steamer trunks in the living room by the hall door were knocked away during the night; the killers didn't do it. There was a long trail of blood extending down the side of the upper trunk onto the slid-askew top of the bottom trunk. Sebring's blood, yet the killers claim he was killed in one spot and never moved.

The answer is that Manson and a companion returned to the scene of the crime.

During the trial, studying the large blood map of the house, I became suspicious that Manson had gone to the murder scene, and asked defense attorney Paul Fitzgerald to query Manson. He replied, "I went back to see what my children did." Apparently unknown to the others, Manson and a pal drove to Cielo Drive, where they boldly parked not far from the gate. They wiped down Steven Parent's car for prints, then walked into the house and saw the dead bodies. Manson later wrote in his autobiography (as told to Nuel Emmons), "I did not feel pity or compassion for the victims. My only concern was whether it resembled the Hinman killing. Would the police now have reason to believe that Bobby was not the slayer of Hinman?" Plus were any fingerprints left there?

"I'd had thoughts of creating a scene more in keeping with a black-against-white retaliation, but in looking around, I lost the heart to carry out my plans." With towels they wiped every surface clean, leaving a Tex Watson print on the front door and Krenwinkel's on the door leading to the swimming pool. Manson hooded a beige towel over Sebring's head, tucking the ends beneath the rope loops.

They may have done other horrible things; perhaps they moved Sharon's body, and Jay's also, to the front porch, then carried them back into the living room. In support of this, two large pools of blood were left on the front porch, one to the left of the door mat, type O-M, Sharon Tate's, and the other on the edge of the porch, type O-Mn, Jay Sebring's. Parent's, Frykowski's and Folger's blood types were all B-Mn, so none of the blood on the porch could have been theirs. A police report describing the homicide scene stated, regarding the blood of Sharon Tate on the front porch, that "From the amount of blood there it would appear that she remained there for at least minutes prior to movement." There were also spatters of Sharon Tate's blood in the front hall and on the door sill, but never, while the killers were at the estate, was she in the hall. The killers—Linda, Katie, and Sadie—later stated that at no time were Sharon Tate or Jay Sebring near the front porch. If they weren't moved there, how did their blood get there in such quantity?

Manson's associate brought an old pair of eyeglasses used as a magnifying glass to start fires, which he or she tossed down near Roman Polanski's steamer trucks as a false clue. Then Manson and pal were gone.

By the door leading to the hallway to Sharon's bedroom rested the wooden rocking chair Doris and Paul Tate had given their daughter for nursing the baby.

Stephanie, Manson's newfound love, testified that Manson came to her around dawn the morning just after the murders and brought her up into Devil Canyon, likely to the campsite by the waterfall, where she stayed for about a week.

Manson in August 1969

Tex Watson

Susan Atkins

Patricia Krenwinkel

Linda Kasabian

Chapter 12

Night and Morning

There were a number of screams and shots reported in Benedict Canyon during the night, most of the screams were after the murders were committed. Nothing out of the ordinary, just ordinary hot weekend screams.

Between 4:30 and 5 a.m., a delivery man brought the morning *Los Angeles Times* to the Polanski front gate, where he noticed that there was a wire down, draped across the fence. At 7:30 a.m., a resident at 10070 Cielo Drive walked out to get his paper and noticed the wire down and spotted the yellow bug light beaming on the Polanski garage.

The Polanski housekeeper, well-spoken Winifred Chapman, had been working for them for just over a year, beginning when Roman and Sharon had rented Patty Duke's place in the late spring of 1968. At about 8 a.m., Chapman took a city bus to Santa Monica and Canyon Drive at the southern end of Benedict Canyon. Because she was late she was considering calling a cab to get to Sharon's residence on time, but she ran into a friend who took her up Benedict Canyon to the front gate on Cielo Drive. She arrived at 8:30 a.m.

When she pushed the button of the electronic gate, she noticed that a wire was down, gathered the *Los Angeles Times*, and strolled up the drive. She turned off the yellow bug light on the garage, then walked past the three-car garage, then headed right, out of view of the bodies, along the extreme north edge of the house to the back, and went into the house through a service entrance door.

She reached above the door to a rafter and picked up a key from its usual place, unlocked the door, put the key back, strode into the service area, and then into the kitchen where she switched off the back patio light and placed her purse down. She picked up the phone. It was dead.

She went into the dining room, intending to wake someone to tell them there was no phone service. She saw the bouquet of flowers that Linda Kasabian had seen the night before, on a small stand in the dining room.

By the time Chapman arrived at the front hall, she spotted a towel, spotted the steamer trunks, spotted blood, spotted an open front door, spotted the bloody doormat, spotted Frykowski. She dashed out of the house the way she had come in, gathering up her purse on the way. Then she ran shouting down the hillside parking lot, pushed the bloody exit button at the narrowing of the driveway, enabling her to flee. There was no answer when she jabbed the doorbell of the house down the driveway from the front gate. She dashed down the hill to the Asim residence, where she encountered fifteen-year-old Jim Asim. "There's bodies and blood all over the place! Call the police!" Mrs. Chapman was so upset that the young man called up the police emergency number. After three calls, a police car arrived, with keening sirens, followed by another, another, another.

At 9:14 a.m., two LAPD officers, in separate West Los Angeles police cars, were given a call by central dispatch: "Code 2, possible homicide, 10050 Cielo Drive." Officer J. J. De Rosa arrived first, encountering the young man Jim Asim and the visibly upset housekeeper, who told him of all the blood and the body as she showed the officer how to operate the electronic entrance.

With rifle in hand De Rosa strode onto the property and spotted Steven Parent slumped in the Ambassador, motor off, lights off. As De Rosa was checking out Parent's automobile, Officer W. T. Whisenhunt arrived, having "received a call to back up a fellow officer investigating a possible homicide" as he later testified.

They called for an ambulance and verified that Parent was deceased. Then they warily proceeded onto the property again, rifles at the ready. They climbed up into the second story of the garage, where Roman Polanski was going to put his office, and checked it out, but found nothing out of the ordinary.

They passed Sebring's black Porsche and the Firebird and the Camaro in the garage, and then walked across the lawn where they encountered Wojtek Frykowski, wearing colored bell-bottomed pants and a purple shirt, and buckled, brown, high-top shoes. They spotted Abigail Folger a few yards to the south, white gown splotched with red.

Another policeman, Officer Burbridge, was the next officer to arrive, joining the two policemen. The three policemen could see the great amount of blood on the front porch and, of course, the open front door. They hesitated, not knowing what sort of crazed killer might be lurking within. With De Rosa covering, Whisenhunt and Burbridge went around to the back of the house to locate additional entrances, but the back door was locked. Whisenhunt and Burbridge decided to enter the open nursery room window on the far right of the house, the very window that Tex Watson had slashed. The slit window screen was resting against the house.

Not long after, Officer De Rosa observed his fellow patrolmen within the house, so he walked over the flagstone porch into the hallway, avoiding the blood. He spotted the "PIG" on the door, and entered the ghastly ghostly gory desolation of Manson's tableau. They spotted the bodies and the rope and quickly searched the house, the bedrooms, and the upstairs loft. A major task was to protect the scene, making careful note of the original physical circumstances of the area and leaving it undisturbed.

The officers completed their search of the house and were checking out the remainder of the estate—the pool area for instance—walking in the direction of the guesthouse, when they heard barking dogs, after which they heard a male voice within the guesthouse.

Bill Garretson yelled "Quiet down!" as the cops approached and started to get up from the couch in the living room where he had been sleeping since shortly after dawn. He was a short, tanned young man with semilong brown hair, age nineteen, barefoot, shirtless, and wearing pinstriped pants. He glanced out the window onto the front porch and saw an officer pointing a rifle at him. The officer told him to freeze. Christopher, the Weimaraner, was barking furiously. Garretson saw a second policeman leveling a rifle at him from the redwood picnic table on the porch.

Officer De Rosa kicked the front door in and the Weimaraner rushed forward and bit De Rosa's leg. They tossed Garretson onto the porch floor, and handcuffed his hands behind his back. Garretson kept asking, "What's the matter? What's the matter?"

"You want to know what's the matter? Well, we'll show you what's the matter," as they marched Garretson across the lawn to Abigail Folger, who lay upon her back in her nightgown. He thought the body was that of the maid. They marched him over to Wojtek Frykowski. He looked away from the unidentifiable victim. Then they took him to the Ambassador, where he couldn't identify Parent.

Thinking that the first body was the maid, Garretson was shocked when he spotted Mrs. Chapman alive when he reached the front gate. When he asked whose body it had been, he was told in error that it was Mrs. Polanski's.

Chapman and Garretson were taken to a police station by Officers De Rosa and Whisenhunt while Officer Burbridge remained behind to protect the crime scene. Mrs. Chapman became overwrought and was taken to the UCLA Medical Center for sedation and then was escorted to West Los Angeles police headquarters for questioning. Daze-eyed Bill Garretson was led into the lockup and sometime later an officer approached to say, "There's the guy that killed those people."

Print and TV reporters who monitor police radio broadcasts quickly heard that something had happened on Cielo Drive. There was chatter about fires in Benedict Canyon with five people killed and that Sebring was one of the victims, so a reporter telephoned Jay's house and spoke to an employee who had stayed over to paint or to repair the house. After the reporter called, the employee called the vice president of Sebring International, who called Sharon's mother. Mrs. Tate then tried to contact Cielo Drive where, even though the phone lines were cut, the telephone appeared to ring, giving the appearance that no one was home. This was not startling to Doris Tate, because she was certain that Sharon was staying for the night at her friend Sheilah Wells's house.

Meanwhile, six squad cars sped up to the Cielo gate, then more. Aerial photos taken a few minutes after the police arrived show the front gate of the estate glutted with reporters, none of whom was allowed through the electric gate onto the property.

The reporters quick-questioned the police as they entered or left the front gate. The first uniformed supervisor to arrive at Cielo Drive described to reporters the condition of the beds: "All of the beds, including those in the guest house, appear to have been used. . . . It looked like a battlefield up there."

And so the police entering and leaving gave out bits of information. One officer said that the murder scene "looked ritualistic." Those words set the tone for early reportage. The *Los Angeles Times* came on the stands that afternoon with a page-one story about "Ritual Murders."

The police gave out so much information that they were endangering the supply of "poly keys"—polygraph interrogation keys—key bits of information about the murders that only the killers could know, so that on a lie detector test the possible killer could be asked questions about these keys.

One officer told reporters that the victims were attired in "hippie type clothes." Another stated that one of the victim's pants were down. Another opined that it looked like a "typical fag murder." Something led reporters to print that Sebring was wearing a black hood over his head, although there is a great difference between a light-colored bloody towel and a black hood.

Over forty officers, including the chief of the Beverly Hills police department, plus ambulance drivers and four members of the coroner's staff, arrived. They spread upon the grounds, up on the roof, scraping, dusting, making notes.

Police photographers took hundreds of snaps of the inside of the house and the grounds. One of the jobs right away was to learn as much as possible about the victims, emphasizing seeking enemies and those with motives.

At around 10 a.m. the police called Sharon's mother. They obtained from her the name of William Tennant, Sharon's business agent. The police then located Mr. Tennant at his tennis club. He went immediately to 10050 Cielo Drive, arriving about noon, still wearing his tennis attire.

He identified Sharon, Abigail, Jay, and Wojtek, then departed, sobbing and holding back an urge to throw up. He refused to speak to the gathering of reporters at the gate. A TV gossip asked him if it was "really Sharon," to which the anguished Tennant replied, "Oh, don't be an ass."

When Mr. Tennant called, it was early evening in London, and Roman Polanski was at home, preparing to go out to dinner with Victor Lownes, managing director of the London Playboy Club. At first Mr. Polanski thought it was a joke and hung up. Tennant called again. "She was such a good person," Mr. Polanski said over and over during the early shock.

Also at around 10 a.m., West Los Angeles detectives arrived to take charge of the investigation. One of them covered the bodies with sheets. They searched the guesthouse looking for weapons. They checked the main house for signs of robbery and ransacking. They noted there were no drawers left open and Sebring was still wearing his $1,500 watch. They laddered up onto the roof to see where the downed telephone and communications wires led. The glasses were found near the blood-spotted steamer trunks.

An officer gathered up all the cutlery in both the caretaker's house and the main house, to check for blood. Also he gathered Roman's engraved .45-caliber revolver, which had been given to him by the cast of *Rosemary's Baby*. They located three pieces of broken pistol grip from the Wyatt Earp revolver, and removed the spattered American flag from the couch.

Police also visited the Folger-Frykowski house at 2774 Woodstock and confiscated ten address books and notebooks, some or all of which were written in Polish. Also taken were various personal papers of the decedents and a box of "miscellaneous photographs and negatives," as it was listed in item number 65 in the police property report.

A man from the telephone company showed up between 10 and 11 a.m., pushing through the news-pack at the outside rattan fence. He repaired two telephone wires and left two down pending police investigation. The police wanted to know what sort of device had severed the wires, so the phone man took a look at the wires to see what might have clipped it. A police officer cut a foot-and-a-half length of wire containing on one end the actual marks of the instrument used by the killer or killers to sever the wire.

The LAPD's Special Investigation Division brought blood analysts to Cielo. A Sergeant Granado arrived and began to take blood samples from forty-three locations all over the house and grounds. For the later trial, the police created a large blood-map of the murder house, which was useful in determining how the crimes were committed. They checked the bloody barefoot prints on the sidewalk to the entranceway. There were bloody pink ribbons hanging on the front door. There was a blood-soaked purple scarf found near Frykowski.

Unfortunately some police officers themselves tracked blood on the front porch, leaving three red footprints. This created problems later when the police were trying to re-create the original scene. They had to find out what sort of soles officers had on their shoes in order to determine the bloody prints were in fact made by a policeman in the early minutes of the investigation.

What seems to remain a part of the mystery is a bloody boot-heel print on the flagstone front porch that was not made by the police. Whose was it? Likely it was not Watson's or Manson's since they seem to have been wearing moccasins.

Sometime around noon the investigation of the murders was reassigned from the West Los Angeles division of LAPD to the robbery-homicide division of LAPD. Lieutenant Robert J. Helder, supervisor of investigation for the robbery-homicide division, was chosen to take charge. Lieutenant Helder stayed in charge until the arrests on December 1.

Two fingerprint specialists, Officer Jerome Boen and Officer Girt, came to the residence about 12:30 p.m. and began dusting for prints. The ridges of the fingers, palms, and soles ooze with oil and fluid. An impression of the ridge patterns was made wherever surface contact was made. On hard, smooth surfaces the ridge impression can be removed. First the officer powdered the surface with a gray powder, which was brushed away with powder sticking to the ridges of the fingerprint or footprint. The print is then sprayed with iodine and transferred to a card with a special tape. Photographs were made of the precise location of the prints.

Another method of detection was used on those prints where dusting didn't detect the "moisture ridges" sufficiently because of the faintness of the ridges. For that, the officers sprayed on an iodine/chemical mixture and within twenty-four to forty-eight hours the print appeared.

Fifty fingerprints were found, with twenty-two eliminated, plus three were "unmakable" and twenty-five remaining unidentified. Of this twenty-five, a good number were located on the freshly painted window sill of the nursery window, indicating that they were likely left there either the afternoon or the evening of the murders. Several were later connected to the killers.

Dr. Thomas Noguchi, the chief medical examiner of LA County, ordered that the bodies not be disturbed till he and his assistants should arrive at the scene. The nylon rope connecting Sebring and Tate was ordered severed by

The LA coroner Thomas Noguchi was at the crime scene to supervise details.

Noguchi. Later the police cut the sections of the rope to trace source, manufacturer, and possible purchasers.

One of Noguchi's deputies took liver temperatures of the victims as an aid in determining the time of death. Victims' hands were wrapped with bags to save possible hairs and skin from the struggle. Then an ambulance crew brought wheeled stretchers and removed the victims.

Right away officers went to Sebring's home to look for evidence. Several friends of Sebring, including a well-known actor, had rushed over to Sebring's house on Easton Drive to clean it free of contraband, evidently ahead of the police.

Later on, the LAPD brought a van to the Polanski-Tate house and brought a truck-load of stuff down to headquarters for examination. A few days later they brought most of it back and tried to array it in the same order to re-create the original undisturbed crime scene.

The glasses found on the floor were picked up and replaced on the table in the foyer. They were later turned over to Sharon's father, Paul Tate, who kept them for several weeks trying to locate the owner.

At the murder site, the police searched for drugs, finding a half-full baggie of twenty-six grams of marijuana in a living room cabinet. They located thirty grams of hashish in the nightstand in Frykowski and Folger's room, plus ten MDA capsules. Cocaine and marijuana were found in Sebring's Porsche and a vial of coke in his pocket.

William Garretson, meanwhile, was questioned at the West LA jail at 4 p.m. He was read his rights and chose to speak without counsel present. "He gave stuporous and non-responsive answers to pertinent questions," a police report said. Shortly after the 4 p.m. interview, he secured the services of LA attorney Barry Tarlow. Garretson was then transported downtown to the LA police headquarters. He was queried once again, this time in the presence of Mr. Tarlow. Garretson then agreed he would submit to a lie detector test on Sunday, August 10, with his attorney present.

The LAPD animal regulation department removed the dogs and the kitten from Cielo, and police instituted a day-and-night guard on the house that lasted almost two weeks.

Meanwhile Steven Parent's body remained unidentified in the rush and confusion, although a reporter at the electric gate could read the license plate on Parent's Ambassador, so he ran a check on it and got Parent's home address. A priest friend of Parent identified his body, while his parents seemed to have learned of his death over television.

Some policemen got no sleep for three or four days, there was so much to do. There was fear as never before. And rumors as never before. Friends of the victims, some of them with enemies also, asked themselves, "Am I next?" Was there a maniac with a grudge slinking through the heat wave toward their homes?

Mother Doris Learns

"My God, Sharon's been murdered," Doris Tate exclaimed, sinking to her knees. Then she whispered, "My baby's dead."

Friends Learn

Joanna Pettet, her husband Alex Cord, and ten-month-old Damien were scheduled to return to Cielo Drive to swim. Pettet: "We were going to go swimming, Alex and I and Damien, and so I just called Sharon, to see what time we'd get there, and the phone rang and rang and rang. I said to Alex, 'This is odd. They have a maid, and all those people in the house.' I called again, and it rang and rang and rang. Then, my next call was from this lady, Janine Forman (whom Pettet had seen the night before) who said, 'I just heard the news. And I think it's your friend.' I dropped the phone and dropped to my knees. Alex was in the room with me, and he picked up the phone and continued the conversation. And then it was just weeks and weeks and months and months of horror."

Sheilah Wells soon also heard the horrible news. Wells recalls it vividly, "Listen, within two hours, there were private detectives in my house, and some were following the occult, and I'm going 'What are you talking about?' I mean it was just so bizarre."

ES: "As far as the occult, you don't have any memories of Sharon taking part in anything?"

Wells: "No. It was all so innocent and strange—having your palms read, and all of that stuff; it all came out of the sixties, and all of those bizarre interests in health food; it was just another part of the deal. It wasn't anything serious, or strange. It was curiosity. That was just so shocking. I guess they (the detectives) just had to follow different paths."

Her great friend's murder impacted Wells enormously. Afterward, she recounted, "I kind of dropped out. I think it really did affect me more than I knew that it actually had. There was a certain joy, a certain part that just kind of stopped." Indeed, she continued to act, mainly in television throughout the 1970s, and had a memorable role in the *Blues Brothers* movie in 1980, but ultimately left the business. (Today she continues her passion for interior design she had revealed when rooming with Sharon back in 1964. "That's what I do," she told me. "That's my passion. I do private residences, people in the business, from Madonna to Rob Schneider.")

Colonel Tate Heads for Cielo Drive

Colonel Paul Tate, according to his written account, was at his base in San Francisco at the time of the murders. He had seen *The Wrecking Crew* the very night Sharon was slain. The next day, at around 2 p.m., Colonel Tate arrived at Cielo Drive, having been called at Fort Baker by LAPD. He apparently flew from San Francisco, then rented a car.

He had a reputation, as an intelligence officer, of being icy cool, and having served through three wars, he was well used to violence. But this was of course different, and he brushed away tears as he pushed his way through the throng at the electric gate and walked toward the house. He was intercepted by police, including Lieutenant Robert Helder, who was the lead officer in the investigation.

Tate arrived at the end of the driveway where the gate opened to the flagstone walkway that curved to the house's front door. Next to the gate was the wishing well. The colonel could view what the police were doing, searching through cabinets and drawers, through the open French doors. All the bodies had been removed, except for Jay Sebring's. Lieutenant Helder would not allow Colonel Tate to view Sebring, who when he arrived was being loaded into a duffel bag onto a gurney. After a few minutes the colonel departed this desolation toward the desolation of his family's home in Palos Verdes.

Chapter 13

August 9–10: More Carnage and Grief

Saturday in London

When he spoke with Sharon on Friday, Roman decided that he could complete the script for *Day of the Dolphin* in Los Angeles. So he told his wife he was going to try to get a flight the next day, Saturday. "I'll leave tomorrow," he had said, giving her a jolt of happy expectation.

Saturday, the consulate was closed, and he needed a US visa. So he decided to fly to the United States "the following Monday or Tuesday, as soon as the visa was granted."

Also on Saturday came the news that the English nanny, Marie Lee, whom Sharon had selected after interviewing dozens of applicants who responded to an ad she had placed in the *London Times,* would be granted a US work permit.

Polanski had lunch on Saturday with "society doctor" Tony Greenburgh and director Simon Hesera. "Conversation was rather subdued," Polanski later recounted. "We had just learned of the sudden death of a friend of ours, Danielle, Dick Sylbert's ex-girlfriend. She was a beautiful French girl in her early twenties, and the news had come as a shock. 'Makes you wonder who'll be next,' I remember saying."

Then Polanski was back at his Mews house. London was nine hours ahead of LA time, and so it was 7 p.m. in London when the call came in about Cielo Drive. The one making the call was his agent, Bill Tennant.

Andy Braunsberg answered. "I handed the phone to (Polanski) and he literally unraveled in front of my eyes," Braunsberg recalled. "He disintegrated.

He put the phone down without hanging up, rushed into his bedroom and was weeping and crying and banging his head against the wall."

The Marauders Go Forth for Another Night

On August 5, Mr. and Mrs. Leno LaBianca drove with their speed boat in tow from Los Angeles north to Lake Isabella where Mrs. LaBianca's teenage son from another marriage, Frank Struthers, was visiting family friends, the Saffies. They left the boat there for Frank to use and returned to Los Angeles.

On August 9, the LaBiancas returned to Lake Isabella accompanied by Rosemary LaBianca's daughter, Susan Struthers, age twenty-one, to pick up Frank, and to haul the boat back to Los Angeles. They spent the day on the lake, had dinner, and were about to leave, when Frank Struthers was asked by his young friend to stay on till Sunday. Accordingly, Susan Struthers and the LaBiancas left the Saffie residence at Lake Isabella around 9 p.m., leaving Frank there, driving their green 1968 Thunderbird, hauling the ski boat, toward home.

They drove straight to Los Angeles. At 1 a.m. they dropped Susan off at her apartment not far from their own home. Shortly after 1 a.m., John Fokianos, who operated a newsstand at the corner of Hillhurst and Franklin Avenue, near the LaBianca house, observed their green Thunderbird pulling the boat-trailer turn into a Standard station, make a U-turn and pull up adjacent to Mr. Fokianos's newsstand.

Leno bought a Sunday *Herald-Examiner* and the Sunday *National Daily Reporter*, a horse-betting publication. Rosemary LaBianca, reading the horrible story in the *Herald-Examiner*, was disturbed about the murders on Cielo Drive, so Mr. Fokianos gave her a front-section filler from the Sunday *Los Angeles Times* with its "ritualistic murders" page-one story. "She seemed quite emotional about it," Fokianos later told reporters. Mr. and Mrs. LaBianca then drove to their home, parking the car on the street by the house, with the boat still hitched to the back.

The white one-story house at 3301 Waverly Drive lay in a quiet upper-middle-class neighborhood not far from Griffith Park. The house, once belonging to cartoonist and filmmaker Walt Disney, had been owned since 1968 by Leno and Rosemary. Frank also lived in the house.

To the west of the LaBianca residence was the former estate of actor Troy Donahue. To the east at 3267 Waverly Drive was the large house once rented by acquaintances of Charles Manson during the period September 1967 to September 1968, during which time some of the M group had undertaken a group LSD trip.

Leno LaBianca was the chief owner of the State Wholesale Grocery Company that operated the Gateway food market chain, businesses prosperously managed by Leno. Mr. LaBianca held extensive property interests in California and Nevada. He owned an enterprise called Arnel Stables and possessed nine thoroughbred race horses. He formerly was a member of the board of directors of the ill-fated Hollywood National Bank.

At the time of his death Leno LaBianca was negotiating the purchase of a ranch in Vista, California, for $127,000. His financial affairs were amazingly intricate, but one thing stands out: he was rich. Leno liked to gamble, visiting the race track often, wagering as much as $500 in a single day. The LaBiancas had recently discovered that their telephone was tapped. A telephone repairman was called to the home the day before the murders due to some trouble on the line, and he discovered the tap. It is now thought that the phone was monitored because Mr. LaBianca may occasionally have used the services of an infamous bookmaker known as The Phantom who lived just down the street.

Mr. LaBianca was forty-four years old and Rosemary was thirty-eight. She was co-owner of a successful dress and gift shop, Boutique Carriage, located within the Gateway shopping center that her husband owned. She herself was a successful businesswoman, and she speculated in stocks and commodities. She left an estate valued at $2,600,000.

The LaBiancas removed the water skis from the boat and carried them to the back entrance of the house and set them on the fender of Mrs. LaBianca's 1955 Thunderbird, which they had left by the garage. When they went into the house, Mrs. LaBianca placed her purse on the liquor cabinet in the dining room. Both donned sleeping attire, and Rosemary was in the bedroom preparing to sleep.

Leno was sitting in his pajamas in the living room, checking out the *Herald-Examiner* sports section and the racing form, sipping a can of apple beer. His reading glasses rested on the table in front of the L-shaped sectional sofa on which he was sitting.

He looked up and saw a short hairy Charles Manson wearing a black turtle-neck sweater, Levis, and moccasins and waving a cutlass. Charlie told Leno, "Be calm, sit down, and be quiet." He ordered Mrs. LaBianca out of the bedroom to the living room, where he ordered them to stand back to back. Then he tied them together, making a double square knot, with two forty-two-inch leather thongs from around his neck. He told them that everything was okay, and they weren't going to get hurt. He sat them down on the divan, and then he walked over to the liquor cabinet, took Rosemary's wallet from her purse, and walked out the front door, leaving it unlocked. Charlie returned to the car parked outside, the same 1959 Ford used the previous night to drive from the Spahn Ranch to Cielo Drive. Inside sat his hand-picked trio of killers—Tex, Leslie, and Katie, plus driver Linda Kasabian—waiting. He said there were two people in the house and that he had tied them up. He told them that the people were calm and not to instill fear in them. Then, to kill them. Afterward they were to hitchhike back to the ranch, where Katie was to go to the waterfall encampment. The killers got out of the Ford, and Linda Kasabian then drove Manson back to the Spahn Ranch.

Kill them they did, in a most horrific manner, leaving blood-writing on the walls, strange words and phrases such as "Rise," "Healter Skelter," and "Death to Pigs."

Then they departed. One of them treated herself to a shower, and to a container of chocolate milk.

Autopsies and Sleuthing the Maze

The initial investigation of Sharon Tate's house was, for the most part, a maze of blind alleys and repetitious and sometimes tedious questionings. All address books, personal papers, sweepings of house and grounds, everything, even the wastebaskets, had to be gathered and examined carefully for leads, enemies, motives, and possible killers. Some investigators searched the brushy hillsides of Benedict Canyon looking for the murder weapons. Others began to look for the type of revolver to fit the bloody bits of walnut pistol grip found in the residence. 10050 Cielo Drive was kept under continuous police guard for about two weeks.

The LA County medical examiner, Dr. Thomas Noguchi, supervised the autopsies of the victims on Sunday morning, August 10, with Noguchi himself conducting the examination of Tate. Tate joined such luminaries as Robert Kennedy and Marilyn Monroe, who were also autopsied by Noguchi. Several LAPD homicide investigators were on hand during the autopsies. Also at the autopsy were Sergeant Paul Whiteley and Detective Charles Guenther of the sheriff's homicide department, who were investigating the Gary Hinman murder. They approached the officers handling the Polanski murders and told them about the similarities between the two sets of murders: writing in blood, wounds inflicted by knives, and so on. The officers of the Tate investigation considered the similarities insignificant, however, since there had already been a suspect arrested for the Hinman murder when the later murders were committed.

Guenther and Whiteley Approach Tate
Detectives During Autopsies: August 10

When writing this book, I asked Sergeant Paul Whiteley to describe approaching the Tate detectives during the autopsies. He replied: "After hearing news reports that there was blood writings at the Tate home and that the autopsies were scheduled for that day, Guenther and I went downstairs to the morgue. Upon entering we saw three of the victims, including Sharon Tate. I remarked to Charlie how beautiful she was even in death. There was about six LAPD robbery-homicide detectives in the autopsy room. I approached Lieutenant Robert Helder and identified myself. I started to relate to him our investigation of the Hinman case, and he directed a Detective Buckles to talk to us. We stepped outside the autopsy room, and I related that we had arrested Robert Beausoleil just days prior for the Hinman Murder. I told him of the blood writing on the wall of 'Political Piggy.'

"At this point another LAPD detective came out of the autopsy room and joined us (he never identified himself). Detective Buckles asked us what Hinman did for a living, and I told him a music teacher. He then asked what Beausoleil did for a living and I told him he was part of a hippie group and wannabe musician. Detective Buckles said their investigation had led them to a Caribbean dope deal that was big-time and couldn't be connected to our case. He further stated that the victims in his case were very important people and they wouldn't be involved with any hippies. We left and went back upstairs to prepare a wanted bulletin for (Beausoleil's girlfriend) Kitty Lutesinger."

Only a few weeks later, when Sadie/Susan Atkins was arrested for Hinman's murder and it was discovered that she was not in jail the night of Sharon Tate's murder, did the connection spark to life.

Newspaper articles describing the autopsy noted that the baby had been perfectly formed, partly to quell any speculation pertaining to Polanski's most famous movie. At the same time, the wildest assertions appeared in national publications about the physical state of the victims, based on inaccurate information apparently leaked from someone at the coroner's office. In Los Angeles, reporters in unusual number gathered at police headquarters, snatching for data.

Because everything any officer said was being published, they had to be careful. On Sunday, August 10, Lieutenant Robert Helder, the head of the investigation, informed a news conference that efforts to find the perpetrators were focused on acquaintances of the caretaker William Garretson. Another police source stated that they were "not entirely satisfied" with Garretson's answers. That afternoon Garretson was given an hour-long lie detector test, in the presence of his attorney, Barry Tarlow.

A lieutenant from the LAPD scientific investigation division administered the polygraph in the late afternoon of August 10, at the Parker Center police headquarters. They found Garretson "stuporous and vague," as if he were under the influence of some kind of narcotic. During his polygraph interrogation Garretson still seemed confused and unable to remember things.

For instance, the caretaker was very vague about what had gone on at the Polanski residence the evening of the murders. The polygraph revealed that someone seems to have arrived at the residence immediately prior to Garretson's trek down to the Sunset Strip where he bought food. Garretson: "And so I stayed home all day Friday, August 8, and I cleaned up the house a little bit and did the dishes and everything, and they came around 8:30, nine o'clock, somewhere around there. And I went to get something to eat, and I went down on the Strip; I had something down there, and I could see her light all the way down from Cielo—not Cielo, but Benedict Canyon, all the way down to the Strip."

One question, who are the "they" who arrived about 8:30? The victims returning from dinner at the El Coyote restaurant? Or guests? Garretson was also vague about what he was doing during the murders. At the trial he testified that he spent the time writing a letter to a friend named Darryl and listening to The Doors and a Mama Cass album. During the polygraph he admitted he might have gone out in back of his house, which was out of view of the main house and grounds, so perhaps he hid there. In spite of inconsistencies, his answers regarding his innocence were shown on the polygraph to be truthful, so Garretson was eliminated as a suspect.

Garretson's attorney, Barry Tarlow, secured the services of a private investigator who conducted a separate polygraph examination of Garretson, and compiled a tape about Garretson and the scene at 10050 Cielo Drive.

"I felt very strongly that he had heard someone that night," the private investigator later told my investigator, Larry Larsen, during the murder trial.

One thing Garretson claimed was that Sharon Tate had given Garretson marijuana for Garretson and Rudy Altobelli to smoke. "Altobelli sent him over for it, and he got it in a little tin foil and brought it back," said the private eye. "He showed truthful in the polygraph except for what he could have heard."

When I later visited Sharon Tate's mother, Doris, she too was perplexed about Garretson. She wondered, where was the caretaker during the murders? Patricia Krenwinkel told her attorney during the trial that she remembered entering the caretaker's house but finding no one there. Yet the caretaker swore he was there all night, listening to records, smoking pot, and sleeping. Mrs. Tate had doubts. It was a mystery she wanted to be cleared up.

Doris believed that the Manson group had advance word that Sharon Tate was not going to be at the house that night. Back in 1971, Larry Larsen had interviewed Jay Sebring's business partner, from whom we learned Sharon had intended to spend the night with a friend. Mrs. Tate verified that during my visit.

Manson associate Vern Plumlee had told us that he'd heard the Family thought Sharon wouldn't be there. Doris Tate believed, she told me, that someone might have tipped the Family off. She wondered if someone saw that Sharon's red Ferrari was gone (it was in the repair shop) and called Manson, and then the attack began.

At the time, I was sending question lists to Manson in prison, and she suggested I tell him I'd visited her. She thought that maybe that would jog his memory.

Steve Brandt, who was a good friend of the Polanskis' as well as their former press agent and a legal witness for their 1968 wedding, arrived in Los Angeles on Sunday, August 10, from New York. He was questioned in detail by police investigators and provided "voluminous information," according to reports at the time, about Sharon Tate and her circle of friends and about dope and Frykowski's ten-day mescaline experiment.

The owner of Cielo Drive, Rudy Altobelli, arrived from Europe Sunday evening. Since the residence was sealed off, he went to a place where he felt he would be safe—to Terry Melcher's Malibu beach house! Only later did he realize the irony. He was interviewed by the police. They asked him about the party in March where Roman Polanski threw a person out. Early speculation held that the "PIG" on the front door was actually "PIC," the nickname of one of the men thrown from the party. They also asked him questions about any possible marital problems between Mr. and Mrs. Polanski.

Mr. Altobelli was asked at the trial when he, Altobelli, first thought that Manson might be responsible for the murders. Altobelli replied that he thought of Manson as a suspect on the plane trip back to the United States just after the murders. In a tragic hesitation without which Manson might have been caught right away, Altobelli testified he did not volunteer the information to the police because he was not asked about it.

Later on Sunday evening, August 10, Roman Polanski arrived at Los Angeles International Airport from London, traveling with friends, including Richard Sylbert, and was silent coming through customs when the reporters crowded about with quick questions, disconcerting lights, and pushing microphones. His friend and associate, Gene Gutowski, read a short statement to the press that condemned sensationalistic printed rumors of rituals and marital problems that had filled the front pages and television screens of Europe and America. Roman Polanski at once was taken into seclusion in an apartment within the Paramount Studios complex.

Robert Evans, in his book, *The Kid Stays in the Picture*, described it: "I arranged for (Polanski) to be driven to Paramount and installed in the suite that had recently been Julie Andrews's dressing room for *Darling Lili*. There he hibernated for a few days, heavily sedated by a Paramount doctor."

Polanski's friend Andy Braunsberg recounted how Polanski was protected at Paramount by bodyguards. It was safer that way, rather than at a hotel, since the killers were still aroam. "It was like the monster from the black lagoon. People believed this would not be the last of the killings," remembered Braunsberg. Polanski was "in a state of complete shock and breakdown."

Late Sunday night police found Sharon's 1967 red Ferrari, license number VAM 559, in a body-repair shop where it had been taken after her fender-bender with her mom—thus removing the possibility that it may have been used as an escape vehicle by a robber-killer or killers.

About the same time, the artist named Witold K. called a friend in New York from a phone booth in Los Angeles, talking nervously in Polish, stating that he knew who the killers were and that he was in fear. Then New York acquaintances contacted a *New York Times* reporter in Los Angeles and related Witold K.'s claim. The reporter called the Los Angeles police, who promised Witold twenty-four-hour protection if he would talk. His friends called Witold K. back at the phone booth where he was waiting, and he agreed to the protection. Three police cars picked up Witold K. and delivered him to the apartment at Paramount Studios where Roman Polanski was in seclusion.

Witold K. told police that Frykowski was offered an exclusive dealership in the Los Angeles area, to distribute the drug MDA. Quarreling occurred, and one of the suppliers threatened to off Frykowski. Witold K. claimed not to know the names of the possible killers but that he could recognize them, and also that they were Canadian. Mr. Frykowski, said Mr. K., kept a diary, written in Polish, and also kept voluminous notes and jotted many phone numbers and addresses. The artist told the police that the identity of the killers was likely to be found in these notes and diaries, but that "it would take two weeks" for him to locate the killers' identities from the notebooks. One close friend, writer Jerzy Kosinski, told me in an interview that Witold K. went around, escorted by police, to the prestigious addresses in Frykowski's notebooks to try to locate the killer—always careful to leave his business card.

Witold K.'s career as a painter was temporarily boosted by his cooperation with the police. One newspaper account showed a picture of Witold K. posing with several of his paintings on the Polanski front lawn. Kosinski claimed that Witold K. even sold a couple of his paintings to two investigators.

This is typical of the hundreds of leads followed vigorously by the police that led to blind walls of cool, silent traffickers in dope. And few things are more hidden than the big-league dope trade.

Finding the LaBiancas

Rosemary LaBianca's sixteen-year-old son, Frank Struthers, was driven home from his vacation at Lake Isabella on August 10 in the evening close to dark, and was dropped off in front of 3301 Waverly Drive. His mother and stepfather's Thunderbird, with boat attached, was parked on the street. He spotted that the window shades were drawn as he walked up the driveway. He continued to the garage, and knocked on the back door, no answer. It was locked. Water skis lay on the fender of the other car, by the garage. He rapped on the den window. Again, no answer. He walked down to a nearby public phone and called the house, but there was no answer. Next he called his sister, Susan Struthers, and told her he was worried.

Susan and her fiancé, Joe Dorgan, arrived at 3301 Waverly Drive, where they met Frank. They retrieved the house keys from the ignition switch of Mrs. LaBianca's Thunderbird and entered the house through the back door. Susan stayed in the kitchen while Frank Struthers and Joe Dorgan made their way through the dining room into the living room and saw Leno LaBianca "in a crouched position" on the floor. Something was wrong, very wrong, so the two turned around and rushed away. Dorgan picked up the phone in the kitchen, then dropped it. They ran into the yard yelling for help, and a neighbor called the police. At about 10:45 p.m. police cars raced, sirens blaring, to the driveway.

Quickly the house on Waverly Drive became glutted with reporters and homicide detectives. The *Los Angeles Times* covered it with a page-one story bearing the headline "2 Ritual Slayings Follow Killing of 5," linking it to the murders of Friday night.

Police released to the public many of the major details of the murders. Newspapers mentioned the knife and fork impaled in Mr. LaBianca and the word "war" scratched in his stomach. They told of the white "hood"—the pillowcase—over his head. Not released to the media were the bloody words "Healter Skelter" scrawled on the ice-box doors, although police did note that there were words in blood on the refrigerator doors. The *Los Angeles Times* story, for instance, mistakenly related that "the words 'Death to Pigs' had been smeared on the doors of the refrigerator, apparently by the heel of a slayer's hand."

Manson's friend Gregg Jakobson was questioned right away because of his association with Cielo Drive owner Rudy Altobelli. Had the words "Healter Skelter" been released to the media by the police, Jakobson, who was one of scores of people who knew what the words meant, right away would have informed the police about the Manson Family, and Manson and crew probably could have been arrested right away. It is likely, however, that investigators, wanting a number of polygraph interrogation keys retained, withheld "Healter Skelter" as well as the bloody word "rise" that was found in the living room.

Police Backing Away from Linking Cielo Drive and the LaBiancas

On the afternoon of August 11, the Cielo Drive caretaker, William Eston Garretson, was set free after being held for two days, walking out of custody facing a row of cameras.

That same day, police pulled back from connecting the Cielo Drive and Waverly Drive murders. "There is a similarity," remarked a LAPD Sergeant, "but whether it's the same suspect or a copy cat, we just don't know." The two sets of victims, how they had differing friends, differing lifestyles, and no apparent connections, helped separate the cases. By August 12, police officially ruled out any link between the Tate and LaBianca crimes.

The LaBianca investigation team was headed by Lieutenant Paul LePage and detectives from robbery-homicide, including Sergeant Phil Sartuche, Sergeant Manuel Gutierrez, and Sergeant Frank Patchett, all of whom played considerable parts in ultimately cracking the case.

The LaBianca investigation initially focused on business affairs and the extensive gambling activities of Leno LaBianca. It was determined that about $200,000 was missing from Gateway Markets, one of Mr. LaBianca's businesses. Mr. LaBianca collected rare coins; his collections were worth thousands. A rare coin collection, believed to be Mr. LaBianca's, was found in a house on Waverly Drive a couple of blocks from the LaBianca residence—a place owned by the bookmaker The Phantom, which had been abandoned by him a week after the murders.

Some friends of Mr. LaBianca denied the possibility that the Mafia had contracted his death. If it had, they said, they would have heard about it. Police made an activity chart divided into half-hour increments showing the activities of Leno and Rosemary LaBianca between August 4 and August 10. They conducted lie detector tests on a good number of acquaintances of the victims.

Twenty-five finger prints were found in the LaBianca house. Nineteen were eliminated, six remain unidentified. 41,634 suspects were checked against the print on the liquor cabinet where Manson had taken Mrs. LaBianca's wallet. The LaBianca investigation team arranged so-called M.O. runs with the State Bureau of Criminal Identification and Investigation (CII) computer, in Sacramento. The CII computer stored a large amount of information regarding crime and criminals. An M.O. run collects all crimes committed with the same methods. A police agency could get a list of every murder where the killer tied up the victim, and/or wrote on the wall, in order to obtain the identity of potential suspects.

On the Polanski residence murders, one of the problems facing the police was the overwhelming number of suspects. The decedents' lives were replete with relationships that could have spawned violent grudges. The Cielo Drive murders provided impetus for a great number of narcotics arrests. Some individuals, however, were promised immunity from dope prosecution if they would provide information about the deceased and possible culprits. Three LA homicide detectives went to Vancouver to help the Royal Canadian Mounted police organize a dragnet for the Canadian dope dealers that Witold K. and others had fingered. The dope dealers were believed headed toward Edmonton, Alberta, or already holed up in the western Canadian woods.

US Treasury agents investigated aspects of drug traffic to see if there was a pattern of interstate trafficking. In the days following the murders there were large-scale cocaine arrests around the country that have been linked to the reverberations resulting from the murder investigation. Police traveled around the country administering polygraph examinations. They went to England to interrogate suspects. The US Bureau of Narcotics and Dangerous Drugs (forerunner to the DEA) also investigated.

Films, Videotapes, and Cielo Drive

Police located reels of film and videotapes of interest during the follow-up investigations. Some were found in the Polanski residence in the main bedroom closet. For instance, one videotape was found in a room off the living room loft and was booked as item #36 in the police property report. Other films were taken into possession in Jamaica and in Annandale, Virginia. Some of the films apparently involved an elite underground film group in Hollywood that swapped erotic files of stars and semistars, past and present.

One videotape found at the Polanski residence was of Roman Polanski and Sharon Tate making love. It was not booked into evidence but was returned, after police viewed it, to the spot in the loft above the living room where police had found it.

During Manson's trial, one of the defense lawyers, Paul Fitzgerald, was approached by a television reporter representing a rising movie actress who had left a roll of undeveloped 35-millimeter film allegedly containing pictures of herself getting after it at the Polanski residence on the day of the murders. The representative wanted the attorney to ask Manson if the Family had removed the film from the house that night, because she had been unable to find out what happened to it, and she felt that if the film were publicized her career would be threatened.

Meanwhile, as the police investigation progressed, all forms of wild speculation were passed from mouth to mouth regarding the Cielo Drive murders. There was speculation from close friends of Frykowski that they had been done by the Polish secret police, who took a plane from Los Angeles to Rome right after the murders, in reprisal for Polanski's defection from Poland. There was every form of speculation regarding mutilation and ritual.

There was a flame of violence in Los Angeles in early August 1969 where from Friday, August 8, to Tuesday, August 12, twenty-nine people were murdered. In the two days following the murders, Ken's Sporting Goods Shop in Beverly Hills sold two hundred guns. The Bel Air Patrol, a private security force serving the exclusive Bel Air Area, hired something like thirty extra men. People slept within easy reach of the electronic panic buttons that could summon the Bel Air Patrol. Bodyguards were in great demand. Individuals placed their own homes under twenty-four-hour surveillance by teams of private detectives. People packed guns at the funerals of the deceased.

A Lie Detector Test for Polanski

On Monday, August 11, the day after he returned from London, Roman Polanski took a lie detector test, which he passed. He'd had some Valium earlier in the day. He was shown some photos, only one of which, of Billy Doyle, he recognized. They also showed him an array of knives.

Lieutenant Earl Deemer, the polygraph administrator, purportedly asked him, "Have you dated any airline stewardesses since Sharon's death."

"Yes," replied Polanski, "Well, I haven't dated; I've seen a couple of them."

"Took them out to lunch or something?"

Polanski replied, "I fucked them."

Years later, while Polanski was testifying in a court, a tape of Polanski's 1969 lie detector test was played in which he had told the polygraph officer he had made it with a couple of stewardesses after Sharon's murder, and he claimed that the boast was a lie, done to lessen the tension with the detective conducting the test. Polanski further told the court, regarding making it with the stewardesses, "Not that I object to it, particularly in those times. It would be something I would not miss if I had the opportunity."

Chapter 14
Aftermath and Investigation

A Federal Narcotics Agent Speaks of a "Cult" Possibly Being Involved

The same day that Polanski had his polygraph examination, two reporters for the New York *Daily News*, Michael McGovern and William Federici, met with an agent of the Federal Bureau of Narcotics and Dangerous Drugs (the predecessor agency to the Drug Enforcement Agency) at a restaurant in Los Angeles. The agent at the restaurant supplied the two reporters with some allegations which Federici and McGovern used in a page 2 story in the *Daily News* of August 13, under the headline "Believe Cultist Hired Sharon Killer."

Federici was a well-respected crime reporter who had won the prestigious 1969 George Polk Award, for metropolitan reporting. In a recent conversation with the author, Federici confirmed the accuracy of what he reported in the *Daily News*. Federici recalls being summoned from his vacation to travel to Los Angeles to write about the murders, and that the agent that provided information was a federal Drug Enforcement Administration agent. I asked why the federal drug agent would have known about the Tate murder investigation. (The DEA was established in 1973; in 1969 it would still have been known as BNDD.) "They were involved in this thing right from the beginning," he replied. "The BNDD was part of the whole thing. There was a whole task force." Federici got his law enforcement contacts in New York to get in touch with law enforcement in Los Angeles and ask them to help Federici. Hence the meeting with the federal drug agent. I asked, "The material in the article reflects what you learned from the federal drug officer?"

"Yes," he replied.

The Federici-McGovern story began, "Beautiful Sharon Tate and four others are believed to have been the victims of an assassin hired by a member of a cult which met regularly for sex-drug rituals in her posh Bel Air home, authorities disclosed today.

"It is believed that the principal targets of the hired killer were Sharon, a brown-eyed movie-TV actress, and her former fiancé, hair stylist Jay Sebring. Sebring, a karate enthusiast who held a brown belt, had been feuding with another cultist over a girl.

"Existence of the cult—whose members include top Hollywood personalities and show business executives—was revealed as detectives investigated the tangled, bizarre events of the group's last evening, which ended with the brutal torture murders."

Tell of Whips, Chains

"Discovered in the death house was an assortment of the cult's tools—including black leather masks, whips, ropes, and chains, investigators said.

"Outside in the driveway, in the trunk of Sebring's back 1966 Porsche was a quantity of cocaine, LSD, marijuana and methedrine, known as speed, it was said.

"Police said that the killer may have been inducted recently into the cult and hired by one of the members.

"He is believed to be one of the weirdos and freaks invited by thrill-seekers who call themselves The Swingers, to participate in the rites of the club.

About Fifty Members

"The club has a permanent membership of nearly 50 but was increased with the admittance of strangers picked up at exclusive Hollywood discotheques by Sharon's crowd.

"The group, a throwback to the Hollywood of another era, drew its inspiration from the fantasy world here of the '30s.

"Sharon, 26, was an enthusiastic dancer at two of the inner circle clubs, the Candy Store and the Factory. Only members are admitted. When Sharon wasn't accompanied by her husband of 20 months, film director Roman Polanski, 35, she attended with any of a number of friends."

A follow-up story in the *Daily News* of August 17, by another reporter, had the following text: "A day after [Polanski arrived at Los Angeles International Airport] a source close to the investigation declared that here had been a 'wild party' attended by some of 'the biggest freaks and weirdos' in Hollywood. What's more, probers said Sharon and the other four might have been victims of an assassin hired by a member of the cult that met regularly in the Polanski home for sex-drug rituals." (During the trial in 1970 I became acquainted with Mike McGovern, who was continuing to cover the case for the *Daily News*. He filled me in on the federal source and circumstances of the information he and Federici had received in the LA restaurant. He also said they had been told by the federal narcotics agent that black hoods were found in the house, and some sort of black aprons shaped like a downpointed ace of spades.)

The swirl was swirling.

Another Early Theory

There was another early theory on the killings from my friend, the poet Allen Katzman, who was editor of the underground newspaper, *The East Village Other*. I had finished recording my album, *Sanders' Truckstop*, for Reprise Records, and was about to go out to Los Angeles to plan its promotion just after the murders occurred. Katzman had been in Los Angeles right after the horrible events, and then returned to New York City, where he told me excitedly about some things he had heard about the killings from Dennis Hopper.

Hopper, one of the stars of the recently released *Easy Rider*, was on top of the film world at the time of the murders. He was living with Michelle Phillips of the Mamas and the Papas. In the fall of 1970, he and Michelle were actually married, though only for a few days.

Allen Katzman was in San Francisco the weekend of the murders, and decided to go to Los Angeles right away as the guest of Los Angeles *Free Press* publisher Art Kunkin. Hopper called Kunkin and offered to supply the inside story of the killings. Kunkin and Katzman met with Hopper at the Columbia Pictures studios. They then went to a restaurant, and Hopper explained that he and Michelle Phillips were then living together, and as Katzman described in his autobiography, *The Perfect Agent: An Autobiography of the Sixties*, "through her [Michelle] he had recently been caught in the maelstrom of the Tate murders."

"He explained that the four murder victims had been involved in a sado-maso club run out of Mama Cass's house. A coke dealer had 'burned' Sebring and Frykowski for a large amount of money, and as revenge he was kidnapped by them, taken to Mama Cass's where in front of 25 prominent rock and movie stars he was 'stripped, whipped and buggered.'" Hopper implied his source was Michelle Phillips. After that, the tale went, vengeance occurred.

A. E. Hotchner quoted Terry Melcher, in a biography of Melcher's mother, Doris Day: "I hadn't been in the house since I moved out, but I had presumed that the murders had something to do with the weird films Polanski had made, and the equally weird people who were hanging around that house. I knew they had been making a lot of homemade sadomasochistic-porno movies there with quite a few recognizable Hollywood faces in them." His source was Michelle Phillips, whom he had been dating during 1969 following his break-up with Candice Bergen. (Michelle Phillips has denied telling Melcher about any "sadomasochistic-porno movies . . . with quite a few recognizable Hollywood faces in them.")

The police examined allegations that residents at 10050 Cielo Drive were into collecting humans from Sunset Strip and from various clubs in the area for casual partying at the estate. It was thought initially that the murders might be the result of one or more of these pickups "freaking out."

There were other swirly theories that blew forth into the horrified yet eager curiosity of newspapers, columnists, and TV reporters. There was speculation from Frykowski's friends that it had been done by the Polish secret police, who took a plane from Los Angeles to Rome right after the crimes, in reprisal for Polanski's defection from Poland.

The LA County coroner, Thomas Noguchi, after his autopsies, suggested that the murders could have come about from a "death ritual." On August 15, the *Los Angeles Times* reported that detectives were looking into the possibility that the deaths related to gambling debts owed by one of the victims. A well-known gossip columnist of the era speculated it was some highly placed Satanists who had threatened Polanski during the filming of *Rosemary's Baby*.

Writer Jerzy Kosinski told me, during the later trial, that well-known publisher Bennett Cerf held to the theory that the murders were committed by right-wing Polish nationalists who felt Polanski was a traitor to his country.

Or how about the rubicund necks? Sharon and Roman friend Michael Sarne suggested to a reporter during these fear-spattered days: "We're deciding that there's a group of nasty people with short haircuts who carry their service revolvers around with them and hate the rich and leisured class. A large part of our civilization is being taken over by rednecks."

Meanwhile, *Rosemary's Baby* producer William Castle was in San Francisco when he first heard of the murders. He headed to Los Angeles, arriving after Polanski had flown in from London and was residing, as Castle later described in his autobiography, "incommunicado at Paramount Studios, hidden from the ugly glare of publicity. Security guards surrounded the studio."

Castle was brought to where Polanski was residing. "Alone and stunned," as Castle described the scene, "Roman stared at me. Handing me a piece of paper, he spoke in a monotone, 'Print *PIG*.'

"Confused, I looked at him, 'Why, Roman?'

"'Do as I ask, please.' I printed the word. 'Again, please, Bill, again!'

"Pausing, I looked at him. Then his eyes welled with tears. 'Sharon, my poor Sharon. . . . And our baby.'"

Roman had already begun his personal investigation into the murders, trying to determine who possibly might have written the word *PIG* on the front door.

The photographer Shahrokh Hatami recalls how one day Polanski, when he was being guarded at Paramount, "came to the Chateau Marmont, and took me in his limousine, which Paramount had put at his disposal, and took me to the villa [the Cielo Drive house] with him. I didn't want to go with him; when I was there, I couldn't listen to what he was explaining about what had happened there. Because I was totally dumb and blocked in myself, to hear him. . . . to go to the place and show it to me, 'oh that's what has happened, that's where she was putting her hands on the wall,' describing what had happened.

"But, he was thinking, I think, to bring somebody to the crime scene who could break down, for instance. That . . . somehow when he's bringing me to the house, he's explaining to me what happened, showing, oh that's her hand on this floor, this is her hand there on that wall, he's explaining to me, and I'm thinking that he's watching me with the corner of his eye, but I couldn't hear what he was saying, because as I told you I didn't want to know anything about it."

Hatami agreed with me when I suggested Roman was trying set him up. Hatami: "that I was one of the killers."

On August 13, the day of the funerals, Roman moved from Paramount into Michael Sarne's beach house in the Malibu Colony where he stayed a few days. Sarne was at the time directing the movie *Myra Breckinridge*. Nearby residents of the Malibu Colony put together a petition, with language such as: "The presence in your house of Mr. Polanski endangers our lives."

Shortly thereafter Polanski moved to Richard Sylbert's more secluded beach house on Old Malibu Road, which was built on stilts. Sylbert was very solicitous of Roman's well-being, making him breakfast and in general "mothering" him. "I didn't let on, though," Polanski later wrote, "not even to him, that I was conducting my own private investigation."

The Tate, Folger, and Sebring Funerals

"Stars Attend Services for Slain Actress Sharon Tate—Rites Held for 3 Others," was the headline in the August 14 article in the *Los Angeles Times*, by staff writer Dial Torgerson, on the funerals on Wednesday, August 13, for the victims. In graceful, threnodic prose, the article traced how at Holy Cross Cemetery,

Roman Polanski "stared a long moment at the silver casket, then leaned over and kissed it in a farewell to his wife, Sharon Tate."

And how "Across the city, at an El Monte Church, six teenagers carried the body of their friend, eighteen-year-old Steven Parent, to a waiting hearse" while in Portola Valley, a suburb of San Francisco, a Requiem Mass was held for Abigail Folger.

At Forest Lawn Memorial Park, at the Wee Kirk o' the Heather, a gathering of friends and film stars gathered for services in honor of Jay Sebring.

Given the headlines, the article was careful to note that "investigators denied other rumors that evidence of weird sex rites were found in Miss Tate's home."

Attending Sharon Tate's funeral in the chapel at the summit of Holy Cross Cemetery in Culver City were actors such as Kirk Douglas, Stuart Whitman, Warren Beatty, James Coburn, Yul Brynner, and Peter Sellers. In the front of the chapel sat Paul and Doris Tate, Roman Polanski, and Sharon's two sisters, Patricia and Debra. The family sat quietly as the Reverend Peter O'Reilly of Good Shepherd Church in Beverly Hills started a brief service.

Father O'Reilly noted how Sharon "was a fine person, and we were in no small measure devoted to her." Doris Tate, wearing black gloves, placed her arm around Roman Polanski when he cried, and patted his head.

Mother Doris retained her outward calm until Father O'Reilly, when the service was completed, went up to the casket and said: "Goodbye, Sharon, and may the Angels welcome you to heaven, and the martyrs guide your way." Doris then broke into sobs, and when the family stood to say a final farewell in front of the closed casket, Roman helped Mrs. Tate to her feet.

In a later article, Mrs. Tate recalled an event that occurred at the funeral that helped her keep her composure. She approached Sharon's closed casket. "I went over to kiss it," she said, "and I heard her say as plain as if she was standing beside me. 'Mother, that's not me.' That's what saved my sanity and that's what gave me strength, because I do believe in life after death. I feel Sharon's presence here in the house and I am certain that, somewhere, some day, we will be together."

At the close of the service Roman kissed the casket, and the funeral director handed Doris Tate five pink roses from a large array of roses and carnations atop the casket, after which the family left the chapel. Thereafter the 150 or so attending the service began to file out. Flowers sent by friends were piled on the lawn in front of the chapel.

Sebring's funeral, two hours later, drew an overflow crowd of fellow hairstylists and a number of Sebring's customers who had become close friends.

Sharon's Funeral at the chapel at Holy Cross Cemetery

Among them were Steve McQueen, who delivered a brief eulogy, Henry Fonda, Peter Fonda, Paul Newman, Alex Cord, George Hamilton, and Keely Smith. A friend, Alvin Greenwald, also eulogized Sebring as "an individual human person who earned and deserves the trust and respect of us all."

"Many mourners—men and women—wept openly as they were ushered from the flower-banked Chapel," the article concluded. "In a black limousine in a funeral procession, three beautiful young women sat sobbing, their mini skirted legs stretched before them, crossed and bare footed, on the lowered jump seat."

The Police Face a Difficult Investigation

The police investigation was complex and fact-packed. Officers put together reports of strange noises, gunshots, and screams from the nearby canyons and hillsides during the night. In spite of the "ritual" appearance of the crime scene, drugs were the early focus. After clearing the caretaker William Garretson, police concentrated on four individuals with whom Wojtek Frykowski had been connected in the drug trade, and who had been visitors to Cielo Drive during the summer before Sharon returned from London. An LAPD lieutenant polygraphed all four, and they too were cleared.

The American flag that lay stretched across the divan in the murder room was taken by the police as possible evidence.

Among the hundreds the Los Angeles Police Department interviewed in the days after the murders was Jay Sebring's on again/off again girlfriend (and the future wife of Polanski's set designer, Richard Sylbert), Sharmagne Leland-St. John. The author asked Leland-St. John about her interview, and she replied by e-mail, "I was 'grilled' for 6 hours. Apparently at that point they were following the 'witchcraft lead' and some asshole told them I was a witch! I was a suspect because of the ritualistic aspects of the murder, the fact that I was Jay's girlfriend, the fact that I had spoken to him that afternoon." Also interviewed by the police was rock star Jim Morrison. Why is unknown.

Meanwhile, money hunger prevailed as quickly the movies in which Sharon Tate had performed were reissued. *Valley of the Dolls* went into twelve theaters in the Los Angeles area, with Mrs. Polanski receiving top billing. Also showing up in theaters was *The Fearless Vampire Killers,* starring Sharon and Roman Polanski. And also resuscitated was a movie made in 1966, called *Mondo Hollywood,* a portion of which was devoted to Jay Sebring as hairstyler of the stars. Also in a brief section in *Mondo Hollywood* was Bobby Beausoleil, who portrayed Cupid addressing his bow. His role in the film was the origin of Beausoleil's nickname, Cupid.

Void-Scan at the Murder House

Two lawyer friends of Jay Sebring, Harry Weiss and Peter Knecht, hired a Dutch psychic named Peter Hurkos to void-scan the murder scene in order to try to pick up vibrations regarding the identity of the killers. Accordingly, on Sunday, August 17, Peter Hurkos, accompanied by an assistant, Roman Polanski, a writer named Tommy Thompson, and a photographer named Julian Wasser went to the house at 10050 Cielo Drive to enable the psychic to undertake a death-scan. It was John Phillips, the songwriter, who talked Roman Polanski into allowing Hurkos into the house. Mr. Hurkos crouched down in the blood-stained living room, picking up the vibes, while Roman Polanski gave Mr. Thompson a running narrative about the crime scene. The photographer took Polaroid snapshots and some color photos of the event. The entire event was written up for a photo spread in *Life* magazine several weeks later.

After his void-scan, Mr. Hurkos announced that "three men killed Sharon Tate and her four friends—and I know who they are. I have identified the killers to the police and told them that these three men must be stopped soon. Otherwise, they will kill again."

(Later, during the Manson trial, I spoke to the photographer, Julian Wasser, about Polanski's visit to the murder house. He said he had asked Polanski why there was a portable Sony video camera with a battery pack in the house. Polanski replied that it was used in *Rosemary's Baby*. There were also video tapes lying around, said Wasser, and a video viewer by the TV, but not hooked up.)

In Sharon's bedroom, Polanski opened an armoire that was fairly stuffed with a bassinet, some diapers, formula bottles, and books such as *Naming Your Baby, Let's Have Healthy Children*, and *How to Teach Your Baby to Read*. There was also a group of photos of Sharon, taken in the front yard. Polanski then paused to cry at length.

The *Life* magazine article was titled "Roman Polanski Comes Home to the Scene of the Sharon Tate Murders—a Tragic Trip to the House on the Hill." One whole page was taken up with a full color shot of Roman wearing a white pullover and sockless white loafers sitting on a porch chair, with the stone walkway spattered with blood, the word *PIG* clearly visible on the white front door, with dark swatches of fingerprint dusting still in evidence on the wood above the door knob.

According to Barbara Leaming in her *Polanski, The Filmmaker as Voyeur: A Biography,* "After his first visit to Cielo Drive, with the *Life* crew, he returned several times as if there might be some explanation hidden there for what had happened. He had moved from the apartment at the Paramount Studios to Robert Evans' house, which had been surrounded with round-the-clock armed protection. Polanski was making every effort to keep his suspicions and his investigations to himself, as he told the police, largely because he continued to believe it was someone he and Sharon knew."

The day that Roman visited Cielo with the *Life* writer and Hurkos, he took his personal possessions away from there, and gave everything of Sharon's, including her Ferrari and estate, to her father.

Monday, August 18, was Roman Polanski's thirty-sixth birthday.

Polanski's Press Conference, Plus Sleuthing into Voodoo and Dope

August 19, Roman Polanski conducted a press conference at the Beverly Wilshire Hotel in Los Angeles wherein he stoutly deprecated the lurid news accounts of the murder house: "A lot of newsmen who for a selfish reason write unbearable for me horrible things about my wife. All of you know how beautiful she was and very often I read and heard statements that she was one of the most, if not the most beautiful woman of the world but only a few of you know how good she was. She was vulnerable." He decried public speculation about orgies and dope, acknowledging the occasional smoking, as in almost every house in Hollywood, of cannabis. He denied that his wife used drugs and that there had been any marital rift, saying: "I can tell you that in the last few months as much as the last few years I spent with her were the only time of true happiness in my life."

In spite of Polanski's defense of his wife, nothing could prevent speculation that the alleged lifestyles of the victims brought on the carnage, with the result that the catch-phrase, "live freaky, die freaky" entered the language.

Shortly after his press conference, Mr. Polanski and John Phillips flew to Jamaica to continue an investigation into drugs and voodoo, according to a reporter named Min Yee. At the end of the month, an LAPD polygraph expert also went to Jamaica, where he spent about a week investigating. According to Barbara Leaming's biography of Polanski: "He flew to Jamaica, the West Indies, with John Phillips to scout locations for *The Day of the Dolphin*, but also to find out about Frykowski's drug connections there. The trip, however, was abortive on both counts. Polanski dropped his film project, unable to concentrate sufficiently to work. He had found no clues."

It was felt that possibly the Canadian dope dealers involved in that Jamaican grass-trafficking were also involved in a Jamaican voodoo group that was somehow connected with the crimes. According to the reporter Min Yee, he and John Phillips went to a voodoo astrologer, who informed them that midnight August 8–9 was a fitting time for a voodoo sacrifice. There was also indication that one of the voodoo adepts had threatened Wojtek Frykowski a few days prior to his death.

One girlfriend of Sebring later alleged that John and Michelle Phillips were into a certain kind of voodoo.

Polanski departed Jamaica the end of August, to New York City. He stayed at the Essex House on Central Park South, where he had purportedly resided during the NY shoots of *Rosemary's Baby*. And, according to Barbara Leaming's biography of Polanski, "was seen about town with friends: lunching at P. J. Clarke's with columnist Steve Brandt, visiting Warren Beatty at the Delmonico." Richard Sylbert was with him in New York City. He then flew to London, "but the press was full of the killings—and Polanski," so he returned to "California, moving into Richard Sylbert's Malibu beach house. Sylbert found him distraught."

Here's one woman's recollection of a visit to Sylbert's Malibu beach house while Polanski was staying there: "As I recall it was on the Old Malibu Road. Which is different than the Colony Road. He and Roman shared the house. I went there only once (after the murders) with Carol G . . . and Mary D . . . , Roman and Warren. I believe we had all been at some club and then went to Milton F. Kreis (drugstore and luncheonette) which was in the Beverly Wilshire and a favorite place to have breakfast after clubbing. I was hoping to see Sylbert, but he didn't return home.

"Mary, whom we used to refer to as 'Mary Mattress,' was having sex with Roman on the living room floor, Warren and Carol had gone off into a front bedroom, and I had stayed in the kitchen at some sort of a breakfast bar which gave a bird's eye view of the living room. I was a little surprised that Roman a recent widower was so casually fucking this girl whom he had just met. Warren was trying to get it into Carol who was teasing him but nothing more. She came out and said she was leaving. She was our driver that evening. A tussle broke out with Warren trying to get me into the bedroom, and when I finally extricated myself from his attempt, I told Mary to put her clothes on and meet us in the car or she'd have to walk home. I remember she kept saying to Roman, 'Oh, you're just like a little teddy bear!'"

A faithful memory?

Polanski's Secret/Not-So-Secret Investigation

As we have noted, after Roman Polanski passed his lie detector test, he began a secret investigation of his own. He worked for a few weeks looking for the culprit among his acquaintances, mingling among them casually, trying to keep them unaware of his sleuthing.

Polanski was provided with the prescription of the pair of myopic glasses found in the house. He used a professional lens-measuring device, with which he stealthily checked out his friends' glasses, looking for the mate to the fire-starting glasses Manson had left as a deceptive clue in the house.

Polanski: "And when Bruce Lee told me he'd lost his glasses, I suspected him. So I accompanied him to the opticians to see if his glasses matched those found in the villa after the crime." (From *Roman Polanski: Interviews*, 1984, p. 108, an interview with Franz-Olivier Giesbert.)

Polanski also did handwriting analyses of friends. He was struck by the word *PIG* written by the killers on the front door of the house—it was Sharon's blood-type.

Polanski became suspicious of singer/composer John Phillips, with whose wife, Michelle Phillips, Mr. Polanski had conducted a one-night stand in London apparently while Sharon was filming *The Thirteen Chairs* in Rome. Polanski wondered if Phillips had suffered a jealous flip-out and took part in the murders. In his autobiography, Mr. Phillips wrote that his wife, from whom he was separated, "had also had an affair with Beatty in London, too. I had phoned Warren once and . . . I warned him, in a drunken, stoned stupor, to lay off other guys' wives or he'd get himself seriously injured. Warren must have related that conversation to Roman, who must have been impressed with my anger and potential for violence."

One night Polanski entered Phillips's Bel Air garage and apparently chemically checked his Jaguar for bloodstains, with no results. He found a machete in the trunk. Another time he was alone in Phillips's Rolls convertible and rifled through Phillips's Gucci diary. "I noted that all the entries, from first page to last, were printed in block capitals. What chilled me was that the lettering bore a distinct resemblance to the word 'PIG' that had been scrawled in blood on the door . . . I quickly photocopied some sample pages and sent them, together with photographs of the 'PIG' inscription, to a handwriting expert in New York." This bore no results.

The conclusion of Roman's investigation of Phillips, according to John Phillips, occurred at the Malibu beach house of Michael Sarne, for whom Mr. Phillips was composing music for his movie *Myra Breckinridge*. Phillips remembers there was a full moon, which would have meant it was the very day that just a few miles away the Manson spores were burying the remains of one of their victims, stuntman Shorty Shea.

Phillips: "We were all helping to prepare dinner. Roman was chopping vegetables with a cleaver. I was sitting on the couch, still in my bathing trunks. Suddenly I felt a powerful hand clutch my hair from behind and yank my head back with a violent jerk. I felt the razor-sharp edge of the cleaver pressed against my throat. I recognized the shape and strength in the hand from countless arm-wrestling bouts. Roman grunted.

'Did you kill Sharon? Did you?' "

Mr. Phillips countered, no, indeed he had not.

The extensive carnage on Cielo Drive would have meant that the killers or killer would have likely had blood on their clothes, hands, and arms, so that they likely would have smirched blood upon the seats and steering wheels of their automobiles. The luminol chemiluminescence reaction is responsible for the glow of lightsticks. The reaction is used by criminologists to detect traces of blood at crime scenes. In this test, luminol powder ($C_8H_7O_3N_3$) is mixed with hydrogen peroxide (H_2O_2) and a hydroxide (e.g., KOH) in a bottle. The luminol solution is applied where blood might be found. The iron from the hemoglobin in the blood serves as a catalyst for the chemiluminescence reaction that causes luminol to glow, so a blue glow is produced when the solution is applied where there is blood. The blue glow lasts for about 30 seconds before it fades.

Polanski acquired a container of Luminol, then surreptitiously swabbed the automobiles of certain friends to check for blood. One night he was going into John Phillips's garage with the Luminol, when two officers came to check out what he was up to; Polanski said he'd left a bag in Phillips's automobile, and the officers let him off the hook.

On September 2, a well-known broadcaster, Rona Barrett, asserted on a Metromedia station serving Los Angeles, that Roman Polanski had received $50,000 from *Life* magazine for the photos and story from the murder house. The charge was hotly denied by Polanski and his attorneys. The owner of the murder house, Rudy Altobelli, became so outraged over the alleged $50,000 that he sued Roman Polanski and the estate of Sharon Tate for around $668,000 dollars, charging "trespassory conduct" in that Abigail Folger and Wojtek Frykowski had dwelled in a house rented for one family residency. He also sued for back rent, damages (lots of blood), and emotional distress.

Mr. Peter Folger, Abigail Folger's father, according to a number of people interviewed, initiated an intense investigation into the matter. Roman Polanski was assisted by several famous LA private investigators. "Polanski worked on it himself. But Polanski didn't realize it was hippies. He was working in his own area," reported one of his investigators. For a while, Polanski was protected constantly by two armed bodyguards. In all, at least ten private investigators in Los Angeles were used extensively throughout the investigation of the case, both by private parties and by the district attorney.

The Reward

Early in September, Peter Sellers, Warren Beatty, Yul Brynner, and others announced the establishment of a reward of $25,000 for the arrest and conviction of the murderers. "We handed the money over to Roman Polanski and his lawyers in the hope that that would bring the killers to justice," stated Mr. Sellers.

Why would Yul Brynner, star of *The King and I*, fork over money to the award fund? Because he was at Mama Cass's for the torment session?

One possible answer was provided by a police photographer named Don Dornan, who a little more than a year later, talked with attorney Paul Fitzgerald. I had heard previously that Don Dornan had copious materials, including police reports, many photos, interviews, hours of tapes, maybe even films, all collected together, perhaps for a book on the murders. Dornan had gone to Inyo County in December of 1969, so I had heard, to take photos for both the sheriff's office and for the LAPD. I later learned that Don Dornan was the brother of the future congressman from Orange County, Bob "B-1 Bomber" Dornan, and that he was well regarded among homicide investigators.

REWARD

$25,000⁰⁰

Roman Polanski and friends of the Polanski family offer to pay a $25,000.00
reward to the person or persons who
furnish information leading to the arrest
and conviction of the murderer or murderers of Sharon Tate, her unborn child,
and the other four victims.

**Information should be sent to
POST OFFICE BOX 60048,
TERMINAL ANNEX,
LOS ANGELES, CALIF. 90069.**

Persons wishing to remain anonymous
should provide sufficient means for later
identification, one method of which is to
tear this newspaper page in half, trans-
mit one half with the information submitted, and save the remaining half for
matching-up later. In the event more
than one person is entitled to the reward,
the reward will be divided equally between them.

Notice of the reward, published in the *Los Angeles Times*, September 10, 1969

So, I asked Paul Fitzgerald to call Mr. Dornan, which he did that evening of December 7, 1970. Dornan confirmed he had become involved in December of 1969 when he went to Inyo County to take photos. He also sold photos, he said, to *Paris Match,* to *Stern,* and to a newspaper in London, among others.

Fitzgerald spoke with Mr. Dornan for about a half hour, after which he provided about a ten-minute rendition of the call. I switched on my tape recorder while Paul was describing the Dornan call, glancing at his notes while he spoke:

"He says that the tapes were found in the closet the next day. He says that there is an underground film club in Hollywood of prominent people; it's like a lending library, they exchange tapes. Polanski did not know who the participants in the films that happened to be in his closet were.

"Apparently he hadn't seen them or hadn't viewed them. . . . The police apparently confronted Polanski about this when he came back. Polanski at the time was working with an ex-cop in a detective agency who got the tapes back from LAPD." Dornan told Fitzgerald that Polanski then obtained money from Yul Brynner, Peter Sellers, and Warren Beatty for the reward.

I asked, "Who obtained the money?

"Polanski and the ex-cop detective agency guy—$25,000 for the reward. He's an ex-cop, he's an Irishman and he talks with a brogue." Quicksand.

Colonel Tate's Investigation

After the murders, Paul Tate drove his family to Texas for reasons of safety, then he returned to California to put in his retirement papers to the army. The lieutenant-colonel resigned from the service at age forty-six, two weeks prior to his scheduled retirement after over a twenty-year career. He had been stationed at Ft. Baker in Sausalito, California—6th Region Headquarters, Army Air Defense Command. Tate had been involved with protecting Nike-Hercules missile sites. Tate immediately put together a team to investigate the murders.

According to an account the colonel later wrote, he had three men, "all friends from the US Department of Defense," as he later described them, and all seasoned investigators, who gathered at the Tate residence near Los Angeles to help in the colonel's investigation. A person Tate called Guy had been the first to offer sleuth-help. He'd been an FBI agent for twenty years (and not technically in the Department of Defense), plus there was a man named Jake and one named Frankie, who was six foot, eleven inches tall. (It's not known whether these are pseudonyms.)

Colonel Tate worked in subsequent years on a book-length account of his investigation. In September of 1973, a press release was issued from an English publisher, Talmy, Franklin Ltd.: "Shel Talmy today announced his acquisition for Talmy, Franklin Ltd. of the exclusive worldwide publishing rights to Col. Paul J. Tate's personal investigation into his daughter's murder." No such book was ever published. At the time, I called the publisher's New York law firm, and was informed that Colonel Tate was still working on the book. The lawyer would not say that Tate was collaborating with others on the project. My investigator Larry Larsen reported in 1974 that Colonel Tate had formed a security company with LAPD Lieutenant Robert Helder and Los Angeles–based FBI agent Roger "Frenchy" LaJeunesse. Were they assisting in the book project? The record is blank.

There apparently were several versions of Colonel Tate's manuscript. One was located in the 2000s in the hands of the William Morris Endeavor Agency in Los Angeles.

According to Paul Tate's account, his investigation began with a gathering of his team on the same day that former film partner Gene Gutowski defended Polanski at a press conference and also the same day as Polanski's polygraph. The meeting was held at the Tate residence in Palos Verdes. Jake suggested that they follow Polanski and check him out. Guy volunteered to see what Interpol had on Roman, and Frankie was to check on Roman's paper trail.

Later that day the colonel was going through Sharon's check registry looking for suspicious checks. Later, Lieutenant Earl Deemer provided a tape of Polanski's polygraph, which the colonel and two of his team listened to. Jake was on surveillance duty, watching Polanski.

Returning from the Polanski surveillance, Jake reported to Tate's investigators that he had followed Polanski the previous night to John Phillips' Bel Air house. He said he had observed Polanski climb over the gate, and then look within a Rolls-Royce parked near the garage. Then the LAPD showed up, and confronted Polanski just as he was leaving. They checked his ID, and soon he was set free. Jake approached the patrolman writing up the report, who told him that Polanski had claimed he'd left something in Phillips's Rolls, and didn't want to disturb him.

Colonel Tate allegedly paid a surprise visit to Sharon's close friends, Jim Mitchum and Wende Wagner Mitchum. Jimmy told the colonel that Jay Sebring was using a lot of coke. He blamed that on Sharon's pregnancy, that Jay had never expected the marriage to last, and now had lost hope in ever getting back with Sharon.

He further suggested to the colonel that Steve McQueen had cleaned out Jay's house before the arrival of the police. They told Tate about Cass Elliot's friends, Billy Doyle and Pic Dawson, and others, who they said took advantage of Cass. Dawson's father was a diplomat, and Dawson used to light up some marijuana and announce, "diplomatic immunity," because he said he'd smuggled it in in sealed diplomatic pouches. The colonel learned that Wojtek Frykowski had befriended Cass Elliot's friends, and they hung out at Cielo Drive.

Tate then, it is averred, stopped off to see Steve McQueen, who denied cleaning out Jay's house, saying that he had "only made the suggestion." The colonel allegedly chided McQueen for not coming to Sharon's funeral. Colonel Tate also spoke with actor James Coburn, who confirmed there was coke secreted all over Sebring's house. This was shocking to the colonel, who considered Jay like a son to him.

Sebring in Debt

Tate's associate Guy delivered a report on Sebring, noting that he was more than $250,000 in debt. Within the past year, he'd borrowed $6,000 from his dentist, $2,700 from Sharon, and $5,000 from Abigail Folger. Tate wondered if there weren't a debt they had not located.

Tate also had a conversation with Warren Beatty, who returned Tate's call. Beatty recalled the year Paul and Doris had had a bunch of them over for Thanksgiving. That night, after Paul and Doris had gone to bed, Beatty, Jay, and the others stood in the backyard watching for shooting stars. "Someone may have lit a joint, I don't remember. But I do remember we passed that night like so many others—blamelessly. Not like what they're writing in the papers. Jay was a good man; the best friend a person could have."

The colonel apparently then received an anonymous telephone call telling him to contact actress Candy Bergen, who, when Tate spoke with her, was still mightily afraid. Candy Bergen tipped off Colonel Tate to the putative buggering of Billy Doyle. In her version, according to the colonel's later account, Billy Doyle had gone to Jamaica to acquire a significant amount of drugs for Wojtek and Abigail, Bergen continued, and when the money didn't arrive from Los Angeles, Doyle returned in anger over the botched deal. With a gun, Doyle, the story went, stormed to Cielo Drive, and threatened to kill Wojtek. Jay was on hand, and with Wojtek's help, overcame Doyle and took him to Woodrow Wilson Drive to Mama Cass's house, where they tied him to a tree, then buggered him in front of an audience of twelve. Doyle threatened to get even.

Told that, Tate and his crew decided to locate Mr. Doyle, and contacted Lieutenant Helder, who told them Doyle had passed a polygraph. Tate wanted to find out for himself, and Helder suggested he try Toronto.

Tate and the ex-FBI agent, Guy, flew to Toronto. They had a photo of Doyle, and spotted him leaving a business owned by his father. They conducted Doyle to a bar, and questioned him.

Doyle denied threatening Wojtek. Then why, Tate wanted to know, was everybody pointing the finger at him? Doyle: "This mess was started by John Phillips. As I'm sure you know, I was living with Cass Elliot until a few weeks before the murders. I love Cass. We have a lot in common. After the murders, John convinced her that I killed all those people. She believed it and told the police a bunch of false things about me. She has since apologized."

"Why did Phillips have it out for you? Did you ball his wife?" asked one of the team.

"No, but Roman did. Has anyone considered that John did this for revenge?" Doyle also allegedly said, "Michelle Phillips is a cobra. I couldn't be less interested in her. As for John, he's a violent fellow who liked to settle all of his arguments with Cass by hitting her. I stopped that, and he's never liked me since."

Then the investigator allegedly suggested, "Tell us about the time that Wojtek tied you to a tree and balled you in the ass." Doyle replied, "I, uh, he didn't. Wojtek invited me up to the house to do some mescaline. I only remember a bit of the party. I can't give you the facts. I was unconscious. But I wasn't sore there the next day, and I was sore everywhere else."

More from Doyle from the quicksand of memory: "Wojtek and I had been drinking a lot of champagne and we got into a disagreement. He was a Communist and bountifully anti-Nazi. I made the mistake of saying that Asiatic communism was the worst political system in the world. Wojtek became hysterical, saying the Nazis were the worst. After that, I remember Wojtek said he'd given me an overdose; not maliciously, just to kind of get back to me as a joke. I was really high and needed something to bring me down. He brought me some pills that he said were Sharon's—very mild sedatives. After I took about eight of them, he told me they were something else, and started laughing. I went crazy, throwing things and such. They called my friend Charles Tacot. He took me to Cass's house and chained me to a tree for eight hours."

Doyle denied dealing drugs. He said he bragged about having pounds of coke because all kinds of famous people were having parties and there'd be plenty of naked girls, and Mr. Doyle wanted to ball them all, using cocaine as a lure.

"Was this sort of orgy occurring on Cielo Drive?" Colonel Tate asked.

Doyle replied, "Only when Gibby and Sharon were out of town, and then only for the five-week period that Wojtek had run of the house."

Doyle claimed that Abigail was very much in love with Frykowski, but would have left him if he didn't marry her.

Visiting Cass Elliot

Next, Colonel Tate visited Cass Elliot at her two-story Cape Cod on Woodrow Wilson Drive. Cass and the colonel sat in rocking chairs on the front porch. Cass told the colonel she had met Sharon through publicist Steve Brandt, who had done publicity work for Sharon. Elliot said that Brandt had planned parties for Michelle and John. "He must have invited Sharon and Roman to one of them," she said. "After that, Roman was up at their house a lot more than Sharon. He didn't like me so much after I found out about him and Michelle."

Paul asked, "Did you tell John?" to which Cass replied, "No. By that point, we had enough problems in the group. John would have turned it around and made it my fault. He did find out though. Michelle told him during an argument."

Tate then asked, "What made you think Doyle and Dawson were the killers?" Elliot answered that it wasn't she, but John Phillips and Steve Brandt who had made the accusation. Both said that the "PIG" on the door was actually "PIC," for Pic Dawson.

"John blamed me for bringing killers into our group, blamed me for Sharon's death, and said the police were going to arrest me as an accomplice. I was mortified. They completely convinced me that my daughter and I would be murdered next. At that point, I would have said anything to get them behind bars."

While the colonel was talking with Cass, his associate Frankie visited John Phillips. Phillips told Frankie he was sure that Doyle and Dawson were the killers. He said he spent a lot of time on Cielo Drive while Sharon was in Italy. And that when Folger was on hand, things were mild, but when she was away, there'd be around twenty naked partyers doing drugs supplied by Doyle and Dawson.

"What else?" the colonel asked Frankie. Frankie replied that it was difficult to keep from smiling when Phillips denied using drugs, because the odor of pot was in the air. Frankie recalled Phillips's rap. "First, it's Dawson and Doyle, then he says it's the Mafia and he's next on their murder list—hit men have been following him. Then he babbled about drugs, psychics, and some guy out in the desert that steals your soul. I couldn't keep it all straight."

The Colonel Surveils Cielo Drive

It is alleged that Colonel Tate conducted nighttime surveillance of 10050 Cielo Drive from a cul-de-sac located above the driveway. There were lots of visitors. Then one night around midnight, there were two headlights of two motorcycles coming up Benedict Canyon. The two motorcycles stopped at 10050. There were four riders. The colonel couldn't tell the men from the women due to the long hair on all of them. They began scaling the chain link fence, but then two guard dogs leaped toward them, and after a few more minutes, both motorcycles headed north on Benedict Canyon toward the San Fernando Valley.

Colonel Tate allegedly followed the bikes as they wended across the Valley, and then down Santa Susanna Pass road to Spahn Ranch. Did this actually occur?

According to Gene Gutowski, Roman gave the Ferrari to Paul Tate, because Sharon had hoped someday to purchase him a sports car.

Tight Lid on the Police Investigation

Meanwhile, after the initial release of information about the crimes, there was a tight lid kept on information about the police investigation. The LAPD sent only a three-line homicide report to the State Bureau of Criminal Identification and Investigation (CII)—barely complying with the law that requires information about crimes to be collected with the CII. After a month of investigation, law enforcement considered the three possible causes of the Cielo Drive crimes either a residential robbery, a drug grudge, or a "freak-out" of some sort.

First Homicide Progress Report

The *First Homicide Investigation Progress Report* was a thirty-two-page typed document tracing the crimes, the victims, and various suspects, covering the investigation from August 9 (the discovery of the bodies) through the end of

August. There were a number of addenda to the report, including Number 9: "Witnesses. All witnesses are indexed and given interview numbers, starting with one. Investigating officers have included as a part of this report interview numbers 1 through 191 as addendum number 9. Investigating officers are in the process of checking these statements for inconsistencies. We are also plotting the exact location of persons hearing either screams or gunfire on the night or morning of either 8–8/9–69. At the time of this report this phase of the investigation is incomplete and the results will be included in future progress reports."

Showing how exacting the investigation had to be were the following paragraphs in the *First Homicide Investigation Progress Report* regarding the .22-caliber pistol, pieces of whose walnut gun grips were found in the hallway by Roman's steamer trunks, bearing blood type O on them:

"Parent, Frykowski, and Sebring were shot with a caliber 22 long rifle bullet. The probable weapon used was a high standard . . . long horn revolver. It has a 9 1/2 inch barrel and a 15" overall length. It has a nine shot capacity and has a blue steel finish, the catalogue number is 9399. The manufacturer has been contacted and states this weapon has been in production since February of 1967. He has contacted thirty-three west coast jobbers for sale numbers and sales information on all 9399 models. A complete list of all 9399 models sold in Los Angeles since 1967 has been received and is included as addendum number 5 in this report.

"Special Investigations Unit, Administrative Detective Bureau, is in the process of checking all model 9399 sold within a driving radius of two hours of Los Angeles. The results of this investigation will be included in future progress reports."

The report mentions the horn-rimmed glasses left as a false clue by Manson: "The horn rimmed glasses which were found just east of the trunks which were located in the living room near the archway, which separates the entry hall from the living room. Scientific Investigation Division firearms section is attempting to locate the manufacturer of those glasses. Their investigation will be included in future progress reports."

As for the Buck knife lost by Susan Atkins, the *First Homicide Investigation Progress Report* lists it as a clue of "paramount importance": "A 'Buck' clasp-type knife found under the seat cushion of an overstuffed chair, which was located in the living room seven feet south of the north wall of the living room and four feet east of the west wall of the living room. This chair is marked 'C' in addendum number 7."

Second Homicide Progress Report

The nine-page *Second Homicide Investigation Progress Report* covered the period September 1 till October 22, 1969. Like the first report, this one was also directed to Lieutenant Robert J. Helder, supervisor of investigations, robbery-homicide division. This second report focused here and there, but showed an investigation that was going nowhere as it continued plumbing the Los Angeles dope scene.

On October 15, 1969, a letter was sent to the LAPD crime lab listing the names and addresses of twelve humans who had recently ordered replacement grips "that would fit our Double Nine revolver."

On October 17, assistant LA Police Chief Robert Houghton told a press conference that the initial part of the Tate investigation was over and that now the police would backtrack over the entire case and compare notes. More than four hundred police interviews had been conducted to that date.

At the end of forty days of intensive investigation, the chief possible motives for the Cielo Drive homicides were thought to be a drug burn or a drug freak-out.

LaBianca Homicide Reports

The two teams of LAPD detectives that investigated the murders of Leno and Rosemary LaBianca completed two homicide investigation progress reports, both directed to Lieutenant P. B. LePage, supervisor of investigations, robbery-homicide division.

I will not highlight the differences in style between the Tate and LaBianca investigations, but by the twenty-three-page second progress report for the LaBianca case, covering the time period of September 1 till October 15, 1969, Manson was listed as a suspect in the LaBianca case:

"MANSON, CHARLES. Investigators contacted Los Angeles County Sheriff's Homicide Bureau requesting information on murders that were similar to the LaBianca murder. Deputy Charles Guenther informed investigators that he and his partner, Sgt. Whiteley, were presently investigating a homicide that occurred at 964 N. Old Topanga Canyon Road, Topanga (Malibu area), on 7–25-/26–69. The victim, Gary Hinman, lived alone at the above location. In that case the words 'Political Piggy' were written on the wall of the victim's residence in his own blood.

"There are two suspects presently in the Sheriff's custody for this murder. The first, Robert Kenneth Beausoleil, male, caucasian, 21 years; and the second suspect, Susan Denise Atkins, female, caucasian, 21 years; is presently being held in Inyo County on another charge. A hold has been placed on her for murder by Los Angeles County Sheriff's Department."

The homicide report goes on to state, based on information supplied by Beausoleil's pregnant girlfriend, Kitty Lutesinger, that she had been "living with a group of 30 to 40 hippies and motorcycle riders (Satan Slaves) on the Spahn

Ranch in Devonshire Division. She informed investigators, and it was confirmed by other members of her group, that the leader of the people living on the ranch was Charles Manson. Manson was known as 'Jesus Christ' and 'God and the Devil' by the people living on the ranch. . . .

"The Sheriff's crime lab has established that the victim's blood was used to write the words ["Political Piggy" on Hinman's wall]. Investigators believe it is noteworthy that this murder, which occurred on July 26, 1969 was followed by two other murders, to wit Tate on August 8, 1969 and LaBianca on August 10, 1969. All three murders have the unique characteristic of the suspect using the victims' blood to write on the wall. This characteristic takes on a greater significance in that in each instance the words make reference to 'pig' in one form or another. Other similarities between the Hinman and LaBianca murders were the placing of a pillow over the victim's face. . . . Although Beausoleil was in custody at the time of the LaBianca murder, Atkins had not yet been apprehended."

Patti Tate Taunted at New School

Sharon's sister Patti Tate, having moved with her family during the summer to Palos Verdes, near Los Angeles, enrolled in a new school. She was said to have recounted how one day that fall some classmates were gathered around a magazine whose cover bore the headline, "Sex, Sadism, Celebrities—The Sharon Tate Orgies." All of a sudden the classmates, according to the account, began to hurl questions: "Did you go to the orgies? How many guys did you fuck? Did your sister really do it with dead people and animals?"

The issue in question, the November 1969 issue of *Pageant,* was probably available in October or even September. The article, "Those Sharon Tate Orgies," was written anonymously, the magazine alleged "by an actor-friend of Sharon Tate, the man who introduced Sharon to Jay Sebring" and was a neighbor to 10050 Cielo Drive, but "because of concern for the safety of his family, he must remain anonymous." Whereas the article does contain considerable occult assertions regarding Sebring, and states that "Sharon was a student of black magic, voodoo and the occult arts," there is nothing about orgies, or "doing it" with dead people or animals. The apparent taunting goes to show the climate of rampant speculation and fear during the months following the deaths.

Chapter 15

The Manson Group Keeps Killing and Moves to the High Desert Near Death Valley

Robert Beausoleil's attempt to blame the Gary Hinman murder on the Black Panthers—by writing "Political Piggy" in blood on Hinman's wall, and then painting, also in blood, a "panther" paw by the writing, and then Sadie/Susan Atkins's horrific "PIG," written again in blood on the front door of Cielo Drive—had not connected the Black Panthers to the crimes either among police investigators or in the public's imagination.

In the days following the murders, Charles Manson tried to raise money from this source or that, but failed. Twice he visited Beach Boy Dennis Wilson asking for cash, but Wilson turned him down. Members of the Family reached out to supporters, but to no avail. He was in over his head at last, though he waved his knife around his cult in threat upon threat.

Linda Kasabian, part of the kill pack at Cielo, fled to New Mexico, then came back to retrieve her child from Child and Family Services, fled again to New Mexico, and finally wound up with her mother in New Hampshire. And Manson, the heat threatening to burn him down, sought a place to move his Family. He thought of moving everybody to a nearby religious community, the Fountain of the World, but Sadie/Susan Atkins, part of the delegation he sent to make the proposal to the Fountain, called someone a pig, and the delegation was asked to leave.

Meanwhile, law enforcement began paying close attention to Manson's act at Spahn Ranch, not for murder, but for running a hot car operation. Sergeant Bill

Gleason was an expert on motorcycle gangs for the Malibu station of the LA sheriff's office. For a couple of months he had been gathering data about Manson. He knew about the threats to various firemen who had come across Manson. He knew about Manson's alleged shooting of a "Black Panther." He knew about the weapons and machine guns at the ranch and about an incident in the spring where Manson had been accused of raping a girl from nearby Reseda. He knew about the dune-buggy manufacturing line at the ranch and the rumors that the M group was girding for a war with the blacks. He had learned from Beausoleil's girlfriend about the hideous death-threats with which Manson terrorized his followers. The sheriff's office decided to mount a large nighttime land-air operation against Manson, involving helicopters, horses, patrol cars, submachine guns, and 102 law enforcement officers.

At dawn on August 16, a week after the LaBianca murders, the raid on Spahn Ranch occurred, with many sheriff's deputies taking part. Twenty-five were arrested and placed in a circle in the dirt parking area in front of the mock Western town. Two helicopters whirred overhead, creasing the hair below when dipping near. One of the dogs was running around wearing a brassiere placed on it by someone in the Family.

But Manson was not anywhere to be found. "Where's Jesus?" a sheriff's deputy asked, as brother officers began to search about for the Jesus/Devil synapse. Finally, crouching down and beaming flashlights into the space beneath the floor of the saloon among the foundation timbers, a deputy named Dunlop spotted Charlie lying face down thirty or so feet from the back porch. They told Manson to pull himself out. As Charlie stood up, a folder of stolen credit cards fell out of his shirt pocket. They dragged him down the side alley to the front of the building, then they hand-cuffed his hands behind him and carried him to the circle, where they dumped him next to other arrestees. He was barefoot, wearing buckskin trousers and a light-colored shirt.

Manson was certain he was about to be charged with murder. Then he and Krenwinkel looked at one another with smiles of relief when the sheriff's officer revealed the charge—auto theft!

Manson was also charged with burglary, possibly because of all the credit cards that had tumbled out during his arrest. After a few days, Manson and the others were released. Apparently, something was amiss regarding the search warrant under which the arrests were made. Then, on August 22, Manson was arrested in one of the so-called "outlaw shacks" at the Spahn Ranch with a young female follower, and charged with possession of marijuana. He called from the jail and demanded that someone arrive to take the blame for the pot in his shirt. Thus Manson, through will, cunning, threat, and chance, continued to escape.

Sheriffs' officers search the yellow and white 1959 Ford used by the murderers on Cielo Drive, August 16. Officers discovered rifles and bullets.

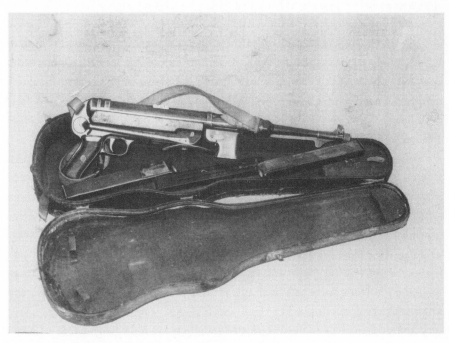

Machine gun in violin case found in August 16 raid

M Group arrested in August 16 raid. Manson on the left, handcuffed.

On August 26, forty-year-old stuntman Donald "Shorty" Shea, a Spahn Ranch hand, was killed by a bunch of Mansonites, and buried in a creek bank near the ranch. While Manson was in jail, "Shorty was doing a lot of nasty talking about Charlie," a Family member told me a year after the murder. Charlie believed that it was Shorty who set up the raid on the outlaw shacks where he and his young follower were arrested.

Some Family members were friendly to the outgoing Shorty Shea, who wanted to become a movie star, and who had at least three friends who allowed him to use their phones as answering services in the event someone in show business should want to call Shea about a movie gig. One important transgression, in the opinion of the Family, was that Shea had married a black dancer whom he had met in Las Vegas. The Family was upset because his wife's black friends began visiting the Spahn Ranch. However much Shea had hankered to force the Mansonites off the ranch, the murder was likely caused because Shorty knew something about the Tate-LaBianca killings.

If the stories circulated by disaffected members are to be believed, key Family members tortured Shorty and, during the torture, tampered with his mental state, as if they were conducting experiments. Manson and his adepts deliberately spread the story that Mr. Shea had been beheaded. Not true. The entire core Family was involved in the offing of Mr. Shea. Some killed, some buried, some burned his stuff, some packed his gear. "By that time, we all had our job to do," Leslie Van Houten remarked, discussing her assigned task of burning Shorty's clothes. They buried him during the night down the creek by the railroad tunnel at the back of the ranch, in a crude, temporary, brush-topped grave. The next day several girls reburied Shorty in broad daylight. The second time, his body was placed down the road toward Simi, and during the years thereafter the sheriff's office occasionally bulldozed the area looking for it. (It was finally located years later.)

By early September, Manson began moving his cult to Death Valley. Somehow, he raised enough money to pull it off. It's not clear how, or from what source. (Did he receive a hefty sum for carrying out a contract killing?) He visited the owner of the Barker Ranch, located high up in the Panamint Mountains reachable from the Death Valley floor by an axle-busting four-wheel-drive trail up Goler Wash, and got the permission of the owner to stay a few days at Barker. The Family stole about seven dunebuggies to replace some of those that were confiscated in the August 16 raid. Charlie drove seven young female members to the mouth of Goler Wash, then dashed up the dynamited waterfalls seven miles to the Barker Ranch. Charlie went back and forth between the Spahn Ranch and Goler Wash in various rented and stolen vehicles.

Ultimately about thirty or forty of the Family were ensconced at Barker. Some settled at the Myers Ranch, near the Barker Ranch, owned by a Manson follower's grandparents, and at an abandoned gold mine along the edge of Goler Wash, as well as in other cabins.

When Manson's recently acquired love-mate Stephanie arrived at the Barker-Myers Ranch area, he handed her a knife. During those days he taught everyone lessons in throat-slitting. He mentioned decorating the Barker Ranch with human skulls, after boiling the skulls in large kettles to demeat them. "We were all sitting around and he asked if we could do it," Stephanie later remembered. "He asked if it came down to it, could we do it and everyone said, 'Oh yeah' and I said, 'Oh yeah.'" At first, Stephanie recalled that she asked Manson, "'How? I don't really know how,' he used me as a live demonstration—how you cut from here to there," indicating throat slit. "Then he said, 'You have to know how to hide everything so no one will find it.' We were down in some canyon somewhere."

Manson talked about General Rommel and desert campaigning. He was going to be the Desert Fox of Devil's Hole at the head of a flying *V* of dune buggies, racing across the desert for plunder. Manson spray-painted his stolen dune buggy and then, while the paint was wet, threw dirt on the paint to create a brown camouflage effect.

They talked a lot about taking over the Death Valley towns of Shoshone and Trona. Manson felt a bit of hostility toward all the desert people, wanting to ping them one by one. Manson talked about terrorizing the police. He talked about killing approaching policemen, removing their bodies from their clothes, then leaving the uniforms and shoes and hats neatly arranged on the desert ground, as if the bodies had somehow just disappeared from their uniforms.

Everybody, even when nude, wore a hunting knife strapped to the leg or waist. The Family was so completely into gore that everybody was armed, not only in fear of the police perhaps, but also in apprehension of possible spontaneous slashing from fellow Family members. Charlie liked to comment on those whom he considered the weak links in the Family. The girls must have been desperate not to be thought of as weak links. Weak links could find themselves on the receiving end of a slash.

And so it went with the Hole in the Universe Gang. For about two-and-a-half weeks the Family swarmed all over Goler Wash and the southwest part of the Death Valley National Monument. Then Manson flipped out and attracted the attention of the park rangers and the California Highway Patrol, so the Family had to go into hiding. But that's why they went to the desert, to hide. Now it was like hiding within the hideaway.

If they hadn't roamed the Death Valley area as marauders, the Mansonites could have lived in that wilderness for years without any trouble. As one of the policemen who arrested them in Goler Wash said, "You could hide the Empire State Building out there and no one could find it."

Late Thursday night or early Friday morning, September 18–19, Manson led his troop out of the vastness called the Saline Valley over the bumpy wilderness trail up the mountain pass, the single headlight on his dune buggy his only guide. At the very top of the pass that would have led him down to the Hunter Mountain campsite, he stopped. Right in front of him were two large wide holes in the dirtway, evidently scooped out by some nearby earth-moving equipment.

Kitty Lutesinger said that Manson, in crazed paranoia, thought the authorities had deliberately dug the holes in his path so that he would crash his dune buggy into them! Manson ordered her and key Family member Gypsy to fill up the large shallow gouge-outs with rocks and dirt. As they did this, according to Snake Lake, Scotty, Tex, Manson, and Clem Grogan removed some gasoline tanks and a grease gun from a nearby and expensive Clark Michigan skiploader. Then they leaked out the fuel oil, poured some gasoline on the wires and the engine, then set it ablaze. The Family raced away and the rest of the night was spent in a roaring roam-frenzy of careening dune buggies.

The burning of the Michigan loader enraged the rangers at the Death Valley National Monument, who owned it. Relentlessly the park rangers, the California Highway Patrol, the Inyo County sheriff's department and, to a lesser degree, agents of the California Fish and Game Commission would begin to track down this uncool group of murderers.

It's always a mistake when a guru makes a claim or a prediction that can never happen. Manson made a big one that fall. He couldn't come up with The Hole. His followers were counting on Manson leading them to it. It was one thing to rap about it around bonfires to one's bedoped disciples; it was another to produce it, especially a Hole with such astounding attributes. According to Tex Watson, this underground paradise zone came outfitted with twelve magical trees bearing wondrous fruit and an underground lake that gave everlasting life. There was a different tree for every month of the year. Plus, most important of all, the sub-desert paradise would have provided a hiding place from the law. Therefore that fall, the dune buggy battalion went Hole-batty. Some hungered for the magical trees of The Hole, others hungered for a safe place from which to maraud forth. There were a few clues, such as great beflittings of black bats that swarmed into Goler Wash at dusk, which the M group was certain had flitted up from the Abyss. They searched everywhere, crawling into old mine shafts, looking for the vein to paradise. But no Hole, no molten Hershey bar factory beneath the Amargosa River. "It began to look," Tex Watson later commented, "as if the Abyss would be harder to find than we'd first thought."

On September 29, Park Ranger Richard Powell and California Highway Patrol Officer James Pursell visited the Barker Ranch area. Manson may have spotted the officers, because two days later he handed Tex Watson a shotgun and told him to squeeze himself into a little crawlspace above the slatted porchway at the side door of the Barker Ranch and wait for Officer Pursell and Ranger Powell to return, then kill them. Watson waited up there until the morning of October 2, at which time he decided, he later wrote, he was no longer going to kill for M. "Even though I was willing to die for Charlie, I was getting tired of breaking my back for him. It seemed as if every day there was less chance of finding the Pit, no matter how much we drove around over the desert, no matter how many abandoned mine shafts we crawled through. We were short of food, we were allowed only one cup of water per day and, worst of all the drugs were running out."

Tex rummaged through the Family's clothes pile to pick an outfit in which he could split into the real world, then drove in a 1942 Dodge Power Wagon down Goler Wash to the Panamint Valley and, running low on gas, attempted a shortcut across the large semidry salt lake toward the Trona Road, where he mired down in the salty mush and soon ran out of gas.

He spent the night sleeping by the side of the road. The next morning, a passing motorist took Watson to the San Bernardino railroad station and dropped him off. Watson said he was going back to Texas, where his parents owned a chain of supermarkets. When he returned to the commune, he was going to bring a truckload of groceries because that was what the commune needed most.

Watson's parents wired him money, and he went home to Texas. He was there for a while, then fled to Hawaii, then back to California, first in Los Angeles, then back to Death Valley, where a prospector told him that in the middle of the night the entire Family, including Manson, had been arrested. Watson's parents again wired him money, whereupon he returned to Copeville, Texas, where he seems to have maintained a routine existence, dating a doctor's daughter, till the end of November, when he was picked up by his cousin, the sheriff of Collins County, Texas, for murder.

When Watson left, Manson was worried and ordered lookout posts and "dugouts" dug where girls hovered under tarps, always on the look for danger. Manson would beat his followers, and with food and water low and intimidation on the rise, girls kept escaping.

Deputies and park rangers in the meantime staked out the Barker Ranch, gradually learning that the Family was only on hand during the night; they disappeared at dawn. Therefore, on October 9, in the dead of night, the police approached the Barker Ranch from two directions: one up the steep and difficult creek/semi-road of Goler Wash and the other from the Striped Butte Valley over Mengel Pass and down the long seven and a half miles to the ranch. The California Highway Patrol gave walkie-talkies to these two advancing parties so that once they got close enough they could communicate with each other. The two parties planned to converge on the Barker Ranch at dawn.

The party of officers proceeding from the Striped Butte Valley parked their four-wheel-drive vehicles at the summit of Mengel Pass, then walked down the steepness toward the ranch.

Just before dawn the two teams of officers achieved walkie-talkie contact. The team of officers arriving from the west, from the Panamint Valley up Goler Wash, encountered, sleeping on the creek bed between blankets, Clem Grogan and a youth named Rocky. Clem's sixteen-inch sawed-off shotgun and twenty-four rounds of ammunition lay next to him.

The officers awakened them and put them under arrest for having a sawed-off shot-gun and for arson and grand theft auto. The officers then left their four-wheel-drive vehicles in a small draw not far from the Barker Ranch. One officer positioned himself high on the south slope across from the Barker Ranch up above what was called "the bunker." Shortly after dawn, Sadie/Susan Atkins, wearing a red hat, emerged from the hidden bunker to relieve herself. She was evidently spotted by the cops. The cops, according to the girls, fired a shotgun blast on top of the metal hidden bunker roof, causing the rest of the girls to come out.

Arrested from the dugout were Leslie Van Houten, using the name Louvella Alexandria; Sadie/Susan Atkins, using the name Donna Kay Powell; Gypsy, using the name Manon Minette; and Brenda/Nancy Pitman, using the name Cydette Perell. Inside the ranch house, the cops arrested Patricia Krenwinkel, using the name Marnie K. Reeves. Also captured was one Robert Ivan Lane, aka Soup Spoon, and they picked up Linda Baldwin, aka Little Patti. Some of the girls were nude, as noted on the arrest report: "When the initial group of female prisoners were arrested, several of the females disrobed. Several of them urinated on the ground in the presence of the officers. They also undressed and changed clothes in the presence of the officers."

Proceeding north in the small draw between the Barker Ranch and nearby Meyers Ranch, the police raided the "spike camp," as they called it, where they took into custody Sandy Good, who was carrying Susan/Sadie's baby Zezo; Ouish, using the name Rachel S. Morse and carrying Sandy Good's one-month-old baby Ivan; and Mary Ann Schwarm, aka Diane Von Ahn. One of the babies had a large cut on his face, and all were burnt raw from the sun.

There was also a "list" allegedly found in Death Valley by law enforcement, which marked out those who were to die. It is not unusual for cults to have a hate list or enemy list. In one report the Family's list contained thirty-four names of stars and businessmen to be killed. Included in the list of enemies were those who had helped out in the past but had ceased to aid them.

A mysterious pack, which may have confirmed visual aids for the preparation of the "list," was taken into evidence by the LAPD from the Family material seized by the police in Inyo County. The "army type pack," as the police report read, contained "64 movie and TV star magazines, 3 bound library books, 1 canvas bag marked 'Federal Reserve Bank of Dallas,' 'No. 3,' (money type bag), savings account pass book. . . . with name of John C. Farnsworth, Los Gatos, California . . . , 1 paperback book *Stranger in a Strange Land* by Robert A. Heinlein." Was this Manson's pack? Was this pack the one Manson brought with him from Los Angeles and did he fib to attorney Paul Fitzgerald?

If movie magazines were in the pack, for ideas on whom to kill, what was a bag belonging to the Federal Reserve Bank of Dallas doing in the pack? This leads to speculation that it might have contained money as payment for a hit.

California Highway Patrol Officer Pursell, Park Ranger Powell, and another ranger went back in to the Barker Ranch area on Sunday, October 12, to look for more dune buggies and check out the various family campsites, looking for illegality. A motorist informed them that a truck had been abandoned in Goler Wash. The officers located the Chevrolet truck still loaded down with drums of gasoline and supplies. They decided that unarrested car-thief nudists, perhaps even Manson himself, had reentered the Barker Ranch area.

So Pursell talked over the radio to other officers. It was decided that then was the time to noose Jesus/the Devil himself. About five o'clock that afternoon police entered the area and took up positions near the Barker Ranch. Meanwhile other officers were on the way from Ballarat, an outpost on the valley near the entrance to Goler Wash.

From their lookout on a ridge up above the Barker swimming pool, Officer Pursell and Ranger Powell saw Manson and a couple of other people walk up the gulch and enter the house. Manson was carrying a guitar case. Another Ranger worked his way around to the front of the ranch so that he could meet the officers who were coming up the Goler Wash from Ballarat. They could hear laughter and conversation from the house, so they knew there were a number of people inside.

The chief ranger for the Death Valley National Park, plus two representatives of the Inyo County sheriff's office arrived and radioed Officer Pursell, who went down the hill in the back of the ranch, then stealth-stalked in under the ivy-trellised side porch, kicked open the side door, and said, "Stick 'em up." He went along the wall, using it as a cover in case any of them should care to attack him, and he told them to put their hands on top of their heads. In slow-motion defiance, the Mansonites complied.

"I ordered the subjects out backwards one at a time where Deputy Ward took charge of them," Pursell told me later. Once again, as in the Spahn Ranch raid of August 16, the officers wondered: "Where was Jesus?"

It was about six-thirty in the evening, and seven disheveled followers of Manson had been hauled out of the ranch house and handcuffed. The quick desert darkness was at hand. Officer Pursell carried the single candle that had been on the supper table around the four-room cabin. He stopped at the small blue bathroom with a poured concrete bathtub and a small blue lavatory. He held the candle's flame near a little cabinet beneath the lavatory and spotted protruding hair. Then he saw wiggling fingers and he said, "All right, come on out, but slowly." A small person uncoiled from the tiny cabinet and said, "Hi. I'm Charlie Manson."

Manson was then held in the Inyo County Jail.

Kitty Lutesinger, pregnant girlfriend of Robert Beausoleil, had been arrested during the Barker raids. When Sergeant Paul Whiteley and Deputy Charles Guenther, LA County homicide investigators working on the Hinman murder learned about Lutesinger, they drove right away to Inyo County and brought her back to the San Dimas sheriff's station for interrogation.

When police officers mentioned the words "gas chamber," it caused some Family associates to talk, and talk plenty. In the beginning, the officers suggested to Kitty that she was one of the girls that had accompanied Beausoleil to Gary Hinman's house. She replied that the girls were "Sadie and Mary" but she was definitely not one of them. She further alleged that they had "screwed up" at the Hinman residence, being sent there by Manson only to acquire money.

Another possible reason that may have caused people such as Kitty to talk was that Manson uttered a few threats over the phone directed against "weak links," either when Clem Grogan had called him down at the Spahn Ranch after the first arrests at Barker or when Manson called from the Inyo County Jail after he was arrested. Kitty really was worried for her life and that of her parents (who lived not far from the Spahn Ranch).

The next morning, October 13, Whiteley and Guenther flew from the Ontario, California, airport to Independence to speak with Sadie/Susan Atkins. They brought with them photos of the Family. The Inyo County Jail was so packed with Family members that interrogation was difficult, so the officers escorted Sadie/Susan to the Lone Pine substation of the Inyo County sheriff's department for Q and A.

During skillful questioning, Sadie/Susan admitted participation in the Hinman murder and shortly thereafter even did some babbling about Shorty Shea. But she declined to tape-record the twenty-five minute session. Then the officers flew with Miss Atkins back to Ontario, whereupon they took her to the San Dimas sheriff's station and booked her for suspicion of murder.

The loquacious murderer was then taken to the Sybil Brand jail in Los Angeles, where she began splashing her secrets.

Chapter 16

The Breaking of the Case

A Nighttime Talk About Murder

After the crazy young murder defendant named Susan Atkins was flown by Detective Guenther and Sergeant Whiteley of the LA County sheriff's homicide to Los Angeles, where she was charged with Gary Hinman's murder, she settled into the gossip-drenched milieu of the women's jail.

On November 6, she held an afternoon confessional conversation with fellow inmate Virginia Graham, jailed for parole violation, followed by breathless nighttime talk with another inmate in the LA County jail, Ronni Howard, aka Shelly Nadell. Howard and Graham were longtime acquaintances.

Virginia Graham and Sadie/Susan Atkins had daytime chores involving running messages here and there in the jail until 3:30 p.m., then they went to dinner, returning to the 8000 dormitory about 4:35 p.m. Virginia was all set to go take a shower when Sadie came over to Virginia's bed and asked if she could sit and talk for a minute. Virginia said okay. They talked. Somehow the subject centered at first on LSD, which the thirty-nine-year-old Virginia had taken for the first time on October 1, a few days before her arrest. Sadie had taken hundreds of trips, so it was something in common to talk about.

Then Sadie began to talk about the Hinman matter, confessing freely to participating in it. Miss Graham reproached Sadie for her loose talk.

"I told her that I didn't care particularly what she had done, but I didn't think it was advisable for her to talk so much," Virginia remembered later. Graham told Sadie she had heard of cases where people in jail were victims of entrapment after confessing to crimes to cellmates who later snitched.

Sadie replied that she wasn't worried because looking into Virginia's eyes, she just knew she could trust Virginia.

Sadie then began to talk about Death Valley and the people arrested up there and the Underground City for the chosen. And she began to talk about Manson. Then Sadie became visibly excited and began to talk quickly. What triggered it off? Evidently a general discussion of crime and murder.

"We were talking about crime and, you know, various murders, and all that," remembered Miss Graham.

And Sadie said, in the course of the conversation, according to Graham, "Well, you know, there's a case right now. They are so far off the track they don't even know what's happening."

There was a pause.

"What are you talking about?"

"That one on Benedict Canyon."

"Benedict Canyon?"

"Benedict Canyon, yes."

"You don't mean Sharon Tate?"

"Yeah," Sadie said. Then she grew even more excited and the baleful words of murd-mania were spewn out. "You're looking at the one that did it."

Several times Sadie raised her voice, and Graham had to tell her to lower it. Out came the horror, the deathly details, the scenarios. And Miss Graham began to ask questions to determine if Sadie was really telling the truth, querying Sadie about the rope, what the victims were wearing, and so on, in order to trip her up. But the story seemed to hold, except that Sadie claimed to have left a palm print on the living room desk and to have lost her knife in the fray, events unmentioned in the media. (And any palm print would already certainly have led to Sadie's arrest.)

For just over an hour they talked. At 6 p.m. there was a jail prisoner count, so their conversation had to stop, but not before Miss Graham's mind was filled with an unforgettable mixture of shocking data. Right away, Miss Graham rushed over to her ten-year-friend Ronni Howard and told her what Sadie had related. They weren't totally convinced, but they planned to try to find out more from Sadie.

"We'll ask her certain questions that only a person would know who had been in on it," Graham said to Ronni. "Try and ask her what color the bedroom was, or what the people had on or anything."

Because Sadie had moved into the bed right next to Ronni, Ronni was able to begin to talk to Sadie, by night, in privacy. Since the prison matrons counted the sleeping inmates each half hour, it was possible by means of a system of lookouts to visit each other intimately for half-hour periods in between head counts.

That same day, November 6, a team of three detectives associated with the LaBianca investigation visited the Inyo County Jail in Independence, near Death Valley, to interview Manson Family members being held after the October raids on their desert hideout. They were Sergeant Frank Patchett, Sergeant Philip Sartuche, and Lieutenant Burdick, all with the LAPD.

Charles Manson answered with a gruff "No!" when asked by Sergeant Sartuche if he'd been involved with either the LaBianca or the Tate homicides. At 1:30 p.m. Lieutenant A. H. Burdick of the scientific investigation division of the LAPD, the gentleman who ninety days previous had administered a lie detector test to William Garretson, interviewed Leslie Van Houten. He outlined, in a report to the LAPD robbery-homicide division, that Miss Van Houten indicated to him that there were "some things" that caused her to believe that someone from her group was involved in the Tate homicide but that she denied knowledge of the LaBianca homicide. At that time she declined to indicate what she meant and stated that she wanted to think about it overnight, and that she was perplexed and didn't know what to do. The next day, Miss Van Houten had gained her composure and refused to speak any more about the matter.

November 8 or 9

Virginia Graham didn't want to rouse Sadie's suspicions, so she waited to bring up the subject of murder. Approximately two or three days after the bedside conversation, she told Sadie this: "Hey, you know . . . " revealing to Sadie that she and her former husband years before, around 1962, had been to the residence at 10050 Cielo Drive to see about renting it. "Is it still done in gold and white?" Taking a shot in the dark, because she had never actually seen the interior.

"Uh huh," Sadie replied.

On November 8 or 9, Sadie came to Virginia's bed carrying a movie fan magazine. The magazine was opened to a picture of Elizabeth Taylor and Richard Burton. Sadie seemed jolly as she disclosed to Virginia a list of future victims, including Richard Burton, whose groin was to be trimmed of appendage, Elizabeth Taylor, Frank Sinatra, Tom Jones, who was singing over the jail radio at that moment, and Steve McQueen—although Sadie said that she hated to have to do in Tom Jones because he turned her on. She also expressed enmity for Frank Sinatra Jr. Sadie told Virginia she planned the most hideous and butcherous of deaths for those on her list.

On November 12, Virginia Graham had a parole hearing, where it would be decided to send her back to Corona State Prison for Women. Just before she left, following Sadie's return from her own court appearance, Virginia had a brief discussion with Ronni Howard about what to do about Sadie's confession.

Ronni said that she had been talking every night to Sadie, adding, "Boy is she weird." Ronni came up with an idea how to tell if Sadie's allegations were true. Ronni said she knew what it was like to stab someone, since she had once stabbed her former husband. Ronni said she'd ask Sadie what it was like, physically, to stab someone, and make a judgement by her response.

Virginia said that one way might be to start out by talking about LSD trips, since that seemed to get Sadie going. As Virginia Graham left to go to Corona, she suggested to Ronni that if she found out more, she could then go to her parole agent.

Ronni replied that there were always homicide detectives arriving at the jail, and that since she worked in receiving, she'd just tell one of them. Virginia added that, if Ronni decided to tell anybody in authority about the matter, Virginia could be contacted at Corona State Prison.

Lights-out in dorm 8000 at Sybil Brand Institute was 9:30 p.m., and that very night Sadie and Ronni Howard were talking face to face. Later Howard described her method of getting Sadie to talk: "Oh, how I got her to tell me about it; I told you we were talking about an acid trip. You know, because not too many of the girls take acid in there and I guess I was one that she could talk to."

Ronni had taken acid twelve times. Sadie told her that there was nothing that could shock her, nothing that she hadn't done. Then upon the urging of Howard, the subject shifted to bloodletting, and Miss Atkins started to confess, whispering in the dark dormitory. Ronni scoffed at Sadie's contentions and asked enough questions to cajole Sadie to reveal all the details.

For five or six straight nights, from November 12 through November 15 or 16, Ronni Howard lay down with Sadie Glutz in the gloom, gathering information. Sadie disturbed Ronni the most when she told her that the deaths were going to continue, and that they were going to occur at random!

Susan Atkins, October 1969, just after she was brought to Los Angeles and charged with murder

Around November 14, Virginia Graham, already transferred to Corona State Prison, decided to talk about what Sadie/Susan Atkins had said. She filled out a "blue slip" or request to speak with a staff member and sent it to the prison psychologist, Dr. Vera Dreiser, along with a note: "Dr. Dreiser, it is very important that I speak with you."

Dreiser sent a "blue slip" back indicating that Miss Graham was to talk with Dreiser's supervisor. Finally about twelve days later she told her jail counselor, Miss Mary Ann Domn, about the Manson Family and Atkins's blurt-outs.

November 17, a Hearing in Santa Monica

Ronni Howard had a number of pseudonyms—among them were Shelley Joyce Nadell, Veronica Hughes, Veronica Williams, Connie Johnson, Connie Schampeau, Sharon Warren, Marjie Carter, and Jean Marie Conley. She had an appearance in Santa Monica Superior Court regarding a false prescription charge.

In California a defendant is allowed a phone call for each separate court appearance, so Ronni called the Hollywood division of the LAPD, because she believed that the Hollywood division was handling the Tate investigation. She told them about Sadie's confession.

After court, Miss Howard returned to Sybil Brand jail, and LAPD Special Investigators Brown and Mossman came to Sybil Brand and talked to Ronni in a private room for about an hour and a half. She supplied them with most of the information that Sadie/Susan had given her, except she left out some of the names involved. What really impressed the officers was that Sadie had told Ronni things only the killer could have known, such as the Buck knife that she said she lost in the house.

By November 17, apparently only one lieutenant and five detectives were still assigned to the Polanski residence case. Right away after Ronni Howard snitched, the full investigation involving two lieutenants and sixteen men was reactivated. With the evidence supplied by Howard/Nadell, the biker Dan DeCarlo, Kitty Lutesinger, Gregg Jakobson, and others, it was all over.

November 23

In the evening, LAPD detectives, Sergeants Patchett and McGann, interviewed Ronni Howard aka Shelley Nadell at the Sybil Brand jail in Los Angeles. The next day, Howard was removed from the dormitory where she was sleeping alongside Sadie Glutz/Susan Atkins, for she could not continue to stay in the same dormitory lest it appear to the court that she had attempted to entrap Atkins to confess.

November 26

There was a hearing for Sadie Glutz/Susan Atkins in Santa Monica on the Hinman case. Richard Caballero, a former assistant district attorney, was appointed to represent Miss Atkins, at county expense. Mr. Caballero conducted a lengthy discussion with Atkins, where she was confronted with the considerable evidence against her from her cellmates. Her attorney convinced her that the evidence against her was overwhelming. She was told by her attorney that only if she made a full confession to all the murders and cooperated with the police could she hope to avoid the gas chamber. She agreed to tell all, and thus the case was truly broken.

On the same day, Sadie's former cellmate Virginia Graham related to her counselor at the Corona State Prison for Women what Miss Atkins had told her about the homicides. The same afternoon, Sergeant Mike Nielsen of the LAPD taped an interview with Graham at the Corona State Prison.

November 28

Colonel Tate filed Sharon Tate's will for probate. The papers listed the value of Sharon Tate's estate: $37,200 in cash, no stock, no bonds, an auto worth $5,700, for a total of $45,400.

That same day, Sergeant Mike Nielsen, of LAPD robbery-homicide division, telephoned Joseph Krenwinkel and asked where his daughter Patricia was. Joseph replied that she was to be found in Mobile, Alabama (where she had hastened after the arrests at the Barker Ranch and being asked about the LaBianca murders in the Inyo County Jail). She would be picked up several days later in Mobile, where she was staying with an aunt.

On November 30, Charles Denton Watson was picked up in Copeville, Texas for murder.

December 1

At 2 p.m. on December 1, LA Police Chief Edward Davis held a press conference in an auditorium at Parker Center, the LA police headquarters.

Paul Whiteley and Charles Guenther of sheriff's homicide, who had been key in bringing the Manson group to justice, were on hand but not allowed to attend the news conference where Chief Edward Davis announced the solution of the Tate-LaBianca-Sebring-Folger-Frykowski-Parent homicides.

Facing about fifteen microphones and a knot of jousting cameramen, Chief Davis said that 8,750 hours of police work had brought down the house of Manson. Followed by worldwide headlines, the case was broken.

Paul Tate wanted to watch Manson being brought in. Lieutenant Robert Helder of LAPD allowed it. One account states that a friend drove Tate to where Manson would be walked, but couldn't find a parking space, so the colonel went by himself. The friend apparently insisted that Sharon's father leave his pistol in the car.

Ten deputies guarded Manson—two on each side, three in front, three behind. Paul Tate thought Manson would recognize him, so he pulled down his sunglasses, and then locked eyes with M. As he later wrote, "Three feet beyond me, Manson twisted around, walking backward in order to continue the staring match."

Something was over, but not the horror and mourning of memory. And nothing could bring back the fresh young mother-to-be in her house of fresh-painted nursery, fresh-purchased baby clothes, and well-used rocking chair freshly brought by her mother in which her daughter intended to nurse the soon-to-be-born baby.

Coda

O Sharon
Your son'd be
    what
well into his 40s by now
& you'd be
    if still acting
playing comedic grandmother roles

which wd be Just—
What's not
is the unthinkable calamity
that befell you

and its loose threads
like an unraveling shawl
    of antique lace
that puzzles us
all these decades later

—**Ed Sanders**

Sharon in the Sky

Afterword

Loose Threads in the Weave

One of the greatest lingering mysteries is why the Manson group went to Cielo Drive that hot, baleful night. Sharon Tate's own mother, when I visited with her in 1989, over twenty years after the murders, was perplexed. She believed that the Manson group had advance word that Sharon Tate was not going to be at the house that night. She felt, she told me, that someone might have tipped the Family off. Doris Tate wondered if someone saw that Sharon's red Ferrari was gone (it was in the repair shop) and called Manson, and then the attack began. And where was the caretaker of the property during the murder? These are mysteries she longed to have cleared up.

In the over forty years since I first became involved in writing and researching this case, some things have never made sense. I am ever reminded of a quote from Graham Greene's novel, *The Third Man*, wherein an intelligence agent comments, "One's file, you know, is never quite complete; a case is never really closed, even after a century, when all the participants are dead."

One loose thread in the story's weave is the role of the mysterious English satanic cult that was active in Los Angeles in 1967 and 1968.

Ace Manson follower Bruce Davis was sent, apparently by Manson, on a strange trip to England in 1968 and 1969. He was associated over in England with the head honcho of the satanic cult, an Englishman who cofounded the cult. This fact was given to me by retired LA County sheriff's homicide detective Paul Whiteley, who, as much as any other officer, was responsible for bringing down the house of Manson.

When I interviewed Robert Beausoleil at San Quentin following his conviction for the murder of Gary Hinman, he stated that the Manson group met the English satanic organization at the Spiral Staircase in Topanga Canyon. Patricia

Krenwinkel later confirmed that. (The Spiral Staircase was a secluded house at the mouth of Topanga Canyon near the Pacific Coast Highway. It was located behind the Raft Restaurant on Topanga Canyon Lane. This place acquired its name from the spiral staircase at the entrance. It has since been torn down.)

The female defendants charged with the Tate-LaBianca murders used to embroider the symbol of this English satanic cult in jail during their trial for murder.

Dianne Lake, in the fall of 1967, was an emancipated child of fourteen who lived with her parents at the commune called the Hog Farm outside Los Angeles. She met the Manson Family in Topanga Canyon at the Spiral Staircase and joined up. She was with them all the way to the mass arrests in the fall of 1969—although she was still just seventeen years old.

She became a star witness at the Tate-LaBianca trial, and during the trial was a ward, because she was underage, of Inyo County district attorney investigator Jack Gardiner and his wife. She had memories of the English satanic group which she imparted to Mr. Gardiner. The Family, she told Gardiner, received money from the cult, and the cult wanted the Family to join. Unusual sex acts came from the English cult, according to Dianne, and use of drugs as part of the "program," according to her, came from the cult.

Jack Gardiner also told Larry Larsen that other Family members, including Leslie Van Houten and a young man named Christopher Zero, talked about the English cult while in jail in Inyo County in late 1969. Zero, whose true name was John Philip Haught, was shot to death, or shot himself, under very strange circumstances, in a house in Venice a few weeks after being released from the Inyo County Jail.

Dianne Lake may have also suggested to Jack Gardiner that there were murder victims buried at the Barker Ranch, located in the mountains above Death Valley, where Manson and his group were arrested in October of 1969. In 1974, Gardiner sent an Inyo County detective to look about 150 yards behind the Barker ranch house, where Manson was arrested, for four gravesites. The detective complied with the order, but no gravesites were located.

John Phillips, the talented but troubled troubadour, leader of the Mamas and the Papas, donated as much as $25,000 to the English satanic group when it was in Los Angeles in 1967 and 1968.

LA private investigator Larry Larsen and I looked into various aspects of the Manson Family's associations and activities, and also the assassination of Robert Kennedy, for years. Larsen was an exceptional investigator—fearless, honest, and very ethical. In August of 1972, less than a year after the publication of *The Family*, Larsen reported on becoming close to an investigative team associated with IRS Intelligence. It was just after the IRS, along with other federal agencies had arrested many associated with Timothy Leary's Brotherhood of Eternal Love (which had paid the Weather Underground to help Leary escape from prison). It was in the course of meeting with associates of IRS intelligence that Larsen was informed that the head of the English satanic organization had recruited Manson. Through Larsen, I was asked to help in the investigation of Timothy Leary, but I refused, saying that I didn't think Leary had done anything to warrant his capture.

Larsen also did research for other writers. In 1974, he was assisting writer Alexander Cockburn in research for an article on Sirhan Sirhan when Larsen learned about an investigation being conducted by an Immigration and Naturalization Service criminal investigator named Richard Smith. The investigation was into the activities of the Satanist group of English origin which had oozed to America in 1967, 1968, and 1969. The investigation delved not only into the activities of the English cult, but also into the Robert Kennedy assassination, the activities of Sirhan Sirhan, and finally into Charles Manson and the murder of Sharon Tate. Larry Larsen provided some reliable information, given to him by Smith himself, outlining Smith's investigation.

Richard Smith prepared a report on the English Satanists around the summer of 1974. Smith was attempting to launch a full-scale investigation of the Satanists, with investigators to go from Frankfort, Germany, to London, England, to speak with Scotland Yard and other sources. Smith proposed to the INS to have the field office in Mexico City investigate the Mexican operations of the satanic cult, but apparently when a superior at INS saw the name of the daughter of a prominent US congressman as belonging to the Satanist society, and other factors as well, he got cold feet. Larsen learned that Smith was told to turn in his files to superiors at the INS office in New York City. Mr. Smith was also denied permission by his superiors to interview Sirhan Sirhan in prison.

Larsen was allowed to read Smith's report. The report stated that English Satanist cult members invited Sirhan Sirhan to a number of parties that were sponsored by television people in the LA area, and that one of the parties took place at Sharon Tate's residence. At these parties, it was averred, sexual and ritualistic rites were reported to have occurred. From Smith's actual report, a copy of which I obtained in later years, it was written that Sirhan Sirhan "had attended some parties given by television personalities in behalf of the organization, where rites took place usually dealing with sexual deviations and heavy drug use. One of these parties took place at Sharon Tate's home."

These assertions were apparently based on an FBI report done during the initial investigation of the Robert Kennedy assassination, which Mr. Smith had acquired. An FBI report with the information linking Sirhan with the English Satanists, though with virtually all of the information blacked out, was received by the Yonkers police department during the Son of Sam investigation decades later. Investigators in Yonkers verified what was in the blacked out sections, and it corresponded with what the INS officer wrote in his 1974 report, regarding Sirhan Sirhan attending parties on behalf of the Satanist English cult, including one at Sharon Tate's place.

CBS television reporter Carl George, whom I met at the Tate-LaBianca trial, alleged that a sheriff's office homicide detective stated he could link Sirhan Sirhan in Pasadena to a member of the English satanic cult.

INS criminal investigator Richard Smith's report stated that an LA law enforcement agency had a female informant who averred that the English Satanist group had commissioned Manson to kill Sharon Tate. Larsen asked Smith about the informant and was told it was a person who alleged that she had been in the same room at the time the Satanists let out an order for a contract to Manson to kill her. The reason for the contract, as Larsen stated in a report to me, was "something that she unfortunately overheard that she was not supposed to overhear either in regards to Sirhan Sirhan or about Sirhan Sirhan."

At this point in the conversation between Larry Larsen and Richard Smith (the conversation had gone on for one-half hour or longer, and Smith had answered every question freely and had shown Larry Larsen every document he had with him), Larsen reported the following: "And then I asked the obvious question, 'What did Sharon Tate allegedly overhear?' and he said, 'I cannot discuss that. It's a matter of national security.'"

Smith elaborated, after a question by Larsen, that it had nothing to do with Colonel Paul Tate and Tate's intelligence activities.

Larsen received this data on October 4, 1974. Smith's list of confidential informers went from L-1 through L-6. The FBI had no number, but Larsen learned it was one of the agencies which provided information.

As we have indicated, the satanic cult had a recruit who was the daughter of a prominent liberal New York Congressman, as a result of which, as he indicated to Larsen, Smith's investigation was terminated, and he was told to turn in his paperwork to the INS chain of command, which he did, but he kept a copy of his "Memorandum to File."

Smith remained in government service and confirmed the facts of his investigation, including follow-up interviews, in subsequent months and years, that were conducted by Larry Larsen. The INS officer was questioned at least twice, in the 2000s, about the assertions of the document, once in 2000 and another time in 2004. During those years I was working on a project with Maury Terry, author of *The Ultimate Evil*. Maury and I figured out a way to approach Richard Smith. Accordingly, I helped prepare a list of questions submitted to Mr. Smith in 2004, at which time he was an INS officer in a large Western city. Smith, thirty years after his original report, still refused to say what Sharon Tate had allegedly learned about the Robert Kennedy assassination that was of such magnitude that it caused her murder and could not be revealed because of "national security."

These matters have disturbed me now for over forty years, and I feel obligated to bring them up in this afterword. (I brought up some of the same issues in an updated edition of my book, *The Family*, in 2002.)

The two houses in which Sharon Tate dwelled at which a party conducted by the satanic organization could have been held are (1) the "Cary Grant" mansion in Santa Monica rented from actor Brian Aherne; and (2) the fourth-floor apartment at the Chateau Marmont Hotel where she and Roman Polanski resided in the late winter and spring of 1968.

There is one individual whom I interviewed, a musician, who claimed to have attended a party at the Chateau Marmont in the spring of 1968, at which he told me he had observed someone he believed to be Sirhan Sirhan. The party, so he alleged, was not at Sharon Tate's suite at the Chateau Marmont, but at the rooms of a photographer friend of Sharon's at the Chateau. Sharon, he said, was there. Everyone was clothed at the gathering and nothing he observed was of a sexual nature. This individual's allegations were in no way connected with Mr. Richard Smith's.

As for Larry Larsen, from 1975 until 1980 Larsen was an LA County deputy supervisor, working for Supervisor Baxter Ward. One of Larsen's duties was to assist Ward's investigation into the death of Senator Kennedy.

Another acquaintance of Larry Larsen during those years was legendary IRS intelligence agent John Daley, stationed in California, who in 1972 investigated Teamster head Frank Fitzsimmons's connections to the Nixon White House. Daley and fellow IRS agents learned from the Teamsters' officials that the Teamsters had given something like $500,000 directly to Nixon, plus other payments to CREEP (the Committee to Re-Elect the President) during the 1972 presidential campaign. Daley and the IRS had learned about the money flowing to Nixon while interviewing Teamsters' president Fitzsimmons and associates, who provided the information hoping to avoid prosecution for other transgressions. After Nixon had won reelection in 1972, there was a meeting between Richard Nixon and Frank Fitzsimmons, in a private room at the White House. Also in attendance was Attorney General Richard Kleindienst, who was ordered by Nixon to review all pending Teamsters investigations, and to make sure that Fitzsimmons and associates were not harmed. This is discussed in Anthony Summers's book *The Arrogance of Power: The Secret World of Richard Nixon*. (Try chapter 28.)

John Daley also developed information on the murder of Sharon Tate. Larry Larsen learned some of Daley's assertions. One, based on information from a woman and her husband in Los Angeles, was that the head of the English Satanist group came through Kansas City, saw "two brothers," then went on to California where he contracted with Manson to kill Sharon Tate. The contract amount, it was alleged, was $25,000. Daley's female informant said she'd witnessed the contract with Manson. I asked former LA County sheriff's office homicide officers Paul Whiteley and Charles Guenther (both now retired) about the supposed informant, and both denied ever interviewing the informant or knowing the informant's name. An LA sheriff's office intelligence division officer, alleged to be one of Richard Smith's sources on the allegation that there had been a contract to kill Sharon Tate because of something she had learned about Sirhan Sirhan, also denied to Larry Larsen that he had been a source to Mr. Smith. Yet in all of Larsen's contacts with Smith, Smith never backed down from his 1974 report.

(Back in January of 1971, during our original investigation for my book *The Family*, Larry Larsen interviewed a woman who had typed reports for private investigators who had been hired to work on the murders of Sharon Tate, Jay Sebring, and the others. She typed reports for a number of months. One investigator looked into locating assets in Kansas City, Missouri, in the name of Susan Atkins, Charles Manson, and on key Manson associate Bill Vance. They also looked in the seacoast town of Corpus Christi, Texas.)

But, all in all, the question is this: Could Sharon Tate have been involved, even in a tangential way, with an organized occult religious group such as the English Satanist organization? It brings to mind the interview that actor Steve McQueen, longtime pal of Sharon Tate, gave in 1980, not long before he passed away. (We have traced this interview earlier.)

The interviewer asked McQueen about going into the occult. McQueen answered, "I was on the ring of it. Jay Sebring was my best friend. Sharon Tate was a girlfriend of mine. I dated Sharon for a while. I was sure taken care of; my name never got drawn into that mess. He was having an affair with the girlfriend of a warlock. It may be for the worse, but I was always against it. I was one of the ones who always felt that I was one of the good guys, but boy I tell you, they did a number on me. I'm against that whole thing."

McQueen went on to say that what attracted him to the occult "was the women, and the dope, and the running around. That's all that was." McQueen insisted that he "didn't know it was the occult. It's bullshit is what it is. No, I really didn't know what it was, and by the time I did, I had never gone to any of the meetings. Never knew anything about it, and was always against it. It was never for me."

What's interesting is the statement: "I had never gone to any of the meetings." What meetings? I asked three people close to Sharon Tate if she had had any involvement with the occult or an occult group. All three—Joanna Pettet, Sheilah Wells, and Shahrokh Hatami—denied that Sharon was involved. Of course, that does not preclude Sharon Tate learning something about the Robert Kennedy assassination that resulted in her own death.

The FBI provided information to INS officer Richard Smith during his investigation. This brings to mind the story, already referred to in this book, that two reporters for the *New York Daily News* wrote, just days after the murder of Sharon Tate, based on conversations conducted with a federal narcotics agent in Los Angeles, who was investigating the murders. Based on information supplied by the agent, the two reporters wrote a story published in the *Daily News* on August 13, under the headline, "Believe Cultist Hired Sharon Killer."

In a conversation with the author, over forty years after the publication, William Federici stood by the material in the article. I asked why the Bureau of Narcotics and Dangerous Drugs (now DEA) agent would have known about the Tate murder investigation. "They were involved in this thing right from the beginning," he replied. "The BNDD was part of the whole thing. There was a whole task force." Federici got his law enforcement contacts in New York to get in touch with law enforcement in Los Angeles and ask them to help Federici. Hence the meeting with the federal narcotics agent. I asked, "The material in the article reflects what you learned from the federal narcotics officer?"

"Yes," he replied.

The Federici-McGovern story has been recounted before in this book, but it bears repeating. It began: "Beautiful Sharon Tate and four others are believed to have been the victims of an assassin hired by a member of a cult which met regularly for sex-drug rituals in her posh Bel Air home, authorities disclosed today." The story claimed that members of the cult included "top Hollywood personalities and show business executives." The story went on to assert that "an assortment of the cult's tools—including black leather masks, whips, ropes, and chains" was found in Sharon Tate's house.

"The club has a permanent membership of nearly 50 but was increased with the admittance of strangers picked up at exclusive Hollywood discotheques by Sharon's crowd. The group, a throwback to the Hollywood of another era, drew its inspiration from the fantasy world here of the '30s."

A follow-up story in the *Daily News* of August 17, by another reporter, had the following assertion: "a source close to the investigation declared that here had been a 'wild party' attended by some of 'the biggest freaks and weirdos' in Hollywood.' What's more, probers said Sharon and the other four might have been victims of an assassin hired by a member of the cult that met regularly in the Polanski home for sex-drug rituals."

I became friends with Michael McGovern while both of us covered the 1970 trial of Manson, Krenwinkel, Atkins, and Van Houten for the murders. He filled me in on the source and circumstances of the information he and Federici had received from the government agent in the LA restaurant. He also said they had been told by the federal narcotics agent that black hoods were found in the house, and some sort of black aprons shaped like a downpointed ace of spades.

Part of the unfair hysteria decried by Roman Polanski and the relatives of Sharon Tate? Indeed, three friends of Sharon Tate—actresses Joanna Pettet, Sheilah Wells, and photographer friend Shahrokh Hatami—all stated to the author that, as far as they knew, Sharon Tate was not upset, in the days before she was killed, about anything she had learned or heard.

Of course, the killers might not have known the real reason for Manson ordering the attack. One or more of them thinking they were starting a race war. One or more of them hypnotized and robotized by extended cult-babble. And some believing they were doing a copy-cat to get off their brother Bobby Beausoleil.

I decided to write once again to Charles Manson, to try to get clarification of what IRS intelligence officer John Daley alleged to Larry Larsen. For an updated edition of my book *The Family,* and at the urging of Sharon Tate's mother, Doris, I had already conducted a correspondence with Manson back in the 1980s. When I first wrote to him, he was very unfriendly, initially sending me a postcard of the devil with a swastika he drew upon the devil's dangling tongue with a red pen. I wrote back, essentially urging him to cool out, and we began a correspondence in which he did supply useful material for the updated *The Family.* In one letter, he wrote, "We knew you were CIA all the time." That was fine with me. In the end, however, he decided to cut me off, writing in a letter postmarked April 24, 1989, that never again would he open my letters, while at the same time he jotted a six-page reply to a question list. In one passage he wrote, "I'm not schooled enough to play words on paper with you but in real life if we could ever meet you would fare about as well with me in real as I do in this game—If I had the power you say & and the command to do such as you write, you would be gone and you know that in your own judgement of me."

Even so, during the writing of this book on Sharon Tate, I wrote him a brief letter, hoping that he might answer. I'd learned that he has been talking, by cell-phone, with a former police officer in California, so I invited Manson to call me. The letter is as follows, with a name deleted:

Dear Charles Manson,

You have written replies to some of my letters in the past.

And I have learned that you have recently communicated by telephone or cell-phone with an acquaintance of mine in California.

My question is this: did _____ __ _____ urge you, and offer you money, to kill Sharon Tate? Yes or no, please.

And if yes he did, could you tell me where this meeting with him to discuss killing her took place? At Esalen? At a house in Topanga Canyon? In LA? Where?

Thank you for answering. You could call me.

Sincerely,

Ed Sanders

So far, no answer, no phone call.

As for the true motive that caused Manson to send his marauders into the house on Cielo Drive, we may never know. And the allegation that Sharon Tate was the target? Indeed, it may all be smoke and mirrors, and ultimately impossible to prove beyond doubt's shadow. Meanwhile, Time's Wingèd Chariot is clacking onward and erasing much of the access to the past.

But, even though the world moves on, decade after decade, that does not prevent loose ends flapping in the multi-decade breeze, and no loose ends can prevent our sense of outrage and anger for the horrible injustice perpetrated upon Sharon Tate and her friends.

Index